The Old Navy

Also by Daniel Pratt Mannix 4th

Hunter
African Frontier Tales
The Fox and the Hound
Black Cargoes

REAR ADMIRAL DANIEL P. MANNIX 3RD

Edited by Daniel P. Mannix 4th

The
Old
Navy

MACMILLAN PUBLISHING COMPANY · New York

To the Officers and Men
with whom it has been my privilege
to serve all over the world.

Macmillan Publishing Company
866 Third Avenue, New York, N.Y. 10022
Collier Macmillan Canada, Inc.

Library of Congress Cataloging in Publication Data
The old Navy.
1. Mannix, Daniel Pratt, 1878-1957.   2. Admirals—
United States—Biography. 3. United States. Navy—
Biography. I. Mannix, Daniel Pratt, 1911-   . II. Title.
V63.M295A36 1983   359'.0092'4 [B]   83-11350
ISBN 0-02-579470-1

10 9 8 7 6 5 4 3 2 1

Designed by Jack Meserole

Printed in the United States of America

CONTENTS

FOREWORD

As a child, I saw my father only once or twice a year and many times not even that often, for he was an officer in the United States Navy, and cruises were cruises in the early years of this century. It seemed to me that he always arrived unexpectedly and at night. I slept in a little room next to my grandparents on the second floor of their Delancey Place house in Philadelphia, and suddenly I would be awake and conscious of a bustling downstairs. I would run along the dark hallway in my white nightgown to the top of the great staircase that led down to the entrance hall, a checkerboard of black and white marble slabs far below me. By the light of a yellow, fan-shaped gas flame I was able to make out hurrying figures as the maids started a fire in the living room barely visible through the hastily opened sliding doors. Mother and my grandparents were already down, and then I would see Bounds, our houseman, open the glass doors that gave onto a tiny hallway beyond which was the massive street door.

Clinging to the mahogany baluster, I would start down the carpeted steps one at a time, terrified of falling but determined not to miss this great moment which rated with Christmas. Long before I reached the bottom, the glass doors would reopen and Bounds would return. After him would come a tall figure with gold lace gleaming on his blue uniform and a boat cape thrown over his shoulders. Then would follow two seamen carrying a huge sea chest big enough to hold a corpse. Under Bounds' direction, they would carry it into the living room, emerging a few moments later empty handed and take their departure after touching their round caps to Father. It behooved me to get there before Father entered the living room and the sliding doors were closed, for it was hard for a little boy to make himself heard through the oaken panels and I would be left standing alone in the cold hallway.

Even in the safety of the living room, no one paid any attention to me, nor did I expect it. Father would first greet Grandmother and

Grandfather as they were the eldest and he was a stickler for seniority. Then he would speak to Mother and, after an embarrassed pause, kiss her on the cheek. Both of them were obviously self-conscious and hardly knew how to behave after so many months' separation. Then, I think almost with relief, Father would turn to me. "Did you take good care of your mother while I was away?" he would ask severely. It was part of my training to know that men always took care of women, no matter what the disparity in their ages might be. After I assured him that I had came the ceremonial opening of the sea chest.

That sea chest was better than all the Christmas stockings in the world. You never knew what would be revealed except that it would be rare and wonderful. One year there was a gush of sandlewood scent as the lid was raised and then, wrapped in palm fronds, were teak elephants with real ivory tusks, a Gurkha *kukri*, alabaster boxes inlaid with semiprecious stones, a hookah, and many more exotic marvels. On another occasion, there was a model full-rigged ship that turned out to sail beautifully when father set the sails (the box she was in was labeled "tres fragile" so I named her that), a set of Black Watch lead soldiers, their kilted uniforms accurate down to the finest detail, and a hand-carved chess set. Again there was a necklace of fresh water pearls from South America, a set of bolas, brilliant serapes, and strange shells. Once after the Russian-Japanese War, Father brought back a human rib from a place he called 203 Meter Hill where, he explained, the ground was too hard to bury the dead. He always had presents for everyone, including the maids, who came up from the servants' quarters to curtsy as they received their gifts.

It seemed to me that Father was never home for more than a few weeks and I saw little of him. Like most well-raised children of that era I spent much of my time in the nursery with my nurse and, except to inquire into my studies, Father seldom spoke to me. I was, of course, destined for the Naval Academy. I was Daniel Pratt Mannix 4th, and every Daniel Pratt Mannix had been in the armed services. It was the only respectable profession for a gentleman. Whenever Father spoke of "civilians," he always did it with a sneer.

As a midshipman, my father served on sailing ships, and he was still an officer in the Navy (although retired) when the atomic bomb was dropped on Hiroshima. During his long career, he met the Empress Dowager of China, the German Kaiser, Edward VII of Great Britain, the Mikado of Japan, and Her Imperial Highness

Zekie, Sultana of Turkey. He fought in eight wars, was awarded six medals, and saw action against the Moro pirates and the Imperial German Navy. He watched the United States grow from an obscure, third-class nation to the most powerful country in the world. Many of the campaigns he described so familiarly I had trouble finding in any historical texts. Today we have no idea how far-ranging was American influence in the early years of this century.

Often I disagree with his dogmatic views, as I am sure many readers will. At other times, I am astonished at his insight. I feel that whether you agree or disagree with his beliefs, it is important to realize that they were the beliefs of many men in this country nearly a hundred years ago, and it was these men who made our nation great. You may be convinced that they were often wrong, but you today are living on their bounty.

After my father's death, my step-mother, Claudia, was kind enough to send me his trunks full of letters, notes, diaries, and photographs. For a long time the task of organizing the material seemed hopeless, but with the help of the Naval History Division in Washington, D.C., I have done my best to reconstruct a picture of the times. I have had to omit a number of his cruises (he sailed the equivalent of eight times around the world) and combined several others (for example, he made three cruises to the Philippines, which I have put together). I hope this has not resulted in contradictions or confusions.

I consider this to be a revealing epic of America from 1880 to 1928, as seen through the eyes of a man who played a role in forming it. If naval officers or trained historians read this, I hope they will excuse any technical errors I may have made. The errors will be mine, not those of my father, Rear Admiral Daniel P. Mannix 3rd. Now I will allow him to tell his story in his own words.

Daniel Pratt Mannix 4th

CHAPTER ONE

Boyhood in China (1881–1885)

Long ago, and far away

My first memories are of China of the 1880's—a China of fat mandarins, of ladies with bound feet, of men with pigtails and of soldiers who carried paper umbrellas as part of their equipment and who never fought when it was raining. Their way of fighting was to frighten the enemy by exploding firecrackers and then suddenly opening their umbrellas on which were painted pictures of devils. It worked quite well on other Chinese but was not nearly as successful against the Russians, French, British, Germans, and Japanese who were invading China. My father, Lt. Daniel P. Mannix, Jr., of the United States Marine Corps, had the task of turning these Chinese levies into efficient combat troops. He had brought Mother, my older sister, me, and Mammy—Mammy who, until the Civil War had been one of our family's slaves—to China with him.

I can also remember, very faintly, myself as a four-year-old boy who ran crying to Mammy because the little Chinese boys laughed at me for not having a pigtail. As always when she heard my cries, Mammy rushed to the rescue and at the sight of her, the Chinese children fled screaming, "First a white devil and now a black one!"

Mother tried to comfort me, saying angrily, "How terrible that these stupid children should be prejudiced against someone just because his skin is a different color than theirs!" I remember Mammy gave Mother a curious look and after a brief pause said, "Yea, Miz Mannix, it sure is a sin."

Mammy soon solved the problem by pinning a false pigtail to the inside of the round cap I always wore. The cap had a coral button on top, insignia of a mandarin, third class, which was the rank that the Empress Dowager had bestowed on Father. I still have the cap and the pigtail.

Father was "loaned" to the Chinese government as the result of an accident. He was Marine officer on board the USS *Ticonderoga* under Commodore Shufeldt who had been sent to the Orient in 1878 to

3

open Korea—as Commodore Perry a few years before had opened Japan—and persuade the king to allow American merchants to trade there. At that time, Korea was a vassal state of China and technically, at least, under the Chinese emperor. The Korean king had refused to receive Shufeldt and the commodore did not wish to use force, although that was customary in those days. While hoping that his majesty would change his mind, the *Ticonderoga* anchored in the Wu long River, emptying into the Gulf of Chihli in northern China. Father was a torpedo expert and to pass the time, Shufeldt had him practice launching torpedoes.

The local villagers regarded the *Ticonderoga* as a treasure trove, and sampans constantly hovered around her. Everything the crew discarded was immediately snatched up for even an empty tin can was regarded as valuable. At that time, self-propelled torpedoes were still under test and development and highly unreliable. The steering mechanism of the first torpedo Father launched proved to be faulty and it ran up on the beach by the village. Naturally, it was instantly surrounded by a curious crowd who had never seen such an object before but were positive it was an important find.

Before a boat could be lowered from the *Ticonderoga* to retrieve the missile, there came the sound of gongs being beaten, and down the village's only street marched a procession of musicians followed by a gigantic, muscular man naked to the waist and bearing over his shoulder an immense sword. This dignitary carefully examined the torpedo and decided that the percussion cap at the end was its most vulnerable part. After ceremonially wiping off the cap with a silk handkerchief, he whirled the sword around his head. The fascinated spectators crowded closer to be in on the spoils when the gleaming tube was cracked open and the Lord High Executioner lowered his sword to wave them majestically away. Then he brandished his weapon again and brought it down with all his strength on the percussion cap.

The village simply disappeared.

Commodore Shufeldt was afraid this incident would cause trouble, but it had precisely the opposite effect. The European powers, together with Japan, were using their battle fleets to seize Chinese cities along the coast as trading centers. Having no coastal defenses China was helpless, and Li Hung-chang, who then held a position roughly equivalent to prime minister, realized that soon China would be dismembered by the predatory foreigners. He heard of the destructive power of the *Ticonderoga*'s torpedo, and it seemed to him that this was the ideal device for keeping enemy warships away. He invited Commodore Shufeldt to call on him in Tientain, his summer capital. Li asked for an American officer to open a torpedo school at the Tientain Arsenal to train Chinese technicians. Shufeldt recommended Father.

It was not unusual then for an under-developed country to "borrow" a military expert from some more advanced nation for an agreed-on period of years. The officer got a quick promotion (Father was made a captain), extra pay, and in return promised to fight with his adopted country against any nation except his own. The United States was only too glad to cooperate with Li Hung-chang, for we had arrived in the East long after the other powers and were hoping for trade concessions. Father sent back to the states for his family, and we arrived in June 1881, at Tientain near the mouth of the Pei-ho River.

As much of the country was cut up into rice paddies, there were almost no roads and we ascended the river in a canal boat, a great barge towed by scores of men. These men were barefoot and left long lines of bloody tracks behind them as they strained at the ropes. When one man collapsed, another took his place. I asked Father why horses or oxen were not used. He replied, "They cost money. Remember that here in the Orient human life is the cheapest of all commodities." I never forgot that.

Although none of us—not even Father—realized it, we were pioneering a new era. For the first hundred years of its existence, the United States had remained in "splendid isolation." Our own vast country supplied us with everything we needed—except for what little was required from Latin America—so the country practiced a sort of Monroe Doctrine in reverse; we did not allow foreign nations to interfere in the Western Hemisphere and we did not interfere elsewhere. Unlike European nations which were armed camps, we were guarded by two great oceans and had no need for armed forces. Our Navy was minute and our Army practically non-existent; it was smaller than Switzerland's. We had no battleships until 1890 when we built three: the *Oregon*, the *Indiana*, and the *Massachusetts*. Two years later we built a third, the *Iowa*. As a result, Europe regarded us as a third-class power, little more influential than Mexico or Brazil. But now the reluctant giant was stirring. In 1881, the United States was on the threshold of greatness. The little boy who ran crying to

Mammy would see during his own lifetime the United States become a vast superpower controlling the destiny of the world. This was the beginning, and he was to play a part in having it come to pass.

Li Hung-chang had given Father a big house in Taku at the mouth of the Pei-ho River. There were a number of European colonies nearby, each flying its own flag, sporting its own club, race track, and church. Every colony was surrounded by a canal or a river to serve as a moat and maintained its own gunboats and troops; they were independent nations on Chinese soil. Their defenses were as much against each other as against the Chinese, for all the foreign nations were rivals. It was only this rivalry that kept them from carving up China as they had already done Africa. The European businessmen in these compounds were called Taipans and their Chinese managers Compradors. Some were fabulously rich but Father looked down on all of them as "counter jumpers" far inferior to the military which was a gentleman's profession. "I would rather have been a drummer boy at Waterloo than the richest businessman in the world," he often said. Father was not popular with either the Taipans or the Compradors.

As we were the only Americans in Taku and Father was an employee of the Chinese government, we saw more of the Chinese than did the other foreigners who took pride in remaining as aloof from the natives as possible. My sister and I had no white playmates as all European children were sent "home" at an early age so they would grow up uncorrupted by foreign customs and manners. We had about twenty Chinese servants, each servant having several assistants. My especial favorite was the mahfoo (groom) so I spent a large part of my time in the stables conversing with him and the stable boys, and I learned to speak Mandarin Chinese before I could adequate English. Perhaps there was something in the European notion of protecting their children from Chinese influences for once while Mother was entertaining some missionaries and their wives, I burst into our "parlor" and rattled off a few sentences. Mother, who could speak only a few words of Chinese, said proudly, "Doesn't he talk the language well?" The missionaries looked at her with popeyed horror until one of the gentlemen managed to blurt out, "Do you know what he SAID?"

Chinese is a very difficult language for a foreigner to learn because it is a tonal language; that is, the significance of a word depends on how it is accented. One word usually has several meanings so the way it is pronounced is all important, much as a note of music can be told only by the pitch of the singer's voice. Foreigners learning Chinese would memorize a word and then always pronounce it in the same way as they would French or English. This often led to confusion. A newly arrived missionary entering the house of one of our Chinese friends would say, in what he thought to be fluent Chinese, "How kind of you to invite me." What he'd really said was something like, "I have a face like a pig's behind." The host and hostess were far too polite to ridicule a guest, but we children and the servants would burst into howls of laughter, to the visitor's bewilderment.

Nowadays we hear a great deal about "all men being brothers" and "everyone being alike in spite of the color of their skins" and so on. To my way of thinking, nothing could be more untrue, and I have spent more time abroad than I have in the United States. One of our greatest problems in dealing with foreigners is that we take for granted that they will think and behave like Americans. When they do not, we are puzzled and angry. The Chinese, on the other hand, considered all foreigners as "crude barbarians" and insisted on following their own customs even when these were obviously disastrous.

The Pei-ho River was the natural roadway to Pekin, the capital, which lay some 80 miles inland. Any attack on Pekin where the emperor kept his court had to be launched up the river as the country was made up of rice paddies and twisting roads impractical for troop movements. The Chinese had built two forts to guard the mouth of the river which they had only finished on the side facing the ocean. The Chinese had never bothered to complete them as it was considered unethical to attack a position from the rear. Pekin was defended only by 48 wooden shutters with painted cannon muzzles on them.

Foreigners regarded the Chinese as barely human. This was not as bigoted as it sounds. Coolies always walked in the streets; they were not permitted to use the sidewalks. If it became necessary to answer a "call of nature" they would do it in plain view of everybody, just like animals and, so strong is custom, the white ladies would pass paying no more attention than as if they really were animals. Public beheadings were common. Human heads, suspended by their pigtails, were displayed everywhere as a warning to others, and criminals with wooden boards around their necks studded with papers describing their crimes wandered the streets.

White people stayed close to Taku for fear of dogs and the Chinese. The country around the town was flat and very wild. It was infected with packs of dogs so vicious that whites never walked in the more desolate parts. They rode horseback and the men carried whips, not for the horses but for the dogs and for another menace still more unpleasant, that is, if anything can be more unpleasant than being eaten alive.

At the gates of the various villages groups of beggars would establish themselves and, on the approach of a white man, surround him while screaming for money. Some of these beggars were actual lepers and others simulated leprosy by painting their faces and bodies ghastly colors. These lepers, real or fake, would crowd around a horseman and, if he didn't at once commence giving them money, they would threaten to touch him, commencing to paw at his legs and working their way upwards toward his face.

I once had an encounter with these beggars that still makes my flesh crawl. One of Father's friends was a general in the Chinese army named Lo who must have weighed over three hundred pounds. General Lo came to visit us and Mother offered him some ice cream. Now the Chinese never ate or drank anything that was iced. The general took a big swallow of the ice cream, dropped his plate, grabbed his stomach and commenced screaming that he had been poisoned.

Forgivingly, General Lo later presented me with a Manchurian pony whom I named after him as the pony was also extremely plump. One afternoon we were entertaining a husky English pilot named Baxter. He was interested in the country so he and Father set out on horseback, taking me with them. I was riding General Lo. Baxter wanted to see one of the villages and in spite of Father's warning, rode over to the gate. Instantly the beggars attacked him. I'll say this for Baxter, he didn't hesitate. He struck the leader of the beggars with his whip raising a bloody welt, wheeled his horse and fled "belly to the ground." Since then I have read of the difficulty of contracting leprosy by mere touch. Maybe, but I still think Baxter showed good judgment.

As I was not welcome in the European compounds and the countryside was unsafe, I seldom left our own yard. Perhaps as a result of this, I learned to read at an early age. Luckily, Father had taken along a considerable library and I read all of them, especially enjoying

Dumas and Stevenson. As a man, I have always taken along a supply of books on cruises if at all possible.

Mammy was a great help to us. Everyone was afraid of her, even, I think, Father, and she ran the household. An enormous woman (she was nearly as big as General Lo) she terrified the Chinese. She was strict unless I was in trouble when she instantly became a crooning, tender mother. She had more to do with raising me than did my parents. I was clumsy as a child, always falling down, and Mammy nicknamed me Bumps. Many years later when she was living in Washington with my sister and her husband I sent my son, Dan, to the kitchen to see her. The way to the kitchen led down a twisting flight of stairs and Dan fell down it. Without looking up from her cooking, Mammy remarked, "Bump's boy."

My only toy was a large rowboat which was mounted on cradles in our backyard and where I used to play for hours. In the bottom were three circular holes which, of course, were supposed to let the water out when the boat was hoisted and to be stopped with plugs when it was lowered into the water. It was one of the mysteries of my child-hood how that boat could float with those holes in it.

The Torpedo School was at Tientsin, a village a few miles from Taku at the junction of the Pei-ho and Hun-ho rivers. Here gunpow-der was stored and the newly trained Chinese mechanics turned out excellent Remington breech loaders. Father showed them how to make mines that could be electrically detonated and explosive shells. Occasionally as a great treat he would take us with him to Tientsin. We traveled by horse litter. These were like sedan chairs with one horse in front and another behind. They swayed up and down and had a tendency to make one seasick. Another means of travel was "Pekin carts," two-wheeled affairs with metal tires and no springs. After a short trip on one of them a traveler felt as though every bone in his body had been broken.

Mother and my sister never walked because Chinese ladies never walked. Chinese ladies couldn't. As very young children their feet were encased in bandages that prevented their growth, resulting in a complete change in the form of the foot. They might totter a few steps but that was all. This was considered graceful, like a white woman mincing along on high heels. For a Chinese lady to show her unbound foot was simply unspeakable. It was just as well. I once saw a woman's unbound feet and didn't want to see any more.

By 1885, even I could tell that war between China and the foreign powers was imminent. The British had occupied Burma which was part of the Chinese Empire. The Russians had taken Turkistan, also part of China. Now Japan seized the Licuchiu Islands. The country was being torn apart. Only a navy strong enough to stop the invaders could save it as they all came by sea. Even the Russians found it easier to invade by ship than to cross Siberia. I can remember at this time there was some dispute with France and for several nights Father remained at one of the forts in anticipation of an attack which never came. Father, in accordance with his oath, was perfectly prepared to die for China if necessary, something few Chinese were equally willing to do.

To me, Father was a giant. He stood slightly less than six feet (as I do now) and always kept himself at full attention. He seldom smiled. He wore an imperial goatee and a mustache like Napoleon III or, as I preferred to think of it, like the Three Musketeers. I can't recall his ever speaking to me except to give an order or a rebuke. I am quite sure he did not mean to be unkind. His whole life had been spent in the armed services and to him I was not a child but a junior officer. Junior officers had to be kept in their place and trained for a career in the service. There was never any doubt that I would enter either the Navy or the Marines.

This was natural for our family had been connected with the military for three generations. We were originally Irish. My great-grandfather had come to the United States in the early days of the nineteenth century, bringing with him his wife and little son who was to be my grandfather. Great-grandfather's name was Daniel Patrick Mannix, but when he arrived in America he found there was considerable prejudice against the Irish, so he changed it to Daniel Pratt Mannix. As he was to become an American citizen, he intended to conform to American customs and attitudes.

During the Civil War, Grandfather was a Colonel of Volunteers and was killed at Shiloh, April 6, 1862, when the Confederates under General A. S. Johnston (who was also killed) all but succeeded in driving our army into the river. My father entered the Navy at eighteen as an acting master's mate, later became an acting ensign and still later a second lieutenant in the Regular Marine Corps. During the war, he served on the *Mississippi* under Farragut. He was at New Orleans and at Vicksburg. In April 1865, he was on duty at the

Washington Navy Yard when Lincoln was assassinated. As commander of the Marine Guard, Father guarded Lincoln's body until it was sent west for burial. He never removed the piece of crepe he tied to the hilt of his sword in mourning for the dead president. I still have the sword with the crepe attached. Later, he became a torpedo expert and in that capacity was assigned to the *Ticonderoga*.

Everyone knew that the attack on China had only been postponed, not abandoned. A weak nation was regarded as public property. In fact, China was hardly a nation at all. Two hundred and fifty years before, the country had been overrun by the Manchus pouring down from Mongolia who flooded almost without opposition over the Great Wall built to hold them back. To my way of thinking, no static barrier has ever been able to stop a determined enemy, as witness the Maginot Line in World War II. The Manchus established themselves as a ruling class, much as the Normans did in England after 1066. The Chinese hated them and they looked on the Chinese with contempt, forcing them to wear the pigtail as a symbol of servitude. Naturally, the emperor and his court in Pekin were all Manchus.

Although there was an emperor when we arrived in China, he was a nonentity. The real ruler was the old Empress Dowager, Tzu Hsi, one of the most remarkable women in history. To understand the events of the next few months and why Father's efforts to save China failed, you will have to know something about this strange woman.

She was born in 1835, a Manchu, and when the emperor died in 1850 she, together with a number of other respectable Manchu girls, was presented to the emperor's son, a nineteen-year-old boy who had assumed the throne. Hsien Feng, as he was named, was married to a noble but not too intelligent lady named Sakota. However, it was taken for granted he would need several concubines as well. Tzu was not especially beautiful but, according to the story, she was clever enough to pretend indifference to the young emperor. The spoiled Hsien Feng was so intrigued by the idea of a woman who was not immediately overcome by his charms that he made her a concubine. Years later, Wally Simpson used the same technique to interest the Prince of Wales.

Sakota, the queen or royal consort, had had only one child. This was not surprising as the emperor, in spite of his youth, was so worn out from dissipation and probably venereal infection that he was virtually impotent. Unluckily for Sakota, the lone child was a girl.

Tzu, however, soon gave birth to a child who was (luckily for her) a boy. The baby was almost certainly the son of the handsome, capable captain of the Palace Guard, Jung Lu, but no one dared to suggest this possibility. Certainly Jung Lu was the only person Tzu ever seemed to care for throughout her long career. So even though Tzu was only a concubine, and a concubine of the fourth class at that, she was now elevated to the rank of queen mother as her son would inherit the throne.

Soon Tzu was virtually running the country. The court lived in the Sacred City, a walled section of Pekin where only a few select individuals were allowed to enter. The Sacred City was run by hundreds of eunuchs who controlled even the emperor. Their power lay in the fact that all the nobles were suspicious of each other, each fearing that his peers might have the emperor assassinated and then seize the throne. A eunuch could not be emperor as they were incapable of founding a dynasty and China was dedicated to ancestor worship, so they were allowed to dominate the government. Many of these eunuchs had willingly had themselves emasculated so they could achieve high positions. They were utterly unscrupulous and lived for wealth and power. Tzu was able to gain their favor by giving them a completely free hand. Her favorite eunuch was a man named Li Lienying who was second only to her. I saw him once. He looked exactly like a fat old woman and terrified me although I didn't know why.

In 1860 came the so-called Opium War. England was making a fortune by selling Indian opium to the Chinese and finally the court in Pekin tried to stop the trade. England declared war on China and a number of other European nations joined her. Tzu had the amazing effrontery to insist that all European embassies enter Pekin through a gate reserved for subject states; this to give credence to the Chinese claim that China was the supreme world power and all other nations were her vassals. As the European countries were busy cutting up China at the time, this was equivalent to a woman being raped demanding that her attackers first bow to her. The European powers quickly captured the Taku forts by sending landing parties to attack them from the rear, and then, sailing up the Pei-ho River, sacked Pekin and burned the beautiful Summer Palace built on a lake and one of the great architectural wonders of the world. The court fled to Jehol, some 150 miles away. Here a conspiracy was formed to overthrow the weak Hsien-Feng but Tzu frustrated it by stealing the royal seal without which no edict could be made. Soon afterwards Hsien-Feng died. Tzu made a treaty with the Europeans giving them all they demanded and returned to Pekin with her five-year-old son. She promptly declared herself regent until her boy was old enough to rule.

Father never despised the Chinese as did most Europeans but he bitterly resented their attitude toward the military. Just as the Chinese worshipped the scholar, Father worshipped the fighting man. It outraged him to see a general magnificently attired riding ahead of unshaven, dirty troops who kept no formation and were armed with a museum collection of spears, blunderbusses, halberts, and pikes. These men's idea of warfare was to blow trumpets, beat gongs, wave banners, give their war cries, and fire off rockets. As for me, I learned at this early age what happens to a country that allows her armed forces to deteriorate. After the First World War, an epidemic of pacifism swept the United States. There were to be no more wars, the League of Nations would insure peace, wars were caused only by munition makers, and such like nonsense. I wish these pacifists could have seen China as I did. Once a nation weakens her defenses, others fall on her like wolves on a crippled animal. China with her awe of scholars, reverence for diplomacy, and hatred of militarism learned her lesson too late.

The imperial court's troubles were by no means confined to foreigners. The Chinese peasants rose in rebellion against their Manchu overlords. They banded together under the title of Taiping (General Peace), refused to wear pigtails, let their hair grow (the Manchus contemptuously referred to them as the "long hairs"), and prepared to take over the country. They believed in a strange mixture of Chinese conceptions and the Christianity introduced by the missionaries. Their leader, a man named Hung, claimed to be Jesus Christ and surrounded himself by a general staff called the Twelve Apostles. Most Chinese conceived of Christianity as some sort of magic that made the white man powerful and adopted it to give them supernatural strength. I don't think the well-meaning missionaries ever realized how confusing their doctrines were to a people with entirely different ways of thought.

The Manchus had once been great fighters but they had so deteriorated that the Taipings won victory after victory. Then Li Hung-chang took the field against them. Li was a Manchu and a noted scholar—to the Chinese the highest of all callings—but he became a

soldier—to the Chinese the lowest of the low. Li was wise enough to
know his own limitations as a military man so he put a professional
soldier in charge of his hastily organized army: an American named
Ward. If the United States had supported Ward, we could have
controlled Asia, but our government was too provincial to realize this
great opportunity. Ward was killed in the fighting so Li put another
foreign professional in command: an Englishman named Gordon who
was ever afterwards called "Chinese Gordon." Gordon was a highly
capable fighting man and soon his force came to be known as the "ever
victorious army." The Taipings made a last stand in Soochow in
1864. When they saw that it was all over, Hung killed himself and the
Twelve Apostles surrendered to Gordon with his promise that their
lives would be spared.

Li Hung-chang was having none of that. As soon as Gordon's
back was turned, he had all twelve men beheaded. Gordon was
furious when he heard the news. He stormed into Li's presence,
denounced him for having betrayed the word of an English gentleman. To Li, keeping one's promises was ridiculous. No one in China
ever kept his promise. When Gordon stamped out of the room, Li
remarked casually to one of his aides, "He can say what he will but he
can't bring those accursed Twelve Apostles back to life." This was
one of Father's favorite stories and he often told it, chuckling. Father,
being a practical man, sympathized with Li. Still Li paid a high price
for the death of his enemies. Gordon left his service and went to Egypt
where a few years later he was to die in Khartum. Tzu made Li
viceroy of Chihli, although I don't think the empress ever really
trusted him. He was too sympathetic to foreign ideas and the empress
hated foreigners and all their works.

In 1873, Tzu's son, T'ung Chih, was declared emperor. He was a
weak young man, dissipated like all the emperors, and dominated
entirely by his terrible mother. He died in 1875. Many believe that his
mother had him poisoned as he was married and his wife was pregnant. If his wife, the royal consort, gave birth to a son, she would have
been more powerful than Tzu.

Now there was no ruler. In this emergency, Tzu appealed to Li
Hung-chang and his troops. With Li's backing, she seized power,
declared a baby boy (her nephew) the emperor and again established
herself as regent. T'ung Chih's widow either committed suicide or
was murdered, leaving Tzu with a free hand. The new emperor,

although only a child who owed his position to Tzu, hated her. When he was nine years old (in 1880), he had an open break with her. It was at this time the *Ticonderoga* came to China and fired its historic torpedo which made Father head of the Chinese Torpedo School and introduced the United States to Chinese affairs.

It was extremely difficult for Chinese and white men to work together as they had no idea of each other's culture. The Chinese were hopelessly confused as to the nature of white men, simultaneously regarding them as savages yet crediting them with more than mortal powers. Once an American cruiser put into Taku with a petty officer on board who had some talent as an artist. This man made a number of sketches and a local mandarin saw one. He was greatly interested as it was so different from Chinese art and demanded to go on board the cruiser to meet the artist. He was piped over the side with great ceremony as he was an important man and after being given a chair—there was some problem finding one large enough to fit his ample stern—he explained that he wanted the petty officer to make a painting of his father. The petty officer was flattered and asked when he could see his subject. "Oh, that is impossible," the mandarin explained. "He's been dead many years. That's why I want a picture of him because none were made during his life."

This was a puzzler. The captain tried to explain the difficulties involved but the noble wasn't having any of it. "If you people can perform so many miracles, surely it would be a small matter for you to go to heaven and see my father," he said angrily. The captain solved the problem in the age-old manner of the Navy. Turning to the petty officer he snapped, "Draw a picture of this gentleman's father. That's an order!" The petty officer made the only possible answer. He said, "Aye, aye, sir!"

Lacking any other model, the artist used a newspaper picture of William Howard Taft as a subject. When the painting was completed, the mandarin was invited on board the cruiser for the unveiling. After the cloth was withdrawn from the painting, the mandarin stood staring at it in astonishment for some time. Then with a deep sigh he remarked, "My, how father has changed!"

In addition to her other shortcomings, the empress was wildly extravagant. She had a passion for elaborate theatricals which Li Lien-ying, her head eunuch, staged for her, and she was busy rebuilding the Summer Palace in even greater elegance than before. I don't

believe that she knew anything about money and quite probably had
no knowledge of even simple mathematics. As far as she was concerned, it was enough that she desired unlimited funds to have them
supplied. Li Lien-ying was only too happy to oblige as he took a hefty
"squeeze" from all sums he collected for her.

Father soon discovered that much of the funds that Li Hung-
chang was raising for the new Torpedo School was being stolen by
the head eunuch for the empress. Li Hung-chang also knew it but he
did not dare oppose "the old Buddha" as the people affectionately
called the empress. Father called her "the old devil" openly which was
a dangerous thing to do. He realized that she was imperiling the
whole country by her extravagance, something the empress was incapable of grasping with her ignorance of finance and her inborn
conviction that a ruler could do no wrong.

The empress had spies everywhere and of course she soon knew
how Father felt. She ordered Li Hung-chang to bring him to Pekin
for an interview. I remember well how distraught Mother was; she
was positive the empress was going to have him killed. I believe Li
was also alarmed. Father was only angry and actually seemed to look
forward to meeting his enemy face to face and telling her what he
thought of her which would have been a very bad idea. The United
States wasn't strong enough to protect him and the empress must
have known it.

Off they went and were gone for several days during which time
Mother was nearly out of her head with anxiety, and my sister and I
crept around like mice to avoid bothering her. Father returned late
one evening. After Mother had flown into his arms, I piped up, "How
was the old devil, sir?" sure that I was saying the right thing.

Father strode over to me and stood staring down from his gre
height with a savage frown on his face while I cowered with terror,
wondering what I had done. At last Father spoke in his most menac-
ing quarterdeck voice. "Never refer to that noble old lady like that
again," he admonished me fiercely. Then turning to Mother he said
proudly, "She has tendered me a decoration of the third class, second
rank Order of the Imperial Double Dragon." While we were still
recovering from this, a file of coolies supervised by a minor court
official entered carrying packages. When opened, they revealed a
magnificent silver service set. The teapot was in the shape of a dragon,
there were silver cups and saucers, sugar bowl and cream pitcher. The

tray on which all these wonders stood also had a dragon engraved on it and was so heavy it took two men to carry it. "Notice all the dragons are five-clawed," Father pointed out delightedly. A five-clawed dragon was a symbol of nobility.

After that, no one dared to say anything against the empress in Father's presence. I heard him telling Li Hung-chang what a brilliant person she was. Li replied briefly, "She certainly understands men."

The empress had bestowed another honor on Father which seemed to give him even more satisfaction than his new rank. She had confided to him, in the strictest confidence, that only Americans really understood the Chinese. "The Europeans are nothing but stupid bullies—especially the English," she told him. "But you are a sensitive people with whom we can communicate. You are the only foreigners with whom China can be friends."

A few days after this great event, Father and Mother attended a dinner party at the British Embassy. Father was subdued for a long time after and one afternoon I heard Mother telling Philo Norton McGriffin, a young American who held a commission in the newly created Chinese Navy, the reason. The British ambassador had had a little too much to drink that evening and in a very un-British burst of exuberance, had taken Father into his confidence. "I say, old chap," the ambassador had explained, "I was speaking to her nibs, Tzu Hsi, and she told me, quite openly, that only we English understood her people. 'You have a long history of dealing with Asians,' she said. 'In you alone I feel the deep sensitivity needed to know our people. The Americans are too raw and new to grasp our ancient culture.' So you are simply wasting your time here, trying to nudge your way in between us and the Chinese."

Yes, Li Hung-chang had been right. The empress certainly knew how to handle men.

I've mentioned Philo McGriffin. He had graduated from Annapolis in the Class of '82. In those days, the Navy was so small that only the first fifteen men in each class were commissioned in the Navy or Marine Corps; the remainder were given an Honorable Discharge, one thousand dollars, the blessing of the Academic Board and were set adrift. Philo was one of those set adrift.

Somehow or other, Philo had reached China where he taught seamanship and gunnery at Tientain. He had even managed to persuade Li Hung-chang to build some modern warships. I remember him especially because he was always so nice to my sister and me and spent a lot of time with us, playing games and telling us stories. One of his yarns was about an American businessman visiting China for the first time and being dined and wined by a Chinese associate. One particular dish took his fancy, he found it so delicious that he fairly stuffed himself. He could not identify it so, turning to his host, he asked interrogatively, "Quack, Quack?" His host shook his head and replied, "Bow Wow!"

Philo, like Father, stood in great awe of the Japanese. They had thoroughly modernized both their army and navy and were a most dangerous adversary. Father, Philo, and Li Hung-chang often discussed the Japanese menace and how to protect China against it. Lying in bed in the next room I listened to their conversations although most of it was over my head. Li believed in diplomacy for he knew China would stand no chance against Japan in a war. Father and Philo reluctantly agreed although Philo felt that the new navy Li was having built with whatever funds the empress let him keep could give the "dwarf bandits" as the Chinese called their enemies a good fight. I remember they made up a doggerel verse about it:

> King Solomon couldn't have been so wise or he'd never
>   have married a thousand wives.
> He had trouble with his wives perhaps but he was wise
>   enough not to fight the Japs.

Politically, the situation grew constantly more tense. Japan coveted Korea and encouraged the king to revolt against his Chinese overlord. The empress was furious and ordered Li to send troops to put down the rebellion. This Li was very reluctant to do. He knew it would mean war with Japan, and China was not ready for such a war.

Father also knew that such a war would be suicidal. He had been willing to fight with China against the French but not against the Japanese. He resigned his position at the Torpedo School and made plans to return to the United States.

Philo McGriffin came to bid us good-bye. Father urged him to leave too but Philo refused. "I've been made second in command of the new battleship *Chen Yuen,*" he explained. "Admiral Ting in command of the fleet is an honest, capable man and his staff are first-rate officers. We have good ships and crews and don't need to be afraid of the Japs."

"Remember King Solomon," said father, only half joking.

Philo laughed. "I haven't any thousand wives so I'm smarter than he was."

In September 1885 we left on a German tea steamer, the *Mossa*. We were the only passengers. The route was across the Indian Ocean, the Red Sea, Suez Canal, and the Mediterranean. As we had sailed for China from San Francisco, this meant a circumnavigation of the world, which not many people had done in those days.

We went on to Washington where Father reported to the Marine Barracks for further duty. He had several long conferences with the State Department and I believe his account of the situation in the Far East influenced our government's thinking. I do know that a short time later he was sent on a cruise to the South Pacific on the *Brooklyn*, one of the first—if not the first—such tours sent out by the United States to obtain information about this potentially important area.

I saw Philo McGriffin a few years after the Sino-Japanese War. In the war Japan had quickly annihilated the Chinese Fleet in the Battle of the Yalu River in September 1894. Within a year, Japan had captured the key cities of Wei-hai-wei and Port Arthur. China was forced to acknowledge the independence of Korea, cede Formosa and the Pescadores Island to Japan, and pay a heavy indemnity. The empress announced that Li Hung-chang was responsible for the disaster and sent him into exile. The war had an even more disastrous effect for China, for it revealed the country's weakness so vividly to the world that the European powers threw aside all restraint and moved in on the wretched land from all sides.

At the end of the war, Philo returned to this country and came to see us in Washington. He was a different person from the jolly, optimistic young man I remembered. He was shrunken, nervous, and bitter. He told us that in the battle the Japanese Fleet, composed of lighter and faster vessels, commenced circling and pouring in a paralyzing fire. In a few minutes the Chinese ships, those that were still afloat, commenced a retiring movement that was very like a flight. The captain of the *Chen Yuen* was killed so Philo took command and tried to fight it out alone.

Father said in amazement, "God, but you showed sand!" a popular term for courage.

Philo shouted at him, "Don't say SAND to me!"

He explained that his shells even when they struck the Jap ships,

did not explode. Meanwhile his ship was the target of the entire
enemy fleet. Nearly all his crew were killed, and he himself was
wounded and had both eardrums ruptured by the detonation of the
Jap shells. Finally he followed the retreating Chinese ships to Port
Arthur and later to Wei-hai-wei.

Here he had a chance to examine his unexpended ammunition. His
shells had been filled with sand instead of gunpowder.

The Chinese Fleet attempted a last stand but their position was
made hopeless by repeated destroyer attacks and the fire of their own
forts, now in enemy hands. Admiral Ting sent a message inviting him
to a dinner on the flagship.

"I sent back a message that this was no time for dinners,"
McGriffin told us. "I was going ashore and I intended to find out who
had loaded our shells with sand and kill the villain if it was my last act.
Ting sent back a flowery reply saying he understood perfectly and as I
was not Chinese there was no reason for me to attend the dinner. I
didn't see what my not being Chinese had to do with it, but later I
found out."

Wei-hai-wei fell and the boarding parties from the Jap Fleet scaled
the sides of Ting's flagship. Gaining the deck they hurried aft to the
admiral's cabin where they found the door locked. Peering through a
porthole set in the upper panel they could just make out, in the gloom
of the room, a group of men who appeared to be quietly sitting in a
circle. A blow from a boarding axe split the door from top to bottom
and they forced their way inside. There they were, the Chinese
admiral and all his captains waiting for them. The snarling order of
the Jap officer being ignored, he flashed the light of his lantern in
Admiral Ting's face; as he did so one of the silent figures slipped from
its chair to the floor. The Chinese officers had refused to survive the
destruction of their fleet; sappuku, the "happy dispatch."

McGriffin went on, "I spent some time trying to find out who had
doctored those shells. I realized some of the palace eunuchs would
know. They knew everything as they seem to be the only people the
empress trusts. Of course, they had to be bribed. You take that for
granted. Finally, one of them told me it had been done secretly by the
empress' orders. Li Hung-chang didn't know anything about it at the
time but after the Yalu, he found out the truth and dared to reproach
the empress to her face. I think this is why she had him exiled. She
told him irritably, 'Sand looks just like gunpowder and it's a lot

cheaper.' She used the money she'd saved to build a marble houseboat in a lake at the Summer Palace she was building. I think she still believes that guns are only meant to frighten the enemy by making a loud noise, like the firecrackers the Chinese used when she was young."

"What are you going to do now?" Mother asked.

"I don't know. I'm going up to New York tomorrow and perhaps something will turn up. I'm sorry I didn't commit sappuku with Admiral Ting and his staff. They must have thought I let them down."

After he left, Father said, "Some day we will have to fight Japan. I know it."

Mother objected and pointed out that Japan was on the other side of the world. Father shook his head.

"I know we'll have to fight her. Too bad we won't have China to help us but the country will be dismembered and cut up among the Europeans in a few years."

A few days later we heard that Philo had shot himself in his New York hotel room on February 11, 1897. He had gone to join his Chinese friends as an honorable man should do.

I little thought then that in a few months I would take part in what has been called "the biggest naval battle since Trafalgar" and see an engagement far larger and bloodier than the Yalu.

CHAPTER TWO

Washington and Annapolis (1885–1898)

When we first saw this here campus
Plebes we were as green as grass
Now as gay and festive bilgers
Tread we o'er the verdant pass.

—From an ancient *Lucky Bag*

HARDLY had we arrived in Washington when Father was ordered back to the Asiatic Station as Marine officer of the old *Brooklyn*. During the cruise, the *Brooklyn* visited Japan, Hawaii, Samoa, Guam, and the Philippines. I have before me a letter he wrote Mother dated March 30, 1888. Although Father was shrewd in many of his observations, he was not infallible as this letter shows.

I would really like to know why we were ordered to make this cruise if it was not to get us away from the womenfolk of Japan. We have steamed 6,000 miles without any apparent result except the loss to the government of the wear and tear to the ship and boilers which are not strong at the best and the expenditure of 8 or 10 thousand dollars for coal. The United States has not a cent's worth of interest in any of these Dutch possessions, not even a poor missionary to look up and encourage.

A few years later, most of these islands would be part of America's new empire.

After Father left, Mother and I found ourselves alone in a city that was nearly as strange to us as Taku had been. I was sent to the local public school and promptly became involved in the same sort of trouble I had been in in China. The first problem was my clothes which were cut in a different manner than the American style and made me look like a "dude." Then there was my way of speaking, intoning the words as the Chinese do. Worst of all was my "cholera band"—in those days all Europeans in the Orient wore broad flannel bands under their clothes supposed to ward off fever. I really went through hell and had to endure countless "beatings up" before I learned to conform.

Mother was worried that I would forget my Chinese which I was only too eager to do as I knew what would happen to me if my schoolmates ever suspected I was able to speak a "heathen tongue." Mother was sure America's relationship with China would grow over the years and being able to talk the language would be an important asset to me. She used to talk Chinese to me whenever she could, but I always answered in English or rather in American as the language spoken in the Washington public school was hardly the tongue of Oxford or Cambridge. When she insisted, I would reply angrily, "People will think we're Chinese." The Chinese were despised in America at that time as cheap labor, opium-smoking villains, and laundry men. In a few months I had completely forgotten my Chinese, and years later when I returned to China I couldn't remember a word of it.

When Father finally returned in 1889 he was ordered to assume command of Marine Headquarters near the Navy Yard. In those days the Marine Corps was small, less than two thousand men. The uniform was also very different from the present one. Officers and men wore Napoleonic shakos, the men with a round buttonlike affair on top and the officers with a tall plume of feathers. Even then the "Corps," small as it was, had the same esprit and clannishness that has always marked it. If someone said sneeringly to one of the old timers, "What have the Marines ever done?" the crushing reply would always be, "WHO CAPTURED JOHN BROWN?"

The commandant of the Navy Yard was Admiral Meade. He was one of the "hard-boiled" military leaders who feel that to be efficient one must be profane and generally disagreeable. I remember that one evening he was giving a dinner dance and wanted the Marine Band to play at the event. Instead of asking Father, as courtesy demanded, he went over Father's head to the Navy Department. As a result, Father received an *order* to send the Marine Band to the Navy Yard on a certain date. Father was tempted to refuse and he spoke to the band leader, John Philip Sousa.

Sousa, while he wore an officer's uniform, really had no actual rank. The men used to salute him but only through courtesy. It was his ambition to be given the rank of second lieutenant, surely a modest enough ambition. For some reason, the Navy Department constantly opposed it. The present leader of the band has the rank of captain of Marines. Meade's peremptory manner of demanding his services was an insult to Sousa as well as Father, but rather to Father's surprise, Sousa said he would be delighted to play for the admiral. In fact, he was looking forward to it.

On the date in question when festivities were at their height, there was a crash of drums and brasses that shook the house and through the door marched the entire band of a hundred pieces with Sousa at the head wearing his bearskin shako and waving his baton. The band was followed by a drum and bugle corps of eighty more pieces playing, as they used to say of Sousa in Vienna "with hands and feets." Admiral Meade couldn't make himself heard against that racket but his gestures and the apoplectic tinge of his features gave a hint to Sousa who, his dignity unimpaired, gave the signal for "counter-marching." The band turned itself inside out and marched proudly back to "Semper Fidelis." Shortly after this, Sousa resigned from the service and organized his own band. Whether his encounter with Admiral Meade had anything to do with his decision, I don't know.

That summer (1894) Washington was invaded by Coxey's Army. Coxey was an Ohio horse-dealer who led several thousand unemployed on a march to the nation's capital to demand redress. Washington was, to put it mildly, in a panic. All liberty was stopped at the barracks; the men's equipment ("light marching order") was laid out by each man's cot; ball cartridges were distributed, canteens filled and "iron rations" stowed in haversacks. I was wild with excitement expecting a big battle and so, I suspect, did Father.

When the army finally arrived, a more pitiful aggregation of footsore, dusty, weary tramps could not be imagined. They dragged themselves as far as the capitol grounds where they were promptly arrested by the police for "walking on the grass," to Father's great relief as he had no desire to order his men to fire on such wretched creatures.

I would be sixteen in September and old enough to enter the Naval Academy at Annapolis. I received my appointment from President Cleveland but I still would have to pass the entrance examinations. During the summer I attended a cramming school named Emerson Institute that specialized in getting would-be midshipmen through these exams. The exams were pretty much the same year after year so by collecting the old examination papers, our instructors could tell fairly accurately what questions would be asked. Beyond this, they had few academic qualifications. One of their main tasks was to keep the students in order for they were a tough lot.

Our English professor was named Jimmie Something-or-other. He was a retired pug and his conversation was full of "deses" and "doses," but his school spirit was tremendous. Once a little business-man who had a shop in the same building burst into our classroom during an English session and screamed, "Professor, your pupils have invaded my shop, wrecked my goods, insulted my daughter, and stolen—" With a roar like the Bull of Bashan, the Professor of English Literature bounded to his feet and bellowed, "Get out of here, you _____ _____ _____." The little man fled like a rag on the wind. Professor Jimmie turned to us and, in a dovelike coo, whispered, "Say, youse fellers didn't do dat, now did ya?"

Due at least in part to Professor Jimmie's inspiration I passed the tests and in the autumn of 1895 found myself a midshipman. From then on my parents were relieved of my presence. I very seldom saw them again. The United States Navy took over my life.

The Academy was very small then, not more than two hundred cadets organized in one battalion of four companies. Now there are double that in one class and men graduate without meeting all of their own classmates, while in my day every midshipman knew everyone in all four classes.

The hazing was strict. The plebes were required always to say "sir" to any upperclassman; when they walked upstairs they were obliged to keep very close to the wall; in the messhall they were not permitted to put their hands on the table, nor their backs against the backs of the chairs; they were not permitted to walk in "Lover's Lane" nor to sit on any of the benches in the Academy grounds; they could not attend the hops; and they were assigned certain "duties" by the upperclassmen; for example, one of my classmates was required each day at dinner to intone, "Only two hundred and ninety-seven more days" (before graduation).

However, the system, silly and sometimes cruel as it was, had its good points. NEVER did an upperclassman lay a finger on a plebe. There was none of the paddling that disgraced many universities and, I am ashamed to say, was introduced into the Academy many years later in direct violation of the Articles of War. If a plebe offended in some way he was usually punished by being required to "stand on his head." In this process he put his hands and head on the ground and then proceeded to kick his heels in the air twenty, fifty, or a hundred times depending on the nature of the offense. Nor were the plebes entirely helpless. If a plebe felt that he was being unfairly treated, he could refuse to obey. Then a man of his weight in the upper class would be selected to fight him. These fights would be carried out with all the formality of a duel with seconds, referee, and timekeeper.

Even so, it was unwise to try and "buck the system." Although hazing was illegal, the upperclasses had a certain legal control over the plebes. The cadet officers and petty officers could report a plebe for countless small offenses such as "Shoes not shined," "Late at muster," "Blouse unbuttoned," and so on. Also, rooms were regularly inspected and a cadet could be reported for "Bed not properly made," "Dust on bookshelves," "Chair adrift" (the two kitchen chairs in each room were required to be pressed against the table, one on each side; if there was one inch of clearance the chair was "adrift"). To be reported for any of these offenses meant demerits and a certain number of them meant dismissal. If a plebe got the reputation of being a troublemaker, he could be forced out of the Academy.

Of course the plebes were required to do all the heavy and unpleasant work at drill. For example, we had Artillery Drill in which the heavy 3-inch field pieces were hauled all over the grounds by means of "drag ropes" with sixteen or twenty men to each gun. The plebes were always put on the end of the drag so, while they were straining every muscle to keep the heavy guns running along, the upperclassmen behind them were frequently taking things very easy. Then, if the order was "Sections right about: in battery," the plebes had to dash at full speed around the circumference of a big circle; the upperclassmen, being near the gun, had to take only a few steps.

Being tall, I was on the end of the drag for my entire plebe year and, just as I expected to be relieved, a new drill officer came to the Academy. A humanitarian, he sympathized with the poor plebes and refused to put them on the end of the drag where they belonged. As a result my class had TWO years of it instead of only one.

That spring we witnessed the graduation of the senior class. There were just forty of them. A great deal is written and said nowadays about the "bloated military" living off the poor taxpayers. I don't know what the current figures are, but in those days the attrition rate, especially among junior officers, was high. Within five years, ten of the class we saw graduate that June were dead; one quarter of the class. Darwin Merritt was lost on the *Maine* shortly after he graduated when she was destroyed in Havana Harbor. Breckenridge was swept overboard from a destroyer during the Spanish-American War; Worth Bagley was killed on the torpedo boat *Winslow* at Cardenas, Cuba; Newt Hall as a captain of Marines fell at our legation in Pekin during the Boxer Rebellion; and Davidson was killed in a turret explosion on the battleship *Missouri*.

Although we didn't realize it we were witnessing the end of an era—the era of Sails and Spars; of Wooden Ships and Iron Men. To the old-timers in the Navy who ran things, it seemed incredible that the time would ever come when sails would be completely abandoned. Even the warships of the period still retained their masts and carried sails and spars so if the engines failed, the ships could proceed under sail as they had done since the beginning of seafaring. Each summer the cadets took a cruise on a full-rigged ship across the Atlantic to Funchal, Madeira, off the West Coast of Africa. I took two of these cruises on the *Monongahela*. Her only means of propulsion was her sails; there was no machinery of any kind on board. There was no steam or electricity to do the heavy work; it was all done by the muscles of the crew.

Besides the cadets on the *Monongahela*, there was a crew of regular seamen, a type of men now as extinct as the archers of England. The present enlisted men in the Navy are all very young, except for the chief petty officers, and are more like college boys. When I took command of my first destroyer at the advanced age of thirty-two, I was not only the "old man" figuratively (the officer in command of a ship is always referred to as the "Old Man") but I actually was the oldest man on board.

The sailing ship seamen averaged twice the age of the modern twenty-year-olders. They were much more primitive and caused more trouble ashore than do the modern crews. They were simpler minded and not nearly as well educated as the modern men. Many of them signed the payroll by making a cross, but in physique they were vastly superior.

As an example, the "captain of the maintop" was a petty officer of many years' service; he was probably forty years old and weighed at least a hundred and eighty. I have seen him go hand over hand up the main topsail sheet (a vertical rope, perhaps two inches in diameter, running from the fife rail on deck up to the main yard) and, when he was high above the deck, let go with his left hand and "chin" himself three times with his right. Mind you, he wasn't holding on to anything horizontal like a bar in a gym, but to a thin vertical rope. Think of the grip necessary!

I have always been interested in gymnastics and am a pretty fair gymnast myself. I was on the Academy gym team (if you're ever in the gymnasium at Annapolis, you will see my name on a shield hung on the wall, gym team of 1900). I enjoyed going to circuses and fairs that featured acrobats and then trying to duplicate their feats in the gym. My muscular development was something of a joke at the Academy. In our class *Lucky Bag* (the book each class puts out on graduation) one gag was about my roommate rushing out of our room and when asked what was the matter replied, "Oh, Pratt Mannix is expanding his chest and I came out to catch my breath." (A less complimentary tribute appeared under my picture and went "Pratt Mannix is a great admirer of all things Washingtonian—especially himself." I hasten to add that all members of the class received some such scathing tribute. Afterwards, we threw the *Lucky Bag* staff into the Severn River to show what we thought of them.) My other favorite form of exercise is swimming which I have been able to keep up long after my gymnastic days were over. I did feel that I was in good physical shape but compared to those seamen, I was a complete slob.

On one of our cruises to Madeira a member of the crew fell overboard in mid-ocean. He had been furling the flying jib and hit the water with a tremendous splash. The cry "Man overboard!" came from forward, the officer of the watch grabbed the speaking trumpet and shouted out the preliminary orders for heaving to, at the same time casting a life buoy over the side. On a steam vessel, if somebody falls overboard, the officer on duty, besides letting go a life buoy, has two courses of action open to him. He may either stop the engines and back full speed or else put the rudder hard over, one way or the other, and swing the ship around. Of course, the object in either case is to get the ship back to the place where the man went overboard and to reduce her speed sufficiently so a lifeboat may safely be lowered.

On a sailing ship affairs aren't so simple. In order to stop the motion of the ship through the water it is necessary to "heave to"; the braces must be manned and certain of the yards swung around until the sails attached to them are "aback." On a square-rigger the big main topsail especially is used for this purpose.

In this case, the weather topsail brace was manned by a long double line of men and hands were stationed at the lee brace to tend it as the heavy yard swung around. Meanwhile the quartermaster and signalmen searched the water directly astern of the ship to locate the man. There wasn't a sign of him. The lifeboat was manned and lowered to the water's edge and, as the topsail yard swung ponderously around, the ship's speed rapidly diminished.

The dropped life buoy could be seen bobbing up and down astern but not a sign of the lost man. Just as the watch officer was about to order the lifeboat lowered for what was evidently a hopeless search, he became aware of a queer squelching sound in his immediate vicinity. Looking down, from his vantage point on the bridge, he located the sound; it came from one of the men manning the topsail brace. The officer observed furthermore that every time this man took a step he left a puddle of water on the deck. This phenomenon required investigation so he hailed the moist one and demanded, "How did you get so wet?" The man sheepishly replied, "I fell overboard, sir."

Further questioning disclosed the amazing fact that the victim of the accident had rescued himself. Like most sailing ships the *Monongahela* had two Jacob's ladders hanging over her stern. To an eyesplice in the bottom of each ladder was attached a grab rope the end of which was only a few inches above the water. The man who fell overboard came to the surface just as the stern of the ship was passing him; he caught hold of one of the grab ropes, was towed along for a few seconds and then succeeded in climbing the swinging rope ladder to the poop.

As his head came level with the rail he realized, from the feverish activity of all hands, that a general maneuver was in progress. With commendable discipline he ran to his station, the main topsail brace, and began hauling away with the rest of his shipmates. The advisability of reporting his presence on board never entered his head, nor did he realize that he, personally, was the cause of all this commotion.

He may have been a little slow mentally but the strength and agility shown in his self-rescue, fully clothed and wearing shoes, was really extraordinary.

Compare this man with a Navy paymaster I saw lose his life during a Samoan hurricane. A wave washed him overboard and, drifting aft along the ship's side, he came against a boat secured to one of the stern pennants. He tried to hoist himself into the boat but, being fat and in bad condition, he couldn't do it and was swept out to sea and drowned.

Through hard work and considerable danger we learned our duties. In laying aloft there were two cardinal rules. (1) Always use the weather rigging, never the lee. That ensured the wind's blowing you against the rigging instead of away from it. (2) Always grip the shrouds (the up and down rigging) and never the ratlines (the horizontal "rungs" of the rope ladder you were ascending). If you put your hands on the ratlines the man ahead of you might step on them. There really should have been a third rule. Never go aloft in your bare feet. I did it once or twice and it was like walking on swords. Then, when we were out on the yard, "holding on with our stomachs" while we worked with both hands reefing sail, the man next to me, who was wearing shoes, slid down the footrope and landed on my bare feet.

One of the infernos on that ship was the gundeck capstan. In a steam vessel there is an anchor engine which does the heavy work of "breaking" the anchor out of the bottom mud and weighing it, but on the *Monongahela* this back-breaking toil was done by manpower. Long bars would be fitted in the capstan and manned. Here again the poor plebes would suffer as they would invariably be at the outer end of the bars making the widest circuit while the upperclassmen, next to the capstan would occasionally lift their feet and "ride" around. The upperdeck capstan was bad enough but the hapless souls manning the capstan on the deck below (they were on the same vertical shaft) in making the circuit were obliged to jump over the anchor chain as it came through the hawse pipe; failure to do this was penalized by a whack over the shins and it isn't the pleasantest sensation to be "whacked" by a heavy steel cable.

Those sailing ship days of so long ago made such an impression on me that even today when I see anyone waste ice or fresh water it makes me uncomfortable; I feel that there is something "wicked" about it. The ice on the *Monongahela* lasted about twenty-four hours and for the remainder of the long sea passages we had canned food. Fresh water was so precious that it was limited to "For Drinking Only" and even that was rationed and a guard put over the scuttlebut (water barrel). As for the quality of this drinking water it became so bad, especially when we were delayed by contrary winds or calms, that we were obliged to hold our noses while drinking it, the odor was so terrible.

Water for washing and brushing our teeth came up from the ocean in a bucket. That wasn't so bad as it is excellent for the teeth to brush them with salt water. The main drawback was that it made us thirsty when our drinking water was limited. When we finally got to Funchal, we all invested in "monkey jugs," jars of porous material like those found in Egyptian excavations. Filled with water and hung where there was a circulation of air these would keep their contents pleasantly cool. Like all things, however, this had its drawbacks, as the men having night watches weren't above emptying some other fellow's monkey jug instead of drinking out of their own.

During these cruises we slept in canvas hammocks. This was very difficult for a newcomer, as they were hung about the level of a man's shoulders and if you took hold of the hammock itself in an attempt to climb in, it would promptly capsize and deposit you on the deck with the mattress and pillow on top of you. The only way to get on board one of those hammocks was to grip the deck beams overhead, lift yourself carefully, deposit yourself still more carefully in the hammock and then let go of the beams hoping for the best.

There was a vicious form of practical joking, not very common, fortunately. It consisted in waiting until a man was asleep and then cutting his hammock lashing. If the foot lashing was cut it wasn't so bad as you, the mattress, and the pillow would slide down to the deck feet first, but if the head lashing was cut, you landed on your head.

During the night, at four-hour intervals, the boatswains mate would pace up and down the deck intoning, "All the starboard watch, turn out now, starboard watch." The next time it would be the port watch, as we stood "Watch and watch" (four hours on, four hours off) while at sea. There used to be a story illustrating the slow Navy promotion of those days. The midshipman of the watch shakes the hammock of his relief and says, "Turn out, Father, it's your watch." His relief turns over and replies, "No, it isn't. It's your grandfather's."

At Reveille the call would be, "All hands, turn out! Lash and carry!" We would slip out of our hammocks frequently landing in a foot of cold seawater (the decks were scrubbed in the morning watch), lash our hammocks and carry them up to the spar deck where they were inspected before being stowed in the hammock nettings. If the lashing had not been properly done we had to do it all over again, seven turns of the hammock lashing, clews neatly turned in, etc. Our instructor in this was a fine old boatswains mate named O'Connor.* On a February night three years later he died with two hundred and sixty of his shipmates in Havana Harbor. He was on the *Maine*.

We got so we could perform our drills literally in our sleep. One night Juggy Nelson was the officer of the watch and as the wind was fair and all going well, he decided to get some sleep. An hour or so later our captain came on deck and, observing storm clouds to windward and being unable to locate the officer on duty, seized the speak-

*Enlisted men and noncommissioned officers were referred to by last names.

ing trumpet and shouted, "Topgallant and royal clewlines!" From the depths of the hammock nettings came a voice giving the correct following order, "Flying jib downhaul!" The captain walked over to the nettings and there lay Juggy, still fast asleep. I forget now what punishment he got, but it was enough to keep him awake for a long, long time.

About the only thing I remember of Funchal were the boys who used to come out to the ship and dive for money ("Heave I dive; ten cents I pass the ship,") and the snowless coasting ashore. The streets were very steep and were paved with small stones that were slippery as ice. We would proceed to the high land behind the city and then coast back in heavy sledges. They would dash through the narrow streets and around sharp corners at tremendous speed barely missing the children and dogs who always occupied the middle of the road, the coxswains of the sleds howling warnings like steam whistles in a fog.

There was a big cathedral on the heights back of the city. The day we visited it a group of very pretty Portuguese girls were kneeling in the middle of the vast floor vigorously saying their prayers at the rate of about a hundred and twenty words a minute. As we entered they all looked over their shoulders at us and as we walked around pretending to admire the murals, they followed us with their eyes meanwhile praying as energetically as ever.

I suppose I must be one of the few men alive who can remember what life was like in the American Navy of sailing ships. All those fine old ships have sailed away into the Land of Dreams, mounting the swells like great birds. No smoke, no vibration, no noise except the occasional slatting of a reef point against its sail. They vanished as did one of their number attacked in World War I by that epitome of the modern, a submarine. Her captain reported, "The torpedo struck her forward and she started going down by the head. She disappeared slowly, gracefully, like the lady she was."

When I became a second classman (equivalent to a junior in college) the battleship *Maine* blew up in Havana Harbor on the night of February 15, 1898. People are still disputing whether her magazine exploded by accident or whether the Spaniards with whom our government was at loggerheads over their treatment of the Cubans, deliberately blew her up. My guess is that the Spaniards had Havana Harbor mined and the *Maine* by accident anchored over one of those mines. Some red-hot young Spaniard couldn't resist the temptation and pressed a button that set off the mine. When the news of that disaster reached Annapolis there was wild excitement. For three months we were kept in a constant state of anticipation which culminated when war was declared between the United States and Spain on April 25th. The first or senior class was ordered to sea and the other three classes granted four months' leave of absence to visit their homes.

After three years in the Navy, I couldn't see myself spending the war at home, especially as boys no older than I (I was nineteen) were enlisting. The empire, established by Pizarro and Cortez that had endured through three hundred years of aggression and strife, had at last been challenged. I sent an urgently worded official application for orders to any ship in the Navy and waited breathlessly for nearly a month for a reply. At last it came. I still have it framed on my wall. Here it is:

> Navy Department
> Washington, May 26, 1898

Sir: You are hereby detached from the United States Naval Academy, Annapolis, Md., will proceed, immediately, to Key West, Fla., or to such other port as the USS *Indiana* may be, and report to the Senior Officer present for duty on board that vessel temporarily.

You will regard yourself detached from duty on board the USS *Indiana* at such time as the Commander in Chief may designate, in order that you may return to Annapolis by September 30th next, and you will so return and report to the Superintendent of the Naval Academy not later than the date specified.

Report to the Commandant at Key West for the necessary transportation beyond that port.

> Respectfully
> John D. Long, Secretary
> USS *Indiana*
> Off Key West, June 2nd.

I packed my sea chest and bought a ticket for Tampa. I was off to my first war.

CHAPTER THREE

The Spanish-
American War
(1898)

Hello Dolly, we won't leave you
Something tells us not to go
Something tells us we're not needed
As a target for the Foe.

—Weber-Fields version of "Dolly Gray"

MY EXPERIENCES in the Spanish-American War are largely copied from the diary that I kept at the time and portions are reproduced here. Later observations are in brackets.

TAMPA. JUNE 4, 1898

Here I am at last in Tampa, en route to Key West. It was a terrible trip by train. We stopped every mile so the conductor could chop wood to keep the engine going. I am staying at the Arno Hotel where the accommodations are good. The Tampa Bay Hotel is said to be one of the best in the South but it costs $5 a day; too much for a midshipman.

Tampa is filled with soldiers going around in their shirt sleeves, with sidearms on, and they are a tough-looking crowd; all last night I was kept awake by shouts and howls, while rifles and pistols were going off all over the place. This place is like a Western mining camp in the days of Jesse James. There are also some of the famous Rough Riders wandering around brandishing loaded revolvers. As the Duke of Wellington said about some newly arrived troops, "I don't know what effect they will have on the enemy but by God they frighten me." The streets here are about three feet deep in sand and every vacant lot is crowded with tents, mostly "pup tents." The camp is supposedly under the command of General William Shafter but there seems to be no discipline whatsoever. I caught a glimpse of the general. He is an enormous man and must weigh over 300 pounds. I can't imagine him leading troops in the tropical jungles of Cuba.

I took a train to Port Tampa, where I could get a boat to Key West. There were about five hundred men of the Naval Reserves on the boat, and at our table were three of their officers; they sat up like plebes with their hands in their laps and didn't say a word during the entire trip. I never saw commissioned officers behave like that.

At Key West, I reported to the naval commandant, Commodore

39

Reamy,* and had my orders endorsed but was unable to get to the *Indiana* which, being a battleship, is a long way from shore. There are over a hundred vessels in the harbor, many of them prizes we had captured from the Spaniards.

The next morning, I ran into Thomas who had been a first classman at the Academy when I was a plebe. He told me that the *Indiana*'s launch was at a certain dock so I had my chest taken down there and embarked.

She is a fine ship and I know lots of the people on her. Captain Taylor is splendid; when I reported he shook hands and said he was glad to see me and was very sorry that the junior officer's mess was so crowded, but that we must expect to rough it in war times and that he would do all he possibly could. After being "cussed out" at the Academy it is a pleasant change to be treated like a human being.

We dress anyway we want to; quite a change from Annapolis. The steerage is awfully crowded; there are twenty junior officers quartered here. Some have bunks, some swing in hammocks, some sleep on the transoms and two are on the table. I have been assigned to the navigator's division.

FRIDAY

We have General Quarters twice a day and all hands run up on deck to their stations wearing sidearms. My station is on the bridge to look out for signals; all the navigator's division will be very busy as soon as we get to sea. Went down in the dynamo room today where the temperature is 150; the thermometer was so hot it couldn't be handled. Wonder what it will be like when we have steam up. The *Yosemite* came in this evening and signalled us; there is a rumor that we are to sail on Sunday but no one knows anything definite.

OFF KEY WEST. JUNE 6TH

We expect to get out of here tomorrow and all hands are coaling; in consequence of which we are all completely exhausted. The crews of the secondary battery sleep at their guns which have ammunition ready by them. All the officers carry revolvers and the sentries' rifles are loaded. Why all these precautions are necessary when we are in a home port, I can't imagine. We will all be glad when this monotony is

---

*Officers of higher rank than the author were referred to by their rank.

changed; there is no shore liberty and it gets tiresome. The divers finished scraping the ship's bottom yesterday and as the captain went ashore this morning, we hope to receive orders to sail.

I do most of my work in the chart house which is on the forward bridge. It is made of wood and is covered with a rope net so that if struck by a shell the splinters will not scatter. My station in action will be in the conning tower with the navigator. My billet is to stand by the voice pipe while McDowell in the top with the range finder passes down the range to me and I set it on the range indicator, which is connected with every gun in the ship, and also pass it to the central station so it can be verified verbally.

We have a great advantage over the men stationed in the gun turrets, for if anything interesting happens we will be able to see it, while they won't know anything about it until it is all over.

OFF KEY WEST. JUNE 13TH

We leave for Rebecca Shoal tomorrow at 5. The army transports will meet us there and we will convoy them to Santiago de Cuba, on the southern part of the island. They are to be landed there and will capture the city. We have heard that the Spanish Fleet under Admiral Cervera is in Santiago Bay and may attempt to prevent the troops from landing. If so, we may have a crack at them.

It is very pleasant on the bridges but in the steerage it is frightful. When we wake in the mornings the sheets are dripping wet with perspiration and, as the water has a temperature of 100, there is no relief in taking a bath. We have a sort of progressive euchre arrangement—no man sleeps in the same place two successive nights; the best place is on the dining room table and the worst is on two trunks. I prefer to swing in a hammock, as the roaches crawl over anything stationary.

AT SEA. JUNE 16TH

We are convoying the American Army of Invasion. There are nearly fifty vessels in the fleet and they extend for miles. Every evening we stop for several hours to let those in the rear close their assigned stations and as they are merchantmen we have no control over them. Whether it is fear of collision or merely a desire to drive us crazy it is hard to tell but they should be under Navy command. They are absolutely independent.

These transports are of all ages and every known type of architecture. One old paddle-wheel ferryboat loaded with mules is waddling along like a duck about a mile to port of her proper position. The *Bancroft* and *Helena* are doing their best to nose her back into the column but she ignores them completely.

The days are hot but the evenings are delightful. The *Indiana* is Chief of Convoy so we occupy the van. This morning a torpedo boat arrived from Key West and signalled, "We have mail for the fleet" so we have something to look forward to.

JUNE 18TH

Still at sea. The weather today was very threatening with heavy rain squalls. A number of water spouts were seen from time to time and one large spout was sighted dead ahead. As its presence would have been a danger to the transports, the crew of No. 1 8-inch turret were sent to their guns and a shot fired which hit the spout squarely amidships, demolishing it completely, to the great relief of the soldiers.

Everyone is indignant; there is a lot of mail on the *Dupont* torpedo boat and they won't let us have a bit of it until we get to Santiago and deliver Admiral Sampson's mail first. Admiral William T. Sampson is in command of the squadron guarding the entrance to the harbor. It is official courtesy to give him his letters first so we will run for six days with mail in sight and not get any of it.

We were obliged to go out of our course to get fresh water for the cavalry's horses, but will probably arrive at Santiago day after tomorrow.

JUNE 21ST

We are about ten miles from Santiago and tomorrow the troops will be landed under the guns of the fleet. The entrance to the bay of Santiago is said to be a narrow gut, guarded on the west side by a mortar battery on Socapa Hill and on the east by an enormous fortress called Morro Castle, hundreds of years old, 230 feet high, and built of massive stones. The army is to attack these strong points at dawn while we give them covering fire. After they are taken, the fleet will run the gut and engage Admiral Cervera's squadron in the bay. It should be quite a battle.

One of the transports has just passed within fifty yards of us with her decks and rigging crowded with soldiers. They gave us a tremendous cheer and we replied with all the volume we could muster and shouted, "Who are you?" They answered, "The Ninth Infantry." Someone beside me remarked, "There will be a lot of vacant mess numbers on that by tomorrow night. They're the ones who are to lead the attack on Morro."

(It was this same Ninth Infantry that two years later fought in the Boxer Campaign in China, their commanding officer, Colonel Liscum, being killed at Tientsin. Later still they took part in the Samar Campaign in the Philippines where one of their companies, Company C commanded by Captain Connell stationed at Balanhiga, while at mess, was suddenly attacked by bolomen who had crept through the jungle like red Indians. The Americans were slashed to death, dying to the last man.)

JUNE 22ND–24TH

All plans have been changed as it was decided that the forts were too formidable to be taken by direct assault. Instead, the troops are to be landed at a little village named Daiquiri 18 miles east of Santiago. We are to give them covering fire in case the Spaniards oppose the landings. As it is reported to be an open roadstead with heavy surf, they will have to be ferried ashore by our steam cutters and pulling boats.

All hands were called this morning at four o'clock. We put on clean uniforms, had coffee, and went to our battle stations. At six we sighted the beach and cleared for action. There was a big fire ashore and in a short time it was easy to make out that the Spaniards had set fire to the village where the army was to land.

As soon as we saw there was to be no opposition to the landing, we kept on to Santiago to join with Admiral Sampson's fleet blockading the entrance to the harbor where the Spanish Fleet is at anchor, leaving behind our boats with their crews to put the Army ashore. Soon we sighted the fleet spread out before the long, narrow, winding channel that leads to the landlocked bay. In places this channel is less than 200 yards wide and the Spanish guns on the rocky escarpments on either side of the entrance completely control the narrow passageway. Morro is huge and seems to be carved out of the solid rock of the hill. Ahead of us we could see the *Iowa*, the *Oregon* (which had just made a famous voyage of 11,000 miles from a drydock in

Bremeaton, Washington State, around the Horn to be in on the fighting), the *Massachusetts*, the *New York* and the *Brooklyn* and a lot of smaller vessels.

There is fighting going on all around. Away off inshore the *Texas* is engaged with the Socapa battery; it looks just like a painting. First the battery would fire and we would hold our breath until we saw the projectile strike the water near the ship, and then the *Texas* would let drive and stones, bricks and sand would go flying up in the air from the fort.

We got orders to engage and went to quarters. There were three of us in the conning tower; the navigator, a quartermaster at the wheel and myself. We headed straight for the entrance and the captain gave the order "Fire to the right of Morro" but on the voice pipe it was given as "Fire right at Morro." We fired several rounds before the Spaniards replied. Their first shell went directly over us and only a little high. It is all nonsense about their not being able to shoot; every shot they fired came within a very short distance of us. Any ship that tried to run the channel between the forts would have been instantly sunk.

I had a fine view until the smoke covered everything for in those days we were using brown powder; not the modern smokeless powder. We would hear a whizzing in the air that sounded like a giant bumble bee and then a great column of steam and water would suddenly appear a short distance away. A few minutes after we commenced firing there was a tremendous shock, as if a locomotive had run into the ship; a shell had struck our armor belt just below the port sheet anchor.

The shock threw me against the sharp edge of a projecting steel shelf and I received a violent blow on the right leg between the hip and the knee. It didn't hurt at first; the leg felt numb as though it was "asleep." So many things were happening that I had no time to think of it. [It didn't even hurt for several days, but about four days later I woke with the most excruciating pain in the sciatic nerve of my right leg. That pain bothered me for the next twenty years, not constantly by any means, sometimes it would go away and remain absent for weeks at a time but it always came back again, sometimes light, sometimes severe. Then, finally, it seemed to wear itself out, as physical ills occasionally do but even now, when the weather is bad, it hurts a little.]

Whenever we fired our own 8-inch guns forward of the beam it seemed as though we had been hit by the enemy; the muzzles of these guns are close to the eye slits in the conning tower and the concussions were simply terrific. Clouds of smoke, dust, and solid matter would come surging in filling our eyes, and our eardrums ached so I felt sure they would be broken in spite of the cotton we were using to protect them.

The ship did some splendid shooting, one 13-inch shell going right into a gun embrasure on Morro and knocking down a whole lower wall. It was impossible to see this from the conning tower but the people on the bridge reported it.

After the bugle sounded the Retreat I went down to the steerage to get a drink of water. McDowell was sitting there with his trouser leg rolled up and a big red spot on one side of his calf and a corresponding one on the other side where the bullet had gone out. I couldn't understand how he could have been hit by a revolver at a range of several thousand yards. Then he volunteered the information that he had been so absorbed in measuring ranges from the top that he had dropped his own revolver and shot himself through the leg.

We exchanged signals with the other ships and learned that the *Texas* was struck and had one man killed and five wounded. There is fighting still going on all around and there is no telling when we will be sent to quarters again. They fight all day here, the object being to exhaust the Spaniards. We watched a party of Spanish soldiers trying to destroy a railroad bridge that led to Santiago, obviously fearing our land forces would capture it and use it to invade the city, but the *Vesuvius*, a dynamite cruiser, ran in and chased them away.

We are all very tired, sleepy and dirty; our clothes are covered with a white coating of saltpeter. This powder leaves a residue that settles on everything in sight.

Many of the officers did not get up the next morning until the bugle sounded General Quarters and had to pull on their uniforms over their night clothes, dressing on the run to their battle stations. As the day wore on and it began to get hot, we started stripping and all the clothes I had on when "Cease firing" sounded were a dirty undershirt and a pair of trousers. The men had on absolutely nothing but duck trousers. The heat in the gun positions was awful. I was sent to the forward turret with a message in the midst of the action and found the officer in command wearing a nightshirt with beautiful ruffles all down the front and with a revolver strapped around his waist, pointing and firing the right 13-inch gun.

The insurgents are having a fight with the Spanish troops ashore now and it looks awfully pretty to see the puffs of smoke in bushes; it sounds just like a wood fire crackling.

The Socapa, the Spanish mortar battery, has started firing at us as we are in range. The shells sound exactly like miniature steam engines coming through the air; "Choo-choo-choo-choo" and then a tremendous BANG when they explode.

JUNE 25TH

The troops have all been landed at Daiquiri and we can see their camp fires at night. Falconer, who was in charge of our steam cutter and our two whaleboats that helped to get them ashore, returned this morning. He said the enemy made no resistance. He also told us that several soldiers were drowned in the landings; they went overboard with their knapsacks on and their belts filled with ball cartridges and sank like a shot. "They didn't even have brains enough to let go their rifles," Falconer reported in astonishment. Probably a lot of these men came from inland towns and had never seen a body of water larger than a horse trough. There was a heavy swell running and great difficulty was experienced in getting the soldiers off the transports as, instead of waiting for the boats alongside to rise on the top of the roll, they climbed down the sea ladders and threw themselves in regardless of where the boats were, landing sprawling, rifle and all, usually on the head of one of the boat's crew.

A regimental commander, in getting in his boat, put his foot on her gunwale as she was coming up with the swell; his knee got caught under one of the rungs of the sea ladder and, as something had to give, his leg was broken between the ankle and the knee and he is out of the campaign at its very beginning. Imagine how he must feel!

[At the time I felt very contemptuous of these "stupid soldiers" but now I greatly regret my smugness. At any rate, they WENT! During the First World War there were thousands of slackers who did everything possible to avoid serving their country. They were the people to be regarded with contempt.]

There being no barges to transport the horses and mules, they were thrown overboard, the idea being that they would instinctively swim ashore. Instead, they headed out to sea. A cavalry trumpeter ran down to the beach sounding the Assembly; all the horses swung around as if on drill and headed for the sound of the trumpet. The mules kept on and nearly all drowned.

On June 3rd, two weeks before we arrived, an attempt was made to block the entrance of Santiago Harbor by sinking an old collier named the *Merrimac* crossway in the passage. The hurricane season is coming on and Admiral Sampson was afraid the fleet could not keep station and Cervera would slip out and escape. The dangerous job of sinking the collier was given to a young naval constructor, Richmond Hobson, and a volunteer crew of seven men. The attempt was made at night but the forts saw the *Merrimac* enter the gut and opened fire on her. They shot away her tiller-ropes so she became unmanageable and drifted into the bay before she went down. Her funnel and masts protrude above the water and we can see them but obviously Hobson hadn't been able to swing her sideways so as to block the passage. He and his crew were captured and are being held as prisoners of war. This morning Admiral Sampson sent in a dispatch boat to Morro, flying a tablecloth as a flag of truce, and offered to exchange for Hobson and his men but the offer was refused. The admiral was furious and sent another message that the ships would fire over the forts and into the city of Santiago itself and warned that women and children had better leave the city.

OFF SANTIAGO. JUNE 28TH

The Army has advanced to within three miles of the city, so we will soon have some work to do. From the Squadron Bulletins, published on the flagship every day, we hear of a cavalry fight in which twenty-two were killed and eighty wounded. Hamilton Fish was among the killed. He was a sergeant and grandson of the Hamilton Fish who had been Secretary of State under Grant. His death has made quite a stir.

All sorts of rumors are running around the fleet concerning the fighting ashore. One story is that the "gallant Seventy-first New York" refused to advance under fire. They are a volunteer regiment, not regulars, and had had no training or discipline. As they were blocking the way, they were ordered to lie down and an all-Negro regiment composed of regulars was brought up and charged over their prone bodies.

Another story we heard is that an observation balloon was sent up directly over a body of our troops; the Spaniards opened fire on it and their "lows" created so many casualties among our men that they commenced firing at the balloon too and got it back to earth again as quickly as possible.

We went to General Quarters last night at midnight and remained at our battle stations until two o'clock this morning. Our duty was to run within a mile of Morro and kept our searchlights on the entrance. One ship has to do this every night to make sure the Spanish Fleet does not slip away under cover of darkness and escape. The steam launches are stationed inshore of the vessel on searchlight duty to act as pickets. They are armed with 1-pounder boat guns and have rocket signals ready to fire if they see anything. Their duty is to keep close to the beach, outside of the searchlight beam and make sure that no destroyer can slip out and torpedo the illuminating ship.

Great excitement was caused last night by one of the auxiliaries firing a whole batch of rockets and blazing away with all her guns; every ship in the fleet went to quarters and closed in. The cause of the disturbance reported that she had distinctly seen a strange destroyer speeding along close to the shore. What she did see was a train running along the bank. The commander of our picket launch got so excited that he dropped his 1-pounder gun overboard; it's just as well, for him at least, that the Spaniards were obliged to confine their maneuvers to the railroad tracks.

The dynamite cruiser *Vesuvius* has worked out a great system. Every night, between darkness and dawn, she fires three dynamite shells—no more, no less—into the forts. They may be fired at short time intervals or hours apart. The result being that after one aerial earthquake has landed in their midst, it is only natural for the enemy's garrison to speculate as to the exact time of the landing of the succeeding ones and such speculation is certainly not conducive to restful sleep.

It is a very uncanny performance as the projectiles are not fired from a gun but from a pneumatic tube. There is no loud noise at discharge, only a prolonged whine taken up by the whiz of the body as it goes through the air, then a period of absolute silence followed by a tremendous detonation in the far distance, as if a powder magazine had exploded in the enemy's works.

The Spaniards managed to blow up that railroad bridge last night which caused considerable scurrying among the smaller craft but this time the damage was done before they could get in close enough to drive away the soldiers.

It is the general opinion that the enemy has to be careful of their ammunition as a number of our converted yachts have run very close inshore without having been fired upon, while it would be dangerous for a jackrabbit on the beach to show itself to one of our picket boats.

This evening there occurred an event which has not been given its proper place in history. The hero of this exploit was the redoubtable Juggy Nelson. Personally, I think it surpasses Hobson's feat with the *Merrimac.*

Juggy was serving on the *New Orleans* and was given picket duty on the ship's launch. As it was a hot night, he and the fireman of the launch stripped themselves and went swimming. Not content with that, they swam ashore and started walking along the beach. Their white bodies shining in the moonlight attracted the attention of the Spaniards who, although they had grown reconciled to seeing our pickets close inshore, obviously considered this as going too far. They rushed to the attack from all directions, firing their rifles and even throwing a barrage of stones, bottles, and every other missile they could find. Juggy and the fireman fled down the beach stark naked with the Spanish Army in hot pursuit. As the enemy began to gain on them, they plunged into the surf, followed by rifle bullets, brickbats, and curses in choice Castilian. When Juggy got back to his ship, his captain, who had no sense of humor, put him under suspension for ten days.

[The captain's name was William Folger and the incident made an impression on him, as it would on most people. Many years later I was serving under him on the *Kearsarge* and we were cruising along this same coast passing Morro. I was officer of the deck and Captain Folger was on the bridge. Suddenly he gave a loud exclamation and I naturally sprang forward to see what the matter was. Captain Folger pointed toward the coast and announced, "That's where that damned fool Juggy Nelson swam ashore and had half the Spanish army firing at him."]

JULY 1ST

We have just received notice that our class from Annapolis has had its first battle casualty. William Boardman has been killed at Cape San Juan Light House where he had landed with a party "for the defense of women and children." There is now a tablet to his memory in Memorial Hall at the Naval Academy. He was our first casualty but by no means our last.

This is a Friday and we have been ordered to Guantanamo Bay to coal. Guantanamo lies some forty-five miles to the east of Santiago and was occupied by our forces some weeks ago. Every few days one or more of our ships go there to replenish their bunkers.

We were still coaling at noon when we heard that a combined land and sea attack on Santiago had begun. Of course, we were wild as we had orders not to return until our bunkers were full and the engagement might be over by then. The news of the attack was spread among the men and a feverish activity ran through the ship. Despite the tropical heat they worked until they dropped from exhaustion and then, before they could be sent to sick bay, staggered to their feet and started loading again.

We swung the last bag of coal on board at midnight. The anchor, previously hove in to a short stay, was weighed and we started for Santiago with the coaling booms still rigged, masses of coal still cluttering up the decks, and everyone black as a sweep.

At four o'clock we rejoined the fleet and found to our delight that the action hadn't started as yet. At daylight, we cleared for action and the whole fleet advanced on the Morro. The bombardment, which lasted nearly four hours, exceeded in violence anything I had hitherto seen. One of our shells knocked over the Spanish flag but some brave man instantly ran out and hoisted it again on the stump of the mast. Our ship was not hit although shells from the Morro and Socapa batteries fell all around us.

Again I noticed, as I had in all previous bombardments, the extraordinary spectacle produced by the Spanish shells striking near the ship. An enormous geyser of smoke, steam, and water would rise to an incredible height and then STAY there for an incredible length of time, suspended between sea and sky. We were too busy to watch these geysers but when, in a calm moment, we looked aft, there they would still be, their number being continually augmented by new arrivals.

Our range transmitters were put out of commission by the concussion of our own guns and we went back to the days of 1812 and used the ships' boys to carry messages. I especially remember one little fellow, the liveliest of the lot, who hadn't had a chance to wash his face since coaling the ship the day before. He was having a wonderful time and that black face, with its grinning white teeth and hair standing on end, which kept appearing in the conning tower entrance, made me think of the blackamoor in Punch and Judy.

JULY 3RD

The next morning, July third, was, in the words of historian Frank Freidel, to be "one of the most momentous days in American history." It was the first Sunday of the month and in accordance with Navy custom, we expected to have Captain's Inspection followed by Divine Service and the reading of the Articles of War. These Articles consist mainly of intimations of the unpleasant things that would happen to anyone who "treacherously yields or pusillanimously cries for Quarter" or who "while on shore plunders or abuses the inhabitants" or who "sends or accepts a challenge to fight a duel or acts as second in a duel." I would never have believed it, but a few years later I was to get into trouble over that one myself while in Imperial Germany.

In anticipation of the inspection everyone had on his cleanest white uniform. It was one of those dazzling mornings so common in the tropics; not a cloud in the sky, the atmosphere clear as gin, visibility absolutely perfect.

About 8:45, the *New York*, Admiral Sampson's flagship, ran up the signal "Disregard motions of commander in chief" and started down the coast toward Siboney, about eight miles away. We guessed that the admiral was going to a conference with General Shafter about how best to invest Santiago. Although the army had taken San Juan Hill and controlled the land approaches to the city, Santiago was well fortified and a direct assault would be very costly in men and material. We had heard scuttlebutt (rumors) that General Shafter was insisting that the fleet run the narrow gut leading into the bay, sink Cervera's fleet where it lay at anchor, and then shell the city, forcing it to surrender. But as long as the gut was protected by the Morro and Socapa batteries, and the gut itself was sown with dynamite mines that could be exploded from shore by the touch of a button, this was impossible, as we hoped the admiral would explain to General Shafter.

Admiral Sampson's withdrawal left Commodore Winfeld S. Schley senior officer present and in command of the fleet. Admiral Sampson had been junior to Commodore Schley until recently when for some reason involving Washington politics, he had been promoted over Schley's head. Commodore Schley had originally been in command of the fleet at Santiago until Sampson had been sent out to supplant him, so Schley had not only lost his command but was in the humiliating position of being commanded by a former junior. [This was the origin of what was later to be the famous Sampson-Schley controversy which the newspapers seemed to regard as more important than the battle itself.]

Our captain started his inspection beginning with the quarter-deck. As midshipman of the navigator's division I was on the signal bridge with a clear range of vision covering the entire horizon; we were about two miles to the south and a little to the east of Morro Castle, which seemed much closer owing to the marvelous brightness of the day.

Just as the officer commanding the quarterdeck division ordered his men to open ranks and the front rank to face about, preparatory to inspection, we heard a light caliber gun fired and saw the smoke of the discharge mounting from the *Iowa*'s superstructure. There was a second or two of dead silence; we thought, if we thought anything, that the discharge had been accidental. Then Captain Taylor, turning to the bugler at his elbow, said quietly, "Sound General Quarters."

At the first notes of the bugle the sleepy Sunday morning spell was broken, the ranks dissolved and a mad rush began for hatches, turret openings, and casemate doors, each man struggling to be the first through, regardless of his clean Sunday clothes. As they ran they threw off their neckerchiefs, jumpers, and undershirts, arriving at the gun stations stripped to the waist.

I looked at Morro and for the first time saw Cervera's squadron. The *Maria Teresa*, his flagship, was already clear of the entrance. The brilliant sun shone full on her, she had been newly painted, black smoke poured from her funnels and she was rushing forward with a "bone in her teeth," (a white bow wave). At her masthead was the red-and-gold banner of Spain and, as she swung westward, she fired every gun that could bear. We could see the flickering light of their discharge against the shiny black of her side. Then, as her shells passed screaming overhead or, dropping short, raised great geysers between us and her, we heard the sound of her guns.

Behind her came three other armored cruisers: the *Oquendo*, the *Vizcaya* and the *Cristobal Colon*. As they passed through the narrow entrance between Morro and Socapa they seemed tremendous. In the lee of the *Colon* came the destroyers *Pluton* and *Furor*. They did not follow the cruisers down the coast but came straight for us.

[As we later discovered, the Spanish government had ordered Cervera to come out against his better judgment. The government knew that the fall of Santiago could not be long delayed and then the squadron would be trapped in the bay and forced tamely to surrender. For purposes of national prestige they insisted that the squadron go down fighting.]

By this time we were under forced draft and headed for the entrance. To port of us was the *Iowa* and to starboard the converted yacht *Gloucester*. This yacht was commanded by Lieutenant Commander Richard Wainwright who had been executive officer of the *Maine* when she was destroyed in Havana Harbor. [The Wainwrights have always been fighting men. Commander Wainwright's father, also a naval officer, was killed at Galveston during the Civil War while in command of the *Harriet Lane*, and the General Wainwright who fought so gallantly against the Japanese at Bataan is Richard Wainwright's nephew.]

As the destroyers advanced against us the fire of our secondary battery and the starboard 8-inch turret guns was shifted from the cruisers to them and at the same time we sent a signal to the *Gloucester*, "Destroyers coming out." This signal was misunderstood (perhaps purposely). [The *Gloucester* claimed later that she thought our signal was "Gunboats close in."] She headed for the Spaniards at full speed running directly into our zone of fire and, before "Cease firing" could be transmitted to the secondary battery, we barely missed sinking her. Just before the order was obeyed one of our 8-inch shells struck the Spanish destroyer *Pluton*, and she disappeared in a great cloud of flame and smoke which, as it dissipated, showed a few of her people struggling in the water.

Meanwhile the *Gloucester* engaged the *Furor* at point-blank range; they were almost alongside of each other. We could see the *Gloucester*'s guns tearing her to shreds. Then something happened to the *Furor*'s steering gear and she commenced running around in circles eventually crashing on the rocks.

From my station on the bridge I could look aft down the entire length of our ship. The broadside guns of the secondary battery were mounted along the superstructure rail high above the deck, so high that the crew manning them stood on swinging gratings at least eight feet above the deck level. They had no protection whatever, not even gun shields, and a fall from that height would have been serious under any circumstances. The men were stripped to the waist and the tremendous exertion which they were putting forth emphasized the splendid muscular development of their arms and chest. They made me think of gladiators in a Roman arena.

All this time the 13-inch guns in our forward turret were firing at the cruisers. The leading ship, Cervera's flagship, was clear of the entrance and headed west before we could bring our speed up to maximum but the two following ships, the *Oquendo* and the *Vizcaya*, received the full volume of our fire and that of the *Iowa*. We could clearly see every movement they made; we were so close to them that we could see their crews running around the decks, replacing casualties at the guns and trying to put out fires.

Because we had no smokeless powder in those days, after a few salvos everything and everybody were in the midst of a dense cloud of thick white smoke. It frequently became necessary to sound "Cease firing" to permit the gun pointers to see their targets.

This certainly didn't add to efficiency in gunnery but it did add tremendously to the spectacle. At one stage of the battle we saw what seemed to be a great cloud of smoke traveling at high speed on the surface of the water. The advanced part of the cloud became disturbed and we could see the white foam of a bow wave. Then out of the smoke, breasting the wave, came the bows of a great ship, the *Oregon*, starting the famous race in which she, a battleship, actually ran down a fast cruiser, the *Cristobal Colon*.

The first Spanish ship to give up was their flagship the *Maria Teresa*. There was a tremendous burst of fire from all our ships to which she gallantly responded and then a great wave of flames appeared in her bow rapidly spreading aft as it was fanned by her own speed. Our men cheered wildly as she put her helm hard-a-port, headed for the shore and grounded, her engines still running full speed.

About this time we passed several torpedos floating vertically in the water, their propellers clear of the surface, the only time I have ever seen a torpedo do this. They must have been fired by the Spanish destroyers before they themselves were destroyed.

Meanwhile the *Vizcaya* and the *Colon* had drawn ahead and were being engaged by the *Brooklyn, Texas,* and *Oregon.* We concentrated

On left: Capt. Daniel P. Mannix, Jr., USMC, Rear Admiral Mannix's father. Photo taken when he was founding the China Torpedo School in 1880.

On right: Admiral Pratt, under whom Daniel Patrick Mannix served during the Civil War and whose middle name he later adopted.

Four generations of Mannix swords. From left to right: Rear Admiral Daniel Pratt Mannix 3rd's sword, First World War; Capt. Daniel Pratt Mannix Jr.'s USMC sword worn at Lincoln's funeral, when he was in command of the honor guard; Rear Admiral Daniel Pratt Mannix 3rd's sword worn when he was a midshipman, during the Spanish-American War; Marine Capt. Daniel Pratt Mannix Jr.'s sword worn at the court of the Empress Dowager in China; Col. John Armstrong Wright's (maternal grandfather's) sword worn during the Civil War; Lt. Daniel Pratt Mannix 4th's sword worn during World War II.

Rear.Admiral Mannix's medals. They include: Sampson Medal with 4 clasps (Spanish-American War); Spanish Campaign Medal; Cuban Pacification Medal; West Indies Campaign; Mexican Service Medal; Victory Medal with mine-laying clasp; Mine-laying Medal; Distinguished Service Medal.

Lt. Hung Chang. Painting presented to Capt. Daniel P. Mannix, USMC.

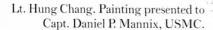

Admiral Ting's card. Admiral Ting commanded the Chinese Navy at the Battle of the Yalu.

Earliest known picture of Mannix, taken at the Emerson "cramming" school in Washington. He is in the second row, second from left, seated.

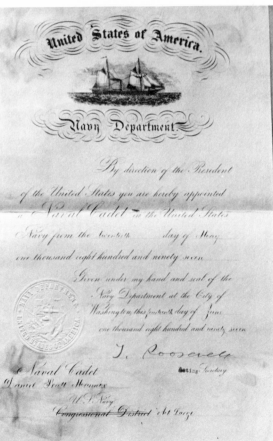

His appointment as a Naval Cadet, signed by Theodore Roosevelt.

Construction Corps.

R. O'Donnell

Mannix, Daniel Pratt. "Armstrong Hobson." *Captain U.S.M.*
Three-striper, Washington, D. C.
"Greater men than I may have lived, but I do not believe it."
Admirer of everything Washingtonian, including himself; double-reflecting, triple-flattering mirror used; Plebe brace; co-efficient of expansion undetermined, but it is considered enormous; Star (3).

Mitchell, Willis Gimmell. "Bill."
Three-striper, *Resigned* Warren. Pa.
"Deceive thyself no longer: thy youth hath fled."
Silent lubricator; Married Men's Club; Req for amanuensis not granted, and stamp supply cut down; calls class-meetings every other night, and brings empty chairs to order; Class President.

Ironic comments about Rear Admiral Mannix in the Naval Academy's "Lucky Bag," the graduation book of the class of 1900.

Mannix and his sister, Romaine, when he was in Washington.

The *Monongahela*, the sailing ship on which Mannix served as a midshipman.

The *Indiana*, on which
nix served during battle,
bombarding Santiago.

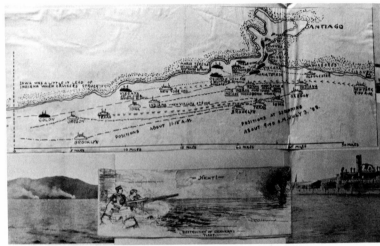

sitions of ships during the
battle of Santiago.

Destruction onboard the
Spanish flagship after the
battle of Santiago.

Newspaper account of battle.

Battle of Santiago.

Victory reception of fleet in New York.

Midshipman Mannix in command of the color company receiving the flag at the Naval Academy.

Ensign Mannix at the Great Lakes.

On the *Kearsarge*. Mannix was in command of turret gun crew that established world record.

A description of Mannix's role in the Pensacola riots.

ENSIGN DANIEL MANNIX RECEIVES DESERVED PRAISE

THE COMMANDER IN CHIEF OF THE FLEET COMMENDS HIM FOR HIS SERVICES LAST SATURDAY NIGHT.

Ensign Daniel P. Mannix, of the U. S. S. Kearsarge, has received from the commander in chief of the fleet deserved praise for the service he rendered last Saturday night in suppressing the riot in the streets of this city, and many Pensacolians will be pleased to learn that he has been commended for his action.

Those who were engaged in that section of the city where the riot occurred, commended the ensign for the very prompt steps which he took at the time, and many commented upon the manner in which he handled the marines under such circumstances. He was alert at all times, and his conduct was such as to encourage those in his command to renewed vigor. The marshal and members of the police department commented, directly after the trouble of Saturday night, upon the manner in which the detachment from the Kearsarge not only suppressed further trouble, but cleared the streets, and they appreciated, to the fullest extent, the as-

makes your action all the more praiseworthy.

"3. Doubtless your presence with the Marines prevented much bloodshed. Respectfully,

"_____ PARKER,

"Rear Admiral, U. S. Navy, Commander in Chief, North Atlantic Fleet. To Ensign Daniel P. Mannix, U. S. Navy, U. S. S. Kearsarge."

(Through commanding officer.)

COMMENDED BY THE ADMIRAL

ENSIGN MANNIX RECEIVES VERY NICE NOTICE FROM COMMANDER IN CHIEF FOR WAY HE HANDLED THE MARINES.

Bravery and voluntary service in the face of danger are closely linked in the life of United States naval officers. They appear on dress parade all right and have a good time, but when the least sign of danger appears these gold-laced, stiffly-uniformed and renowned individuals are over-anxious to be to the front. This has been exemplified in more than one

MOB OF SAILORS MADE ATTACK ON POLICEMEN

AND HAD THINGS THEIR OWN WAY FOR AN HOUR OR MORE SATURDAY NIGHT — MARINES FROM BATTLESHIPS CALLED ON TO QUELL RIOT WHICH WAS EARLY PRECIPITATED.

Enraged at the arrest of a sailor named Cole by a single policeman about three hundred bluejackets, with perhaps a sprinkling of civilians of the more rough class, attempted to actually mob a policeman or two Saturday night at 7:20 o'clock. The attempt precipitated trouble of a serious nature and resulted in the death of one man from Fort Barrancas named Charles Banks and the wounding by pistol shots or clubs of four others. None of the latter were hurt a great deal and soon all outward evidences that they engaged in such rough tactics will disappear.

There were several policemen hurt, being struck by flying missiles. Officer Villar wrenched his leg to some extent while Officer Burnham receiv-

Ensign Mannix at the time of
the riots.

On the *Kearsarge*. Mannix is in the rear rank.

Lt. D. Pratt Mannix with landing party.

Mannix at this time.

American sailors landing in Havana.

Company forming skirmish line on reaching shallow water.

Soldier drowning and being rescued by
naval boat crew.

Naval officers at Mindanao; Lieutenant
Mannix is at extreme right.

our fire on the *Oquendo* and, just like her sister, the *Teresa*, she burst into flames and headed for the beach.

Just then something else attracted our attention. The troopships and other auxiliaries which ordinarily lay at anchor in Guantanamo Bay had all put to sea and were scattering in every direction, tooting their whistles and giving every indication of frantic excitement. One of them, the *Resolute*, bore down on us and, as she passed close aboard, her captain shouted that a Spanish battleship was approaching from the eastward and that she had attempted to attack the *Resolute*, who had barely escaped by clever maneuvering and superior speed.

Following the *Resolute* came a newspaper tug, the *Hercules*, fairly bursting with excitement. Her people shouted that it was a big battleship flying the Spanish flag. Captain Taylor asked if they had made out the stranger's name; the newspaper man replied that he hadn't waited long enough for that.

Just then the *New York*, Admiral Sampson's flagship, passed us heading for the sound of the guns. The admiral had seen the battle from Siboney and was racing back to be in on the fight. Admiral Sampson must have been mad with rage that on this day of all days, he had left his post and now Commodore Schley would get all the credit for the victory. Our captain hailed her and said a Spanish battleship had been sighted and we were going to engage her. The *New York*'s crew gave us a great cheer as she sped past.

As we headed east we wondered what Spanish battleship it could be. The consensus was that it must be the *Pelayo* as that ship had been reported by the papers as having left Spain with the apparent intention of reinforcing Cervera.

Approaching Guantanamo we saw, hull down ahead of us, a great ship evidently traveling at a high rate of speed. She rapidly grew larger, heading straight for us. Our turrets, those that could bear, were swung around until the heavy guns pointed directly at her. Then, in plain view of us, she mastheaded her flag. It was the Spanish flag, red and gold. She appeared to be training her guns on us; the fire control party in our fighting top commenced sending down ranges and deflections; the gunnery officer, on pins and needles, fidgeted; the bugler, his instrument poised, waited for the word to sound, "Commence firing." All of us, our fingers crossed, waited for the blast of fire from the black muzzles of the guns frowning across the rapidly narrowing water between the two ships.

Then, just as the tension had become unbearable, Captain Taylor said sharply, "Look at that flag!" As he spoke, the sun, coming from behind a cloud, shone directly on the banner at her masthead. The flag wasn't red and gold; it was red and WHITE. She wasn't Spanish; she was Austrian. Luckily for her the flag she flew was a new one and the white in it wasn't discolored.

She sent a boarding officer to us; he arrived wearing his cocked hat and epaulets and gazed in amazement at the condition of our ship and our half-naked crew. He was told that the Spanish Squadron had been destroyed and showed polite incredulity; he asked permission for his ship to enter Santiago Harbor to remove any Austrians in the city; he was referred to the *New York* and Admiral Sampson. The moment his boat was clear of our side we headed back to where we could see the *Teresa* and the *Oquendo* burning on the beach.

The only ships nearby, apart from the auxiliaries, were the *Iowa* and the yacht *Gloucester* and we could see boats busily running back and forth between them and the grounded Spaniards. As quickly as possible we got three of our boats in the water to help in the rescue work. I was in command of one of them.

As we approached we could see that the Spanish ships were burning as fiercely as ever and the men who were still on board and who were still alive were crowded up in the bows where a series of splashes showed that they were jumping overboard and endeavoring to swim ashore through the surf. We passed perhaps twenty bodies floating in the water, some close at hand, others drifting out to sea with the tide which had started to ebb. I remember one body particularly; the chest seemed to be tremendously expanded. It reminded me of a Brady picture of the Civil War called "The High Water Mark of the Confederacy." It was taken at Gettysburg and showed the body of a Southern soldier who had fallen well in advance of his comrades. His chest was expanded in the same way, as though by a supreme effort.

Some of the bodies were not resting quietly on the water; they were twitching restlessly but would quiet down as our boats approached. They were being attacked by sharks or other fish.

The Spanish boats had a few head of live cattle on board. These poor creatures were being burned alive when a classmate of mine, Charles Freeman, did a very gallant thing. He had charge of one of the rescue boats and, seeing the animals in the midst of the flames, he climbed the side of the burning *Teresa* and shot the unfortunate things with his revolver, this at imminent peril to himself. [The only recognition he ever received for this gallant and humane act was to be kidded about it by the humorists putting out our *Lucky Bag* who laughed at him for "running an abattoir on the *Maria Teresa*."]

By this time we were quite close to the beach, just outside the surf. We could see a number of bodies lying on the sand but it was impossible to say whether they were living or dead. Then we saw something else. Out of the jungle fringing the shore appeared a group of men. We couldn't tell whether they were soldiers or guerrillas or just plain bandits. They looked like tramps but they all had rifles and they had bandoleers of cartridges slung across their shoulders. They leisurely formed a ragged line, filled the magazines of their rifles, and then commenced shooting at the naked, half-drowned Spanish sailors who were struggling in the surf. A number of them sought "natural rests" (fallen trees, etc.) for their rifles to make their aim steadier.

There were several American boats in the vicinity. I don't think anybody gave an order but they all headed for the beach. Apart from the officers' swords and revolvers these boats seemed to be without arms for, as they grounded and the crews jumped ashore, none of the men had weapons. However, every man had an oar, a boathook or a wooden stretcher.

[Once, many years later, I saw a dog run at a cat. The cat must have been owned by a family who also owned a dog for she showed no alarm, apparently thinking that the dog wanted to play. At the very last moment she sensed something hostile in the rapid approach and, with a wild leap, found sanctuary in a tree. Something like this happened on the Cuban beach.]

The men ashore saw our boats coming but showed no particular interest; they may have thought that our people wanted to join in the fun. However, when our men piled out, each carrying a potentially nasty weapon, a wave of uncertainty went down their ranks; they lowered their rifles and for the first time began to observe our movements.

Then, with a rush, our men were among them. Some vicious blows were struck and the killers seemed, literally, to melt away. One moment they were there, the next, they had vanished and our people found themselves facing each other, their improvised weapons still raised in the air. Not a shot had been fired in this supplement to the Battle of Santiago.

In the course of the afternoon of July 3 I went on board the *Maria*

Teresa and the *Oquendo*. They were still on fire and burning fiercely. Most of the wood on board had been consumed and much of the metal was so hot that it raised a blister when touched. Her wooden decks had nearly all disappeared, and we made our way aft by stepping from one steel beam to the next.

There were many bodies lying around all burned to a crisp. At one gun an American shell, passing through the gun shield, had exploded killing the entire crew. This was an example of a gun shield proving a menace instead of a protection; had it not been there the shell might not have exploded.

[Several years later I saw this same gun at the Brooklyn Navy Yard, near the gate entrance on Sands Street. I remembered how it had looked on the *Maria Teresa* with the charred bodies of its crew around it.]

The crew didn't look like men; they looked like fallen trees, burned absolutely black. One of them had an arm raised in the air; an American sailor tapped it gently with a stick and the arm fell off.

We had been warned before leaving the *Indiana* not to take anything from the Spanish ships but, as always happens, our men did pocket some small, virtually worthless articles. I found a watch with the crystal melted down on the hands (I still have it); another man found about a hundred silver Spanish pesos that had melted together forming a stick about a foot long, which he carefully stuck down his trouser leg. Somebody found ten thousand dollars in Spanish gold. That, however, he didn't stick down his trouser leg; he turned it in to the paymaster when he got back to the ship. I never heard what eventually happened to it.

About two o'clock we went back to the ship as nobody had had anything to eat since early that morning. Hardly had we sat down in the steerage mess when the word was passed, "Here comes Cervera!" and all hands dashed up on deck again.

It had been intended to send the Spanish admiral to us but at the last moment it was decided to send him to the *Iowa* instead.

The pulling boat carrying Cervera passed within twenty feet of us; we could look directly down into it. There was water in the bottom of the boat, as though it had been lowered before the plug had been put in. In the water lay the body of a dead Spanish sailor. Admiral Cervera was in civilian clothes loaned him by Captain Wainwright of the *Gloucester* (Cervera had swum ashore in his underclothing), he had no hat and no collar; his head was lowered in deep dejection. As he approached, our men, lining the rails, gave a tremendous cheer of triumph which was instantly suppressed by the officers and in a dead silence he passed, his head bowed. It made me feel as though I were in church. I was never so sorry for anyone in all my life.

We worked hard transferring the wounded Spaniards to the *Indiana*'s sick bay. Soon it was full and we had to put the men anywhere we could. I especially remember a Spanish officer we had to carry on board as his right leg had been cut off between the ankle and knee. He had been on board one of the destroyers and, when she blew up, had jumped overboard and been caught in the propeller which had cut off his leg as cleanly as an axe could have done. He was a good-looking young fellow, about my age. Our two surgeons laid him out on an ordinary dining room table, their arms already bloody to the elbows (they didn't wear rubber gloves in those days). The table and the deck below it were spotted with strips of flesh and little puddles of blood. The end of the stump looked like a bloody sponge. Four of our sailors held him while the surgeons completed the necessary amputation. Every little while the Spaniard would come to and cry out something in Spanish. He had been wounded at nine-thirty that morning and had received no attention since that time. His wound had been soaked in saltwater and then he had dragged himself up on a sandy beach where the stump had become filled with small shells and other foreign matter.

A few days later, he was transferred to the *Harvard*, which served as a hospital ship. He had been provided with a pair of improvised crutches and appeared on deck pale as a sheet but perfectly composed. As though making his adieux after an enjoyable evening, he thanked us for our "hospitality" (no, he wasn't being sarcastic) and expressed his profound regret for the annoyance that his unfortunate arrival had caused. He was sure we would understand he would not willingly have intruded on us in that condition, but matters had reached a state where he was no longer master of his own movements. He spoke in French, exquisitely pronounced, and very slowly, so we would be sure to understand without being put to too much effort.

I have met men of all nationalities during my years in the Navy; in "good breeding" none of them could equal the upper-class Spaniards.

All that afternoon we were busy transferring the fifteen hundred prisoners to the *Harvard*. On one of the last trips my boat came close to the *Brooklyn*, Commodore Schley's flagship. The officer of the deck hailed and told us to come alongside. When I climbed the sea ladder to the quarterdeck I was told to go to the commodore's cabin as he had some urgent mail to go to the *New York*, Admiral Sampson's flagship.

After the orderly announced me I entered the cabin. The commodore, who was seated at his desk, rose, walked across the room and greeted me with the same courtesy that he would have shown a visiting flag officer.

Mind you, I was an Annapolis undergraduate, something less than a worm. Ever since entering the Academy I had been kicked around and, what is worse, frequently made the subject of sarcastic and biting comment to which I could not possibly reply, like the jokes sometimes indulged in by judges having the Jeffreys' complex. But here a national character, a hero to thousands of people, was treating me with the same courtesy I am sure he showed to the humblest person in his squadron. At that moment I would gladly have died for him.

Many years later when I was to reach command rank, I always tried to model myself on Commodore Schley rather than Admiral Meade, the commandant of the Washington Navy Yard. Only the men who have served under me can say how well I have succeeded.

[Later, when the Sampson-Schley controversy was started largely by the adherents of the two men rather than by the men themselves, the pro-Sampson clique did everything possible to smear Schley. The basis of the dispute was who deserved credit for the victory at Santiago. According to naval usage, as Admiral Sampson was in command he deserved the credit, just as if the battle had gone against us, his would have been the blame whether or not it was his fault. The pro-Schley group insisted that as Admiral Sampson wasn't even there during the fighting, the credit should go to Commodore Schley who had commanded the fleet. The Navy Department took the first view and although both men were promoted, Schley was kept junior to Sampson. During the long sittings of the Court of Inquiry in Washington, every phase of the engagement was discussed and re-discussed a hundred times and a number of criticisms were made of Schley's tactics. Even today historians are debating what should have been done.

I'm afraid that I can contribute little to the controversial features of the battle. The reason is that I didn't see them. There was so much noise and excitement, to say nothing of the smoke which made it virtually impossible to see anything. (My feeling is that most historians don't realize the battle was fought in a fog.) Besides, there was so much happening in our immediate vicinity that we had no time to bother about something that was taking place a mile or two away.

There were two things that were fought over (verbally) for months and years. The first and most important was the turn made by the *Brooklyn*, Schley's flagship, at the beginning of the battle. The *Brooklyn* was rushing at full speed toward the *Teresa* as she emerged from the harbor entrance and when the Spanish vessel swung to the westward, the *Brooklyn*, instead of putting her helm hard-a-starboard in order to come on the same course as the enemy, put it hard-a-port and made the turn AWAY from the Spaniards instead of TOWARD them, thereby increasing her distance by the length of her tactical diameter and also running across the bow of the *Texas,* barely missing a collision. The *Texas*, who like the rest of us, was making a desperate effort to close the range, was obliged at this critical moment to stop and to back full speed to avoid striking the *Brooklyn*. The smoke was so thick it was only by a miracle she ever saw the *Brooklyn* at all.

Sampson's supporters in their efforts to discredit Schley said he turned away from the *Teresa* in "craven flight" which I am sure is nonsense. No one thought of personal danger at that moment; everyone had only one idea—to close with the enemy as quickly as possible.

The *Brooklyn*'s explanation was that had she swung in the other direction, she would have interfered with the fire of the American ships. I don't know the answer but I do know that if she had gone hard-a-starboard and as a result been hit by our fire, then Schley would have been denounced as a fool instead of a coward. In other words, he couldn't win.

I might add that the *Brooklyn* was struck more than thirty times by shells from the enemy squadron, far more than any other American ship. My ship, the *Indiana,* was struck three times. I am not sure about the others.

The other point of contention was the handling of the *Brooklyn* during the chase of the *Cristobal Colon*. The *Colon* was the only Spanish vessel that managed to slip away under cover of the smoke and general confusion. She raced westward along the coast, hotly pursued by the *Oregon*, and shortly afterward by the *Brooklyn*. The *Oregon* followed directly after the fleeing *Colon* while the *Brooklyn* kept her bow a point or two to seaward, thereby remaining considerably outboard of the other two ships.

The *Brooklyn*'s explanation of this was as follows: "Look at the

map of Cuba and you will see that the southwestern point sticks out
considerably beyond the general coast line. The *Colon*, had she continued the course she was on, would not have cleared this point. She
would have had to have come about and put out to sea. We headed for
the point, instead of directly at her, in order to be sure of cutting
her off."

The *Oregon* slowly began to overhaul the Spanish and finally tried
a ranging shot with her bow chasers. When the captain of the *Colon*
saw the splashes ahead of him, he knew the battleship was within
range and surrendered. It is ironic that this, the last of the Spanish
Squadron, should have borne the name of the man who first won for
Spain her great empire, the last remnant of which was now slipping
from her grasp.

Some time after the battle a Board of Experts was appointed to
visit the Spanish wrecks. This Board reported that the American
gunners had aimed so badly they had made only one and a half percent
of hits. This statement has been frequently repeated. Well, to return to
the Oriental habit of speech of my childhood, this insignificant individual offers the worthless opinion that no human being could possibly have told how many or what percentage of hits had been made
on those Spanish ships. If that one and a half percent referred to marks
on the HULLS it is perhaps correct, but the UPPERWORKS had
been, literally, torn to pieces and the ships had been gutted by fire.
Also, another point has, I think, been overlooked. The *Indiana* fired
1,876 shots during that battle and the other ships probably did about
the same. BUT the vast majority of our shots came from small caliber
guns, 6-pounders, 1,744 shots; 1-pounders (top guns), 25 shots.
These small shells might, and probably did, slaughter the Spanish
crews without leaving a mark that could later be identified. The one
American killed in that battle, Chief Yeoman George Ellis of the
Brooklyn, was decapitated by a small caliber shell from a Spanish gun
that passed over the *Brooklyn*'s deck from starboard to port and never
touched the ship.

There was at least one thing about the Battle of Santiago that no
one could criticize and that was the "timing." No Hollywood director
could have done better. The army commander, General Shafter, had
sent a message to Washington that, owing to heavy losses, he would
have to withdraw his troops and give up the attempt to capture
Santiago. Back home, a rumor was circulating that our soldiers were

in danger of being driven into the sea and all through that long, hot Sunday the entire country was tense with apprehension. Then, in the early morning hours of the Fourth of July, came the news of the smashing naval victory. No work of fiction was ever as theatrical or as thrilling as what actually took place at Santiago de Cuba during the first week of that July of so long ago.

JULY 4

The evening of that Independence Day is one that none of us on the *Indiana* is likely to forget. Only a miracle of luck kept us from being casualties. At five minutes before midnight a gun went off and almost simultaneously our alarm gongs began to ring and the bugles to sound General Quarters.

Racing for the bridge, I found that we were under way and headed in for the Morro. The night was intensely dark but the *Massachusetts* had been stationed at the mouth of the gap with orders to keep her searchlight trained on the entrance in case any more Spanish ships tried to escape. By the glare of the searchlight, I could see that something was happening inside the harbor mouth. We learned later that the Spaniards were trying to sink one of their ships, the old *Reina Mercedes*, to block the passage so we could not enter the harbor if we decided to make the attempt.

I heard nothing except some confused, far away noises. Then, out of the night, without the slightest warning, came a shrill scream followed by a tremendous explosion and we on the bridge were drenched by a great wave of saltwater rising, apparently miraculously, from the calm sea through which we were moving. At the same time the ship quivered convulsively as though she had struck something. Then, before we had a chance to wipe the water out of our eyes, came a second and more appalling scream accompanied by a swift rush of air hot as that from an open furnace door and followed by a terrific detonation and a dazzling glare of light from our darkened quarterdeck.

We had been struck by two 8-inch mortar shells. They had been fired at the *Massachusetts'* searchlight and had hit us. The first shell had dished our starboard bow plate and the second, coming down vertically on the quarterdeck, had passed through the deck, through the deck below and had exploded on striking the armored deck.

When we went aft to view the damage it seemed incredible that a single shell could have created such havoc. That part of the ship was a wreck. The projectile struck in the officers' quarters and had we not been at our battle stations every officer on the ship would have been killed. There was a foot of water on the deck in which our belongings were floating in an indescribable state of confusion. Bulkheads had been knocked down and where there had been a line of staterooms was now a great open space with no partitions, littered with fragments of what had once been furniture.

The shell in exploding had set fire to the ship and at the same time had fractured the water main. The water, squirting out under high pressure, had extinguished the fire; the first time in history that a fire had been put out by an automatic sprinkling system!

Our punch bowl suffered a deep dent and when it was repaired a fragment of the exploded shell was mounted on the cover. As for the junior midshipman on board, he was reduced to one pair of trousers. When, six weeks later, he arrived in New York harbor those trousers had absolutely no seat in them. If ladies visited the ship he was obliged either to remain seated, like royalty, or else lean nonchalantly against the nearest wall.

[I have since read that it was ridiculous for us not to have made an attempt to run the passage into Santiago Bay because the only ordnance the forts possessed was some ancient cannon dating from 1668. Very interesting. I can only say that those seventeenth-century cannon balls behaved remarkably like mortar shells. I am sincerely sorry that these experts could not have been our guests in the officers' quarters when those cannon balls struck. Of course, there were some of these old cannon in Morro where they were kept as relics. One of them is now at Annapolis. It is made of bronze and bears the motto ULTIMA RATIO REGNUM—The Last Argument of Kings. Unfortunately for us, they also had modern ordnance and knew very well how to use them.]

For the next few days, General Shafter kept sending letters to General Toral, chief of the Spanish Army occupying Santiago, ordering him to surrender the city, which General Toral politely refused to do. He knew our army was being decimated by various tropical illnesses, especially yellow fever, and could not maintain the seige for long. Finally a plan was worked out which was to end the war.

On the morning of July 10th, the *Indiana* and the *Brooklyn* got underway and proceeded to a point off Aguadores where they dropped anchor. We couldn't see anything except a series of hills enclosing our anchorage. Ashore there was a small detachment of the Army signal corps. First we went to General Quarters which had become as familiar to us as brushing our teeth. Then our heavy 13-inch turret guns were swung to starboard, that is, to seaward as far as they would go. Nowadays heavy guns turrets are balanced so that when they are swung abeam the ship remains on an even keel. On the *Indiana*, however, this was not so and the results of swinging the turrets was to give the ship a heavy list to seaward so that the 8-inch turrets nearest the shore were tilted upward until their guns pointed in air so they could fire over the hills.

The stage being set and various mysterious calculations having been made by our bearded navigator, a range and deflection was sent to the 8-inch guns. I remember the range; it was nine-thousand yards, or four and a half sea miles. We saw the afterturret swing to the left, then slightly back again to the right, a pause, and then the ear shattering crash of the discharge. No wonder so many of the older Navy men are hard of hearing.

As the shell passed out of sight over the summit of the hills it awoke a series of wails and howls that no banshee in Ireland could have equalled, the echoes taking them up until gradually they died away in the distance. Then ensued a long wait followed by marked activity among the little group of signalmen ashore. One of them began waving a flag at us. We used the Meyer system then, not the Morse and it was before the days of the two-armed semaphore. The words of the message were spelled out by waving one flag to the right and to the left. Naturally, the Meyer code being long obsolete and of no value whatever, I remember every word of it.

We read the signal the soldier sent us. "Low and to the right." The range and deflection were corrected and a second shot fired. In a very short time no future corrections were necessary and all through that long Sunday afternoon, at intervals of two minutes, we sent a shot at our invisible target nearly five miles away over the hills.

We were bombarding the city of Santiago de Cuba.

The next day, July 11th, the bombardment was renewed. We kept up the fire for two hours and then an agitated fluttering of flags from our friends ashore bade us, "Cease firing." The Spaniards had had enough. Honor had been satisfied and they were surrendering.

Some of our people who visited the city, reported that our fire had been systematically knocking down the houses, block by block. The actual surrender took place on July 17th but, after that second day's bombardment, the results were certain.

We arrived at New York on August 19th, my twentieth birthday. Before sighting Sandy Hook we were met by an escort of ferryboats, excursion steamers, tugs—everything that could float. More and more arrived until we seemed to be surrounded by the entire population of Greater New York. Everyone was cheering madly.

The Battery was packed by an enormous crowd and, as we headed up the North River, we passed more multitudes covering both shores. As the land grew higher the number of people didn't diminish; they covered the heights and the slopes down to the water's edge. Our ships still wore their war paint and the *Brooklyn* was flying the flag she had used in the battle; it had been torn in many places by the enemy shells and certainly didn't detract from her appearance. We went as far as Grant's Tomb where we fired a National Salute and then turned and headed down river to our anchorages.

Perhaps people were simpler and more enthusiastic in those days; perhaps the Spanish War didn't last long enough for them to get bored and cynical; perhaps the fact that we had no allies made it more personal; perhaps the fact that every man, whether he did well or badly, was a volunteer had its effect but, whatever it was, I never saw anything like this reception again.

When liberty was granted we could not walk more than a block without running into crowds surrounding a sailor whose cap ribbon bore a name now made famous, such as "Oregon" or perhaps "Brooklyn." They were being plied with questions and regarded as heroes.

It is now fashionable to jeer at the Spanish-American War. Even so, it had something. The tropical setting, the background of palms, white surf and blue sky, the chivalry of the enemy, the shortness of the range (in the battle of July 3rd we could see the faces of the people we were fighting), the absence of submarines and the type of warfare they represent, the fact that it was largely a war of movement and things took place out in the open with flags snapping in the breeze, the sea salt in our faces, and our ships speeding through water as blue as turquoise and white with foam, the staccato sequence of events, the fact that when it was all over we knew who had won.

Perhaps most important of all, we were a new country just entering the world arena to test our ability against the old, established nations. Now we too had an empire. Now the sun never set on the

American flag, for we had acquired the Philippines. Now, as Mr. Kipling assured us, we were to take up the white man's burden and rule over lesser breeds. For the first time in our hundred years of history, we were received as equals by Europe. As President McKinley said, rather in astonishment, "In a few short months we have become a world power; and I know, sitting here in this chair, with what added respect the nations of the world now deal with the United States and it is vastly different from the conditions I found when I was inaugurated."

Very soon we were to discover what our new-found responsibilities were to cost us in blood and money—many times over what the war had cost. But in those golden weeks no doubts troubled us. The United States was on its way and nothing could stop us.

CHAPTER FOUR

Life of a Junior Officer (1900–1903)

So we'll drink tonight
To the Midshipmite,
Singing cheerily lads, Yo ho!

—Old song

LOOKING OVER the previous chapters, I have made it appear that a midshipman's life was all hazing, bad water, and hard labor. True enough, it was no life for a mollycoddle, yet thinking back it seems to me that some of my happiest days were spent as a junior officer—first a middy and then an ensign. If we spent long days at sea, we had liberties on shore. Although our pay was only three thousand a year, we lived like kings when on leave. A stein of beer was a nickel and that included the "free lunch" which often amounted to a veritable smorgasbord of twenty dishes or better. The best seats in the theater were $1.40 (balcony 50 cents) and a first-class supper at Rector's or Delmonico's, wines included, never came to more than $30 for you and your young lady. We paid neither board nor rent for we lived on the ship, so we had no "overhead." Perhaps best of all, we were constantly being shipped from one port to another, which was most convenient if you found yourself becoming overly involved with some lovely fair or her too-demanding parents. No millionaire, unless indeed he was able to afford his own yacht, could have led such a life.

Shortly after the war, I received my first decoration: a bronze medal in acknowledgment of my service. Later, I was also awarded five clasps to be attached to the medal's ribbon commemorating various engagements I had taken part in under fire, such as attacks on Morro and mining operations. The engagements deemed worthy of these decorations were those of June 22nd, July 2nd, July 3rd, July 4th, July 10th, and July 11th.

Perhaps best of all was an award of $272.62, prize money for the destruction of Cervera's fleet, the sum being based on the computed value of the ships sunk and my rank. Apart from the fact that as a midshipman I could use the money, I was proud to have this bond with John Paul Jones and the frigate captains of the Napoleonic wars, many of whom after a successful cruise, became independently wealthy, bought a country estate, and lived "disguised as a gentleman" as the cynical saying went. Indeed, many old-time captains were so lacking in interest in their profession that they preferred the command of a frigate to that of a ship of the line (the modern equivalents would be a cruiser and a battleship), for when it came to prizes the slower, heavier line vessel didn't have a chance.

Although the English look down on us for always chasing the "almighty dollar" (I don't think an Englishman can pronounce the word "dollar" without prefacing it with "almighty"), they take a far more practical view of such matters in a military sense than we do. At the end of the First World War, the British admiral David Beatty was not only created a baron and an earl but was given a cash grant of FIVE HUNDRED THOUSAND DOLLARS! The same was done for the army commander, Sir Douglas Haig. A number of other Army and Navy leaders—Jellicoe, French, Allenby and several others—were created viscounts and given a quarter of a million. Contrast that with our General Grant who, while dying from a painful disease, wrote his memoirs lest his creditors remained unpaid.

When the politicians abolished prize money, one remarked virtuously, "It was a relic of piracy." I remember a cynical midshipman at our mess commented, "The politicians used to get half; now they get all."

I should add that there were many cases of outrageous scandals in connection with prize money on the part of the civilians involved. One of my classmates, in command of a prize crew, found the cargo of his captured vessel being openly looted by the local authorities in a certain southern port. He reported it. In return, he received a volley of abuse from the local press. For months afterwards attempts were made to hurt him with the Navy Department. They were ultimately successful for he was forced to resign.

I had a good record at the Academy, and it was generally considered certain that I would be made cadet lieutenant-commander, the highest possible rank for an undergraduate. I remember at a party a few weeks before graduation, we were each given a prophecy and mine read, "I see four stripes" (today, the cadet commander is a five-striper). When the appointments were posted, I was a three-striper, in command of the color company—the second highest honor. I couldn't believe my eyes. After walking around in a daze for some time, I returned to the bulletin board certain I had made a mistake. No, it was still there. It was a small matter, so I am sorry to say it was probably the bitterest disappointment of my life. I was still able to select the young lady who would present the corps with the colors and to receive a kiss from her. Ah well, it is all over now.

After graduation in June 1900, I was ordered, together with several of my classmates, to temporary duty on the USS *Michigan* conducting a hydrographic survey on the Great Lakes. It was thought that all naval officers should have the opportunity to study every branch of the service. I regarded this as rather tame duty, but actually it turned out considerably more interesting than I had anticipated.

The *Michigan* was an institution; she was a side wheeler, built long before the Civil War. The original engines, of the inclined type, were still in her and, amazingly enough, in excellent condition. Her crew were as special as the ship; they were permanent and were never ordered to another ship or station. They were very well off; the bugler was rumored to be a millionaire. All of them were older men and had their own traditions and ways of doing things which were often puzzling and sometimes infuriating to a regular naval officer.

Yes, I committed the standard blunder that all saltwater officers invariably committed when assigned to duty on the lakes. It was lucky I did so. It would have broken my crew's hearts had I omitted it. At the first Abandon Ship drill, I noticed that all the crew had expectant smiles on their faces for some reason I could not fathom. Annoyed, I made a point of carefully checking the ship's boats to make sure that they were equipped with provisions, medical supplies, life preservers, signal flags, etc. I still felt that something was missing. Suddenly I realized what it was. Pointing an accusing finger at the coxswain, I thundered, "Where are your water beakers?" While the crew burst into a roar of delighted laughter, the coxswain picked up a dipper and pointed to Lake Michigan. This was a joke that never failed.

A short time later, I got my revenge although it was unintentional. I had the deck and I ordered our millionaire-bugler, "Bugler, hook on the first cutter"—meaning, of course, for him to sound the call. I then turned to other duties. Suddenly it occurred to me that he had not sounded the call and had disappeared. Looking over the rail I discovered our millionaire down in the boat hooking it on himself and loudly protesting that it wasn't his job. Of course, this seemed as hilarious to us "regulars" as the water beakers business did to the ship's crew.

For the first time I realized the enormous size of the great inland seas on our northern border. In case you don't know it, it is very easy to get seasick on the Great Lakes, humiliating though that is to a deep-sea sailor. When there is a "sea" it is usually an unpleasant, choppy one. Another problem was the traffic. Sometimes I would go on deck prepared to stand the Mid Watch (midnight to 4 A.M.) and find there were twenty or thirty lights in sight, all forward of the beam and most of them having the "right of way" over us. At such times, I longed for the open sea.

It was at this time that Theodore Roosevelt, then vice-president, in a speech at the Minnesota State Fair, uttered the famous words, "Speak softly and carry a big stick." He added, "Build and keep at a pitch of the highest training a thoroughly efficient Navy." Roosevelt instantly became the hero of every Navy man. Later he was to fall out of popular favor as a jingoist but he never fell out of favor with the Navy.

We had two notable experiences that summer, although of very different natures. The Pan American Exposition was being held in Buffalo and President McKinley was there. More important, Wurzburger beer was introduced into the United States for the first time. It was a memorable experience to visit the "German Village" accompanied by a young lady and with your arm around her waist sing, "Down Where the Wurzburger Flows," to the music of a military band. Everything seemed calm and peaceful but as usual in military life, one never knows what will break the next moment.

A few hours after we had left Buffalo, we were overtaken by a frantic tug. The skipper shouted at us through a megaphone, "President McKinley has just been assassinated by anarchists at the Exposition! The IWW has declared a revolution! Rioters have seized the city and it's a national emergency!"

The president had indeed been murdered by an anarchist named Czolgosz. While McKinley was shaking hands with the crowd, the murderer approached him with a bandage wrapped around his left hand. A small revolver was concealed in it. He offered his right hand to the president and simultaneously fired with his left. A senseless, brutal crime.

We spun around and raced back to Buffalo. A landing force was prepared, rifles and ball cartridges were issued, and a corps of "pioneers" was organized carrying axes and crowbars to break through possible barricades. I was the adjutant. We all expected a desperate resistance and when we reached the beach and the anchor dropped, we flung ourselves into the boats unshaven and wearing flannel shirts. The IWW (International Workers of the World) were regarded as murderous fanatics intent on destroying all order and authority and we intended to be ready for them.

After we had charged up the beach like the Rough Riders at San Juan Hill, we found to our chagrin that there were no riots; all we were supposed to do was to escort the slain president's body from Milbourne House to the railroad station. We did it although we were a pretty rough-looking escort. On the way, I saw for the first time a number of men with their caps turned on backwards peering at us through queer-looking boxes and cranking busily away. I had never seen such devices before, but I recognized them as motion picture cameras, having read about these curious inventions in the newspapers. This was the first time I had ever encountered them.

It was natural, I suppose, that the landing force was subject to a good deal of ridicule from both the press and my fellow officers for our dramatic sortie into Buffalo under the impression that we were putting down a revolution. As adjutant, I was prime target. My classmates accused me of "playing soldier"—in the Navy, the worst of insults. I was given the ironic title of "Armstrong Hobson" after the rather flamboyant officer who sank the *Merrimac* in the entrance to Santiago Harbor and later made something of a fool of himself posing as a hero. I was described as a "double-reflecting, triple-flattering" individual who had supposedly rushed up the beach waving a cutlass over my head while shouting, "Follow me, men!" I don't suppose anyone likes to be made a fool of, and I took it rather hard.

Still, the incident, minor though it was, taught me something about organizing and directing a landing force. Getting men into boats, seeing that they all hit the beach at the same time, keeping them together and directing their movements is quite a complicated procedure for which none of us had had any training. Also for the first time I had had to consider what to do if we were confronted by a dangerous mob. The standard order was to fire a volley over their heads to disburse them, but now I realized how impractical this would be. By the laws of physics, what goes up must come down and a bullet fired into the air will descend with the same velocity with which it left the rifle's muzzle. If there were innocent hangers-on milling about behind the belligerents, some of these would surely be hit. If we fired directly into the crowd, we would be sure to kill a number of people, quite possibly women and children. In those few minutes while trying to plan my future strategy, I felt a profound sympathy for the British officer in command of the company which fired on the crowd of drunken patriots in the so-called Boston Massacre of 1770, an act which many historians believe precipitated the American Revolution. In spite of the ribbing I received, I spent a great deal of time reviewing my actions and planning what to do if such a situation ever arose again.

From the *Michigan* I was transferred to the *Dolphin* and spent the winter taking deep-sea soundings near Haiti and Santo Domingo. We were supposed to have found a famous "deep" of some sort. I'm sure it's still there, if you want it. Afterward, I was lucky enough to be assigned to the *Kearsarge* that had New York City as a home port. This was one of the best tours of duty I ever had. After several days cruising up and down the coast running through combat drill, we would return to the Brooklyn Navy Yard for an overhaul period during which we were given shore leave. We never slept. When we were on duty we had regular "heel and toe" night watches to stand (we were not permitted to sit down while on duty) and when we were off we went ashore where it was far too entertaining to sleep.

There were five watch officers and, in order to provide "time off," the watches were arranged like this: starting a tour you came on at midnight and were on until 4 A.M. (the Mid Watch); then you came on once more at 8 A.M. and had the duty until 12:30 P.M. (the Forenoon Watch); then you were on from 4 P.M. until 6:30 P.M. (the First Dog Watch); then from 8 P.M. until midnight (the First Watch); then from 12:30 P.M. until 4 P.M. (the Afternoon Watch); then from 6:30 until 8 P.M. (the Second Dog Watch); and then from 4 A.M. until 8 A.M. (the Morning Watch); after which you were off for two days and nights and then the cycle started over again.

When I say you were "off" I mean that you had no watches to stand but "on" or "off" your regular day duties, drills, paper work, etc., continued. There was no chance to sleep in the daytime; had there been, the noise of the pneumatic riveters would have made it impossible. Time and again, when I finished a tour of duty, I was so tired and sleepy that I determined to stay on board that night and make up some sleep, but when night came it would find me trotting up and down Broadway as usual. The final watch, from 4 to 8 A.M., always was a refresher as decks were scrubbed with sand and we rolled up our trousers and paddled around in our bare feet, looking with virtuous disdain at such of our messmates as were returning, bleary-eyed and often a little unsteady on their feet, from shore.

At the turn of the century New York was wide open and, to put it mildly, TOUGH. The old Tenderloin district, west of Herald Square, flourished, and all along West Twenty-ninth Street there was a series of dance halls that, without injustice, might be termed dives; the Cairo, Bohemia, The German Village and so on. As for the ladies of the trottoir, they operated, not singly as scouts or spies, but in companies, battalions, regiments.

The entire district was spotted with "Raines Law Hotels." State Senator Raines, in an honest effort to abate the drink evil, had sponsored a law restricting the sale of liquor after certain hours to hotels having rooms for hire and requiring guests to register. The unexpected result of this law was that a swarm of places came into being that had the appearance of hotels (somebody called them "hotels for single men and their wives") and, judging from their registers, entertained guests that were both illustrious and extraordinary. The pages of their registers contained such names as "Mr. and Mrs. M. Aurelius," "Mr. and Mrs. J. J. Rousseau," "Benvenuto Cellini and Wife," and "Thomas Katt and Wife."

A famous resort of those days was the Haymarket, located at the southeast corner of Sixth Avenue and Thirtieth Street. It was a big dance hall with a balcony of loges or boxes overlooking the dance floor. Ladies were admitted free; gentlemen for twenty-five cents. There were small tables where drinks were served. There was an elegant and slender floor manager (Ike) but the dominant figure of the establishment was the bouncer, Big Bill. Bill maintained strict discipline; apart from his bouncing duties he saw to it that the ladies of the ensemble conducted themselves in a ladylike manner; any rough stuff, any pilfering or other unfair treatment of male patrons, and the offending fair one was cast into the outer darkness with orders to stay away for a week or whatever her sentence might be.

I recall one lady who had joined a gentleman at his table and the man gallantly called, "Waiter, bring this lady a glass of beer!" The lady, who naturally got a percentage on the price of all drinks purchased for her, coquettishly replied, "Aw, I want a stylish drink," to which her escort shouted, "Waiter, bring the lady a bucket of water."

The furious fair exploded, "You think you're a smart &%#$@, don't cha?" The next moment she was headed for an exit propelled by Big Bill.

I have always been interested in physical culture and it was a matter of wonder to me how a man who lived such an unhealthy life and who virtually never had a breath of fresh air could keep his pristine vigor. Of course, Bill's home life may have been simple and virtuous in the extreme and he certainly was a teetotaler as, indeed, were most bartenders. Whatever it was, he certainly kept his vigor. On one occasion a very famous football player from a very famous eastern university got rowdy in the Haymarket; Bill politely suggested that he go somewhere else; the visitor impolitely replied that he wouldn't, and in a moment the gridiron hero was being dragged toward the door. En route he seized an iron railing that separated the tables from the dance floor; Bill gave a jerk and out came a section of the railing still in the visitor's grasp; then football hero and railing were cast into the middle of 6th Avenue. He didn't come back.

Yes, New York was tough. There were gangs of streetcar rowdies (especially on the cars going to and from Coney Island) who, when the cars were crowded, used to climb through the windows and molest the women passengers, usually spitting tobacco juice on their victims in contempt after having finished with them. If a man whose wife or girl had been molested dared to object, he would be beaten to a pulp; if he was husky the whole gang would jump on him.

This sort of thing was ended by a police captain who, himself, had a tragic end—Captain Charles Becker. Becker was executed for his share in the murder of the gambler Rosenthal. The actual killers were Lefty Louie, Gyp the Blood, Dago Frank, and one or two others I don't recall, but Becker was the mastermind.

Becker, as an old policeman, knew perfectly well that the streetcar rowdies didn't mind being arrested and sent to the "Island" where they had a pleasant vacation at the expense of the city and returned heroes in the eyes of their comrades. What they did dread, like all those tough babies, was to be beaten up themselves. This is something most reformers never seem able to grasp. Becker organized a "Strong Arm" squad composed of the most powerful members of the Force. This squad operated in plain clothes and roamed all over the city. At the first indication of rowdy activity on a car or bus, the vehicle would be stopped and the rowdies dragged out on the sidewalk where, instead of being decorously conducted to the nearest police station, the erstwhile beaters were themselves "beaten to a pulp."

This highly irregular procedure, curiously enough, instead of tending toward anarchy, had the opposite effect and the streetcar rowdies vanished like the snows of yesteryear.

A few vignettes linger in my memory. I recall one morning as we were returning to the Navy Yard I saw two women fighting, tearing each other's hair out, while a crowd of spectators, composed of cabbies and other night hawks, shouted encouragingly, "Go to it, old girl!" On another evening I saw a drunk being assisted into a patrol wagon by a policeman; the officer could not have been more solicitous or careful. Once in the wagon he carefully seated his charge and took the place opposite him. Just then the drunk, with a wild swing, smashed the officer's helmet down over his eyes (yes, the Force did wear helmets then). The officer very gently put him back on his seat, took off his helmet (it required an effort) and smoothed out the dent in it. A spectator near me said, "It's amazing how patient that officer is." Another spectator, more cynical or, perhaps, more knowing, replied "Just you wait until he gets that bum on a back street."

Amid all this chaos, there was one obscure little saloon which was a haven of peace. Nothing untoward every happened there. The reason for this immunity lay in a sign over the bar:

No Discussions on Race, Religion or Politics!
THIS GOES!

Directly below this sign, and within easy reach of the bartender's hand, was a heavy wooden mallet of the type used to loosen bung stoppers in beer kegs. No, there were never any disturbances in that place.

There was a tremendous amount of misery in New York then. In going back to the Navy Yard we used to take the Sixth Avenue El to Park Place and then walk across City Hall Square to the old Brooklyn Bridge. On bitter cold winter nights the benches in the square used to be crowded with men, women, and little children wrapped in newspapers in an effort to keep warm.

There were also pirates in New York, but they had none of the glamor of Captain Kidd or Blackbeard. They operated mainly in the Inner Harbor, Buttermilk Channel, and the East River. Any yacht careless enough to leave a boat in the water overnight, especially if tied up astern, would find by the dawn's early light that cushions, oars ... in fact, everything movable had disappeared. Not infrequently the boat itself would disappear if the anchor watch wasn't on the job.

These pirates even invaded the Navy Yard. You see, that while the Navy had absolute jurisdiction inside the Yard, which was federal territory, if a thief with government property still in his arms succeeded in getting over the wall or fence he was in the City of Brooklyn and could thumb his nose at the US Navy and Marine Corps. If we wanted him arrested we had to send for a policeman. If our Marine Guard or Naval Shore Patrol attempted to arrest him screams of rage would issue from every city official down to and including the dog catcher. The civil authorities are ever watchful for encroachment on the part of the brutal military.

One night a Marine sentry saw a shadowy figure busily engaged in filling a bag with some valuable electrical fittings that had been received at a late hour, too late to be stored properly. The young marine (he was twenty-one), in accordance with his orders, brought his rifle to the ready and challenged: "Halt, who goes there?" Ignoring the challenge the intruder grabbed the bag and fled toward the nearby fence. Twice more the sentry challenged and then, still in accordance with his orders, raised his rifle and fired. The thief, in the act of climbing to safety, fell dead—on the Brooklyn side of the fence.

Well, there was the devil to pay. For more than a year afterwards a three-cornered correspondence was kept up between the Navy Yard, the Navy Department in Washington and the City of New York. The dead man had been a notorious gangster and killer; one would have thought that the city would have presented the sentry with the croix de guerre for the public service he had rendered in ridding the community of his victim. Far from it. The city demanded that the young marine be turned over to them to be tried in the civil courts for MURDER! They never got him but for nearly a year that very efficient young soldier was kept in semi-confinement so as to be available in case Washington decided to turn him over to the tender mercies of a local court and jury. Another example of military brutality.

Of course, had the gangster been killed by a police officer, there would have been no trouble whatever.

The pirates were especially daring and cunning. One afternoon our sister ship, the *Kentucky*, was holding open house and was crowded with visitors. She was moored directly opposite us and only a short distance away. Naturally there were lots of women among the visitors. A group of hoodlums, just outside the Navy Yard fence where they knew they'd be safe, walked down to the East River, took off their clothes and proceeded to disport themselves in and out of the water, stark naked and making indecent gestures. We thought they were merely trying to annoy, but it turned out that they had a strategic reason. Phoning the police did no good, as usual, so the ship, because of her women visitors, hung up some bunting to serve as a screen, their verbal protests having been answered by filth from the hoodlums.

Naturally everybody's attention had been directed to the bathing episode. That being settled, as well as possible, some of us happened to look at the *Kentucky* once more and were utterly amazed to see that a boat, manned by some tough-looking characters, was busily engaged in taking off her scupper lips; scoop-shaped pieces of metal fitted under the scuppers to prevent dirty water from running down the side of the ship. They obviously intended to sell them for old metal.

It was broad daylight and the boat was well inside the Navy Yard and in plain view of half a dozen Navy ships manned by hundreds of men. I must say there was really something sublime in the pirates' nerve. We on the *Kearsarge* commenced screaming at the *Kentucky*, "Look! Look!" The people on board her, thinking we were cheering their party, gaily waved back. Finally, leaning over the side, they discovered what was going on. They commenced throwing holy-stones at the thieves which the robbers caught and threw back at them. Then the nozzle of a fire hose appeared over her side and a stream of high pressure cold water did the job. If ever you want to get rid of rowdies or tomcats, don't use kicks or blows—use cold water. The pirates drew away cursing and leisurely rowed to their landing, just outside the Yard limits.

They didn't get away with their loot for they were pursued by a picket boat which, in direct disobedience of the city authorities, followed them to the landing, took their boat in tow and brought it back to the Yard, followed by curses and cries of "Bring back that boat!" What happened later I don't know but I'm sure the thieves all wrote to their congressmen.

Although I always felt that the Marine guards were justified in shooting trespassers on sight, there was one occasion when I must admit I'm very glad they didn't. Every afternoon we used to receive the countersign for the day from the Marine Barracks. Returning at night, if we didn't know it we might be stopped by a sentry and taken to the guardhouse until our identity was established. One afternoon a number of us went ashore early before the countersign had been received by our ship. We returned about 3 A.M., very tired and anxious to get to bed, so we decided to avoid the sentries if possible and, instead of entering the Sands Street Gate, we went to a place where we knew there was a broken picket in the fence and crawled through, one by one. Just as we straightened up with a feeling of relief, a voice at our very ear cried, "Halt! Who goes there?" We answered "Officers" and advanced confidently. The voice shouted, "Don't come near me! Don't you dare come near me!" We halted dead in our tracks and from the darkness emerged a very young, nervous sentry, his bayonet advanced. He was so relieved to discover that we really were officers that he luckily forgot all about the countersign. I'm glad that one didn't decide to fire.

During our tours of duty, I got to know New York quite well, or at least, the parts of it that would interest a gay young ensign. Among the most popular restaurants were Martin's (very elegant on the Fifth Avenue side, not so elegant on the Broadway side); Murray's (on Forty-second Street), the Café Boulevard (way down on Ninth Street), the Marlborough Rathskeller (very popular Thursday nights for some reason), the Knickerbocker Grill with its famous murals, the Ritz Roof, Terrace Garden (an open air place at Fifty-ninth Street and Lexington Avenue; it was a terrific journey to get there in a hansom) and Pabst in Harlem, way out on 125th Street. I wonder if anyone else alive today remembers these famous spots.

Of course, there were no movies but instead there was continuous vaudeville. In order to discourage the habit that some patrons developed of sitting through several shows, the vaudeville theaters always had one or two acts that were called "chasers." They were so terrible that no human being was supposed to be able to sit through them more than once.

The theaters included the famous Weber and Fields Music Hall with Lillian Russell, Dave Warfield (before his serious days), Fay Templeton and Pete Daley (who was very fat). Hence this sally:

"Be careful or the bugaboos will carry you off."

"Are the bugaboos anything like derricks?"

And, of course, Weber and Fields themselves:

"You are a business man someting like a tief."
"Vat is a tief?"
"Subbose I should come up to you on de street and should take ten tollars
   oudt of your pocket; vat vould I be?"
"You vould be a vonder."

It all seemed very funny then.

Then there was the Old Casino, at Thirty-ninth and Broadway, with a new musical show every year. Here were lugubrious, "dead pan" Dan Daley ("These Johnnies Give Me the Willies") and beauteous Marie George:

How would you like to pet a beautiful gay soubrette?
Oh, you can bet we'd like to pet the gayest soubrette
   that we could get.
How would you like to be, a little bit gay with me?
Oh, Hully Gee, we'd like to be as gay as the very old
   deuce with thee.

At another theater, further uptown, *The Wild Rose* was playing with Evelyn Nesbit in the chorus; Irene Bently was the star and Eddie Foy was the comic:

I fell into a mortar bed from the 42nd Floor.
I never was, in all my life, so mortified before.

There was a patter song in this show, one of the numerous verses went:

Lady gets on street car with a crying baby
Conductor stares at kid which angers the lady
She says "Rubber!" as she hands him pennies five
Conductor says "Is it? I thought it was alive."

Ah well, after a few beers it was a lot of fun.

Then there was the old Hippodrome with its water ballets and elephants sliding down into the tank and splashing us in the front row where we were enjoying a "worm's eye view of the stage." Also the old Madison Square Garden with Diana on top. We saw Sir Henry Irving in the theater there in *Dante* and, a few years later, just missed seeing Harry Thaw shoot Stanford White in the Roof Garden. It was the opening night of a new show; I remember it was called *Mademoiselle Champagne*. I was cruising around with a charming young lady from Maine and we tried to get tickets for the show but the box office was sold out so we went elsewhere. Three hours later, when the theaters let out, the newsboys were crying the murder.

Despite all the attractions ashore, I kept up with my reading. I remember that some of the books out that year were *Mrs. Wiggs of the Cabbage Patch, Kim* by Rudyard Kipling, *Monsieur Beaucaire* by Booth Tarkington, *Lord Jim* by Joseph Conrad, *Graustark* by George McCutcheon, and *The Hound of the Baskervilles* by Conan Doyle. Besides the music hall attractions, there were Richard Mansfield in *Cyrano de Bergerac* at the Garden; Julia Marlowe in *The Countess Valeska, If I Were King* with Edward Sothern, and William Gillette in *Sherlock Holmes*. Among the musicals were *The Wizard of Oz* with Montgomery and Stone, Ethel Barrymore in *Captain Jinks of the Horse Marines*, little George M. Cohan in *Peck's Bad Boy*, and Victor Herbert's *Babes in Toyland*. I watched Houdini escape from a straitjacket at the Colonial and mounted to the top of the newly erected Flatiron Building, the highest in the world at twenty stories. Coming home in the evenings with our girls, we sang, "I Love You Truly," "Mighty Lak' a Rose," "In the Good Old Summer Time," "Bill Bailey, Won't You Please Come Home?" and "Oh, Didn't He Ramble?" We would see horse-drawn fire engines, belching smoke, galloping down the streets, wooden Indians to mark cigar stores (I had taken to smoking a pipe and my particular brand of tobacco—which I kept to all my life—was Prince Albert); watched "Gentleman Jim" Corbett work out at his gym where Gimbel's now stands, and admired Charles Dana Gibson's drawings. I still think the Gibson Girl was the loveliest of all feminine ideals. We enjoyed cartoon strips such as "Happy Hooligan" (who always wore a tin can for a hat and was famous for his team of ultra-polite Frenchmen "Pardon me, my dear Alphonse." "After you, my dear Gaston") and the brattish Katzenjammer Kids. In those days, all small boys had to be portrayed as little monsters.

I spent as much time at the opera as the music halls—well, almost as much. I saw *Il Trovatore, Pagliacci, Aida, Tosca* and many more. I heard the famous Melba (the only singer in history to have a dessert named after her) do the mad scene from *Lucia*, the lovely Fritzi Scheff (who later went into musical comedy) as Zerlina in *Don Giovanni*, the great Madam Schumann-Heink sing *Tristan,* and even—some years later—listened to the most notable of them all, Caruso. I recall that the day before he opened at the Met—I think it was in *Rigoletto*—he had been arrested in the monkey house at the zoo for pinching a woman; an act that would have caused no comment in his native Italy. When he appeared, the boys in the peanut gallery shouted, "Monkey house, monkey house!" at him which notably disconcerted the great tenor.

But my most vivid memory of Caruso was in *La Bohème,* when, carried away by a scene in which the mad, gay students stage an orgy in their attic he took a flying leap onto a bed. As Caruso was a little fat man, built along the lines of Bud Costello, the bed collapsed under his weight and the whole cast had to rescue Rodolfo from the wreck.

I also saw Lina Cavalieri in *Fedora,* a stunning beauty who could have gotten by on her looks even if she didn't sing a note. She had a famous affair with Willie Vanderbilt, and as a result his father—who was one of the directors of the Metropolitan—had her fired. This didn't bother Lina in the least as she promptly married another millionaire named Robert Chanler, first stipulating that he had to sign over all his fortune to her. This the infatuated young man did whereupon Lina divorced him. Chanler had a brother innured in a madhouse who promptly telegraphed him, "Who's loony now?" I missed seeing Lilli Lehmann, one of my lifelong regrets, but on subsequent leaves I heard Galli-Curci and Rosa Ponselle.

Perhaps it is only nostalgia, but it seems to me that these great divas were far more colorful and romantic than the actresses and motion picture stars of today. It was an era of glamorous women. The girls then looked like girls. They had full figures and graceful costumes, not like the skinny flappers of the twenties or the girls of today, all of whom look exactly alike and have no allure. It was so different in New York when I was a young man.

In 1903, the fleet, together with the *Kearsarge*, was transferred to Pensacola, Florida. There I had an experience which convinced me, if I had ever doubted it, of the authenticity of the "miracle cures" of Lourdes and Saint Anne de Beaupré.

I have mentioned that I had a game leg, resulting from an accident I suffered during the Spanish-American War. While the *Kearsarge* was at anchor in Pensacola Harbor, my leg began acting up and by the evening of April 16th the pain became almost unbearable. I was unable to stand on it; when my right heel touched the deck a hot flash of pain shot up my leg from knee to hip. Suddenly we received word that a major riot had broken out in the "red-light district" of the town involving both Army and Navy personnel and civilians. One man had already been killed and half a dozen were down with gunshot wounds. The local police were completely unable to handle the situation. To make matters worse, one of our two Marine officers was on leave and the other was ashore visiting a country house several miles away.

Since the time I had had the bad luck to command the landing force in Buffalo at the time of President McKinley's assassination, I'd done considerable thinking over how to handle troops sent to suppress a riot so I was eager to put my theories to the test. Completely forgetting my leg, I ran on deck and volunteered to take our Marine Guard ashore. As no else cared to undertake this thankless job, Lieutenant Eberle, flag secretary to Admiral Barker in command of the fleet, was only too happy to send me. It was a more delicate mission than I realized at the time (I was only twenty-four), for if we had killed anyone—or if any of the men under my command had been killed or seriously injured—I could have been tried for murder or at least lost my dearly won commission in the Navy.

First, let me explain what had happened. As I have said, the sailors in those days were a far rougher lot than the modern bluejackets. One man from the fleet, obviously drunk, had tried to gain admission to a brothel, which was refused. He then started to kick the door down. The madam called the police and two officers answered the call. By the time they arrived, the man had succeeded in entering the house and was attacking the women. The policemen dragged him out, sent for a patrol car, and were trying to put him inside when a crowd of sailors, hearing his cries, came to his help and attacked the police. They had knocked down one policeman and were trampling him when his comrade and the officer driving the patrol wagon, drew their revolvers and fired, killing one sailor. The crowd drew back, the patrol wagon was able to drive away, and all might have been well had not a petty officer blown his whistle, signaling for help. In seconds, scores of men came racing to the scene . . . not only seamen and marines but also the rougher element from the city slums. The officers were attacked again and forced to fire blindly into the crowd. The furious seamen began to break into downtown shops to obtain fire-arms, only knowing that their messmates were being fired upon. Naturally, local roughs seized on the situation to start a general looting of the town and the whole situation got out of hand.

Let me say that when anyone in authority, be he in the armed services or not, undertakes to lead a handful of men against a mob numbering several hundred rough, dangerous individuals, his first duty should be to his own contingent. The marines put under my command had no choice but to obey my orders, and it was up to me to look out for their interests and not risk them unduly. Too often it seems to me that the general public and a certain type of newspaper reporter regard men in uniform as fair game for any gang of hoodlums who cares to attack them. They seem to think that because the representatives of law and order have guns that fact renders them invulnerable to rocks, bottles, or even bullets fired at them by a crowd outnumbering them several hundred to one. There have been cases when troops attacked by a mob (as happened in the Pennsylvania coal fields) and ordered not to fire have allowed the guns to be torn from their hands by the crowd rather than defend themselves. The natural result was that a number were killed and still others blinded for life when the half-mad crowd gouged out their eyes with bits of broken glass. A gun, if you are forbidden to use it, is of no more value than a stick. I had long ago come to the conclusion that if there was the slightest question of whether one of the men entrusted to my care or a rioter was to die, I would not hesitate in making my choice.

At the same time, I perfectly realized that it was my responsiblity to restore order without bloodshed if possible. It is a great mistake not to train troops for possible riot action because it is extremely easy for an ignorant officer to blunder into a position where he has no option but to fire a volley into his attackers with disastrous results. I had had no training yet after the Buffalo experience, I had luckily turned over in my mind the various situations with which I might be confronted in such an event and how to deal with them.

I had under my command about forty men; consisting of the Marine Guard on the *Kearsarge* plus our master-at-arms who took with him all our available supply of hand irons, our bugler (so signals could be given above the roar of a crowd,), and two hospital corpsmen. I had no idea how large the mob was or how much of the city was in their hands.

It was nine o'clock in the evening when we landed on Palafox Wharf, where we were met by a most excited chief of police. I left a non-commissioned officer and two men on the wharf to guard our boats and make sure our retreat would not be cut off, always an important consideration when your force is greatly outnumbered. We then marched up Palafox Street, dropping off marine guards at each corner to prevent our being attacked from the rear. So far we had seen only scattered rioters and encountered no resistance.

But at the conflex of Palafox and Saragossa we saw waiting for us a large and very belligerent crowd covering both sidewalks and most of the street. They clearly intended to stop our advance and there seemed no way to disburse them except by firing a volley.

The only description of the mental workings of a mob that I had ever read was in Mark Twain's *Huckleberry Finn*. Twain emphasizes that a mob is absolutely dependent on its leaders; once they are eliminated it will break up easily. My trouble was that I could not see any signs of leaders. Then it occurred to me that they would in all probability be well in the background, hiding themselves behind their more excited . . . or drunken . . . followers. The question was how to get at them? I saw a restaurant named Nick's with a second floor balcony so I ordered a non-commissioned officer and two men whom I knew to be sharpshooters to break in the door and take up positions on the balcony. Here they could look down on the crowd and see anyone directing the action.

As soon as they were in position, I shouted to the mob to clear the street or they would be hurt. I then ordered the marines to advance with fixed bayonets. At once a man in the crowd began shouting, "Fire on the bastards!" I halted the guard and directed two privates to make a rush for him. The man turned and ducked back into the crowd, but the three marines on the balcony of Nick's establishment could keep track of him and saw him run into a saloon. Again I ordered the guard to advance. The mob held for a few seconds but their leader had fled and as a newspaper reporter who was present later wrote: "The appearance of the men from the *Kearsarge* with bristling bayonets and rattling chains that they were carrying showed they were not out for pleasure." The mob broke and ran. I sent a corporal's guard into the saloon and they soon returned with their prisoner in chains. I told them to hand him over to the guard at the dock and then return immediately. Meanwhile, we continued down Saragossa to the corner of Baylen.

Here there was another large mob, and I could see several men urging the crowd to attack us. I sent two details into houses at either side of the street with orders to station themselves at windows commanding the intersection and to be prepared to pick off any agitators.

This turned out not to be necessary for as soon as the troublemakers saw rifles trained on them from above making it impossible for them to hide behind their fellows, they promptly lost heart. As the marines came on steadily the crowd disbursed. This was the last resistance. The chief of police now came up to me and requested that we allow "the more orderly people to return as otherwise it would interfere with the business of the saloons and disorderly houses." So we retired to the docks. In all, we took twelve prisoners who were later turned over to the authorities. Not a shot was fired and no one hurt.

I was gratified—and rather surprised—to find that I had become something of a hero. The next day, two newspapers ran headlines praising my part in suppressing the riots. One read: "Ensign Daniel Mannix receives deserved praise. The commander in chief of the fleet commends him for his services." The other ran: "Commended by the Admiral. Ensign Mannix receives very nice notice from commander in chief for the way he handled the marines." *Leslie's Weekly*, a popular periodical, ran a picture of me and a brief description of the riot on a page, "People Talked About." It said, "Young Ensign Mannix led a company of marines with a bravery and discretion which effected a prompt suppression of the riot without bloodshed." Quite different from the "double reflecting, triple-flattering" individual who had led the landing party at Buffalo! And yet surprisingly I was the same person and had behaved much the same on both occasions.

Most amazing of all, the pain in my leg had disappeared and didn't return again for nearly a month. Now, don't tell me that the pain was all in my imagination; it was a concrete thing.

A few days later I received the following letter from Rear Admiral Barker, the commander in chief of our fleet:

> U.S. North Atlantic Fleet
> Flagship *Kearsarge*
> Pensacola, Florida
> April 20, 1903

Sir,

1. The Commander in Chief commends the efficient manner in which you assisted in suppressing a riot in the City of Pensacola on the night of the 16th inst. while in charge of the Marines sent from the *Kearsarge*.
2. I have learned that you were a volunteer for this duty which fact makes your conduct all the more praiseworthy.

3. Doubtless your presence with the Marines prevented much bloodshed.

Respectfully,
A. S. Barker
Rear Admiral, US Navy

Ensign D. P. Mannix   Commander in Chief
USS *Kearsage*   US Atlantic Fleet

At least my presence did prevent my having sciatica for nearly a month! Also, I received my commission as a lieutenant (junior grade) as an additional reward. I was on my way up the ladder.

Shortly after this, the *Kearsage* was ordered to make a "goodwill tour" to Imperial Germany. I was delighted as I had never been to Europe. If I could have foreseen that I would be required to be a second in a duel and also find myself in a scrap that could have easily destroyed friendly relations between the United States and Germany, I might have been less enthusiastic.

CHAPTER FIVE

Imperial Germany (1903)

I vas der Ruler of der landt
Und Me and Gott all dings gommand.

—Hoch der Kaiser

AT THIS TIME, relations between Germany and the United States were strained, to say the least. Many regarded war as inevitable, and a war with Germany would have been a very different matter than a war with Spain. Germany had arrived late on the colonial scene and was trying to make up for lost time. She was determined to seize any lands not under the flag of one of the great powers. There had already been a crisis with her over the Dewey-von Diederich affair.

Immediately after Dewey's victory at Manila, Vice Admiral Otto von Diederich with eight warships had sped to the Philippines "to protect German interests" which consisted of one small export firm. His fleet was considerably stronger than any force that Dewey could muster. Even though our fleet was in possession of the harbor as a result of Dewey's victory, von Diederich sailed into the bay pointedly ignoring an interrogation signal from the USS *Raleigh*, who was stationed at the entrance. The *Raleigh* was commanded by a peppery officer named Capt. Joe Coghlan, noted for being a character. Coghlan's response was to send a shot across the vice admiral's bow. Foaming with rage, the German was forced to heave-to and fly an indentification pennant. Von Diederich then asserted his authority by stopping the insurgents (whom we were supporting) from capturing a Spanish outpost on Grande Island. Dewey arranged an interview with von Diederich and asked him bluntly, "Are you trying to provoke a war?" Von Diederich avoided the issue by replying, "I am obeying the orders of the Kaiser" which indeed he was. As was later learned, the Kaiser had told him to create an incident that would give Germany an excuse to occupy the Philippines. Fortunately at this point a British fleet arrived under Captain Chichester, who moved his ships between the combatants, Great Britain having no desire to see the approaches to Hong Kong, Singapore, and Burma in German hands. For a time, von Diederich was checked, but then the irrepressible Captain Coghlan nearly touched off another crisis by reciting, after a few drinks, a comic poem, "Hoch der Kaiser," better know as "Me und Gott." As the Germans referred to the Kaiser as "the All-Highest" and regarded him as only slightly less than divine, Captain Coghlan's humor took a good deal of explaining away.

Next, an event occurred in Samoa which bade fair to precipitate a full-scale conflict.

Samoa was of importance because of its geographical position. England, Germany, and the United States all had representatives there. We had been able to establish a coaling station in the best port in the islands; Pago Pago—later famous as the scene of Somerset Maugham's *Rain* with the immortal Sadie Thompson. Samoa had a king but the real power lay with the various local chiefs. It was simple for a foreign power to enlist the aid of one of these chiefs by giving him arms or money and then moving in troops to "protect our ally against aggression."

The Samoan king had died leaving two rival candidates for the throne. The tribal leaders elected one of the men, and here matters would have rested had not the losing party refused to accept the decision. It was generally believed that the main instigator of the trouble was the German consul, Rose. Apia, the chief city, soon became unsafe for either Americans or Englishmen. Then fighting started during which two of my classmates, Monaghan and Lansdale, were killed.

A native uprising, directed almost surely by Consul Rose, had broken out. A joint Anglo-American force set out to suppress it. The force was commanded by Lieutenant Freeman of the British Navy and our contingent was under Lt. Philip VanHorn Lansdale, a member of a prominent Pennsylvania family. Our artillery consisted of a Colt automatic gun that was fired by means of an ammunition belt that passed through the gun from one side to the other, "feeding" the cartridges as it went along, one of the earlier types of machine gun.

The line of march of the landing party was through a dense jungle and at one place it was necessary to ford a stream. In carrying the gun across, one of the men slipped and wet the ammunition belt. Nobody thought anything of it at the time.

A little further on, while proceeding single file along a narrow trail, they were suddenly attacked by a large force of Samoans armed mainly with spears but having some firearms. A shot struck Lansdale in the leg disabling him and, in the confusion, the two officers and the gun's crew became separated from the main body. As the Samoans, big powerful men, came charging down on them, an attempt was made to get the Colt gun into action. The ammunition belt, wet and swollen from the stream, started passing through the gun and then jammed. Monaghan could easily have abandoned Lansdale and saved himself, in fact Lansdale urged him to do it, but he stood his ground and drew his pistol. As he fired the first shot the Samoans were on top of him. They threw him down and cut off his head and then that of Lansdale. Mounting the heads on spears they paraded them through the native villages.

While we were at Pensacola in 1903 trouble with Germany came closer to home waters. Castro, the Venezuelan dictator, had refused to meet the financial obligations which he had incurred in his dealings with the European powers and had defied them to force him to do so. Germany and England sent warships to enforce their orders. Some small towns were bombarded, expeditionary forces had been landed, and the custom houses occupied. Needless to say, these operations "lay athwart the hawse" of the Monroe Doctrine. It was thought extremely likely that Germany, especially, hoped to use the incident as an excuse to occupy Venezuela and turn it into a German colony.

While the *Kearsarge* was stationed off Pensacola, we had staged a series of drills with our 8-inch guns. Ever since the Battle of Santiago, gunnery had been a hobby of mine and I had worked hard to train my gun crew. I was in command of the afterturret and we were able to score ten successive bull's eyes in five minutes, firing at a target 1,600 feet away, while the ship was moving at the rate of ten miles an hour. This proved to be a world's record and Admiral Taylor, chief of the Bureau of Navigation, personally commended us. Our government, alarmed by the hostile acts of England and Germany, ordered the *Kearsarge* to proceed at once to Port of Spain, Trinidad, later to be reinforced by the main fleet under Admiral Dewey. It looked like war, and I was eager to see how my gun crew would behave under actual combat conditions.

I have often wondered if the Latin American nations who talk so glibly of "Yankee imperialism" ever stop to consider that the only reason they exist is because of the protection of the United States Navy. Otherwise, Latin America would have been carved up long ago among the great powers as was Africa and Indo-China. In those days, any weak nation was considered fair game by the big powers, although they were seldom willing to risk war in order to gain new territories. Hence the sight of the *Kearsarge* caused a sudden change in the European vessels' actions. Our anchor cable had scarcely ceased rattling through the hawse pipe when signal flags sprang up their masts recalling their landing parties. A few days later the appearance of the main fleet under Admiral Dewey settled the matter and the European vessels withdrew. As one newspaper put it:

> Yankee Dewey's near La Guira
> Yankee Dewey Dandy
> Maybe just as well to have
> Our Yankee Dewey handy!

I doubt if the general public realizes how often a show of strength—and naturally you must have the strength to show—prevents more serious trouble. Except for the arrival of our fleet, the Germans would have unquestionably established a naval base in Venezuela which would have been a nasty business in both the First and Second World wars. Yet little affairs like this hardly receive mention in our history books and so people do not realize the constant need of a battle fleet.

If Germany did not want a war with the United States, neither did we want a war with Germany. So President Theodore Roosevelt decided to send four warships on a friendly mission to North German ports. These "friendship tours" were quite common in those days and paradoxically served a dual purpose: they reminded the foreign power that we had a powerful Navy that could reach their home waters while at the same time allowed the people to meet Americans and learn that we were not all strange, uncivilized barbarians. Of course, it was of vital importance that the ships' companies taking part in these missions do nothing to offend their hosts during their visit.

The *Kearsarge* was designated for this duty and together with three other warships we sailed for Europe on June 3rd, 1903. Rear Admiral Cotton in command of the squadron, transferred his flag to the *Kearsarge*. Shortly after he came on board, I received orders to report for duty as junior aide on his personal staff, which was gratifying but also entailed social and diplomatic responsibilities for which I was ill prepared.

I'll quote from the diary I kept at the time:

KIEL, GERMANY. JUNE 23RD

We arrived at the entrance to Kiel Harbor at nine-thirty this morning and found four German launches waiting for us; one went alongside each of the American ships and an officer of the Imperial Navy came on board to pilot her into the harbor. These men also brought with them a copy of the Harbor Regulations (thoughtfully printed in English), a chart showing the landings to be used by the officers and those for the enlisted men's liberty parties (the Germans took it for granted that officers and enlisted men had to have separate landings) and a summary of what was to be done each day of the ensuing week.

We were accorded the special honor of occupying four of the five inner mooring buoys, the fifth being reserved for the Royal Yacht *Hohenzollern*, due to arrive the following day. It was a splendid berth, just off the Kaiserlich (or Imperial) Yacht Club, built by the emperor at a cost of over a million dollars, and had an excellent view of the flower of the German Navy, forty battleships and cruisers, moored in faultless alignment, ready to receive the All-Highest on the morrow.

Everything, even down to the smallest detail of the ceremonial routines, had been carried out with absolute precision in a way that made our own efforts seem clumsy and amateurish. As one of the younger officers remarked in awe, "If these people make war this efficiently, I hope to heaven we never have to fight them."

Our pilot now produced a letter informing us that each of the ships in our squadron was to be entertained by two of the German's. The *Wittlesbach* and the *Kaiser Frederick II* were to be hosts to the *Kearsarge*, whether we liked it or not.

To avoid numberless official calls, the Germans had arranged that all the admirals and captains of their fleet, headed by Prince Henry of Prussia, would meet at once on the *Kaiser Frederick II* and our admiral, his staff, and captains, would pay their call at the same time, our admiral receiving a thirteen-gun salute on his departure. His call would then be returned by Vice Admiral Prince Henry, plus two rear admirals, who would then come on board the *Kearsarge*. We were warned that their proper salutes were seventeen- and thirteen-guns, respectively. Obviously all this protocol was regarded as vitally important to our hosts, and the slightest breach would be deeply resented. As Admiral Cotton's aide, a large part of seeing that everything went smoothly was up to me, and I would rather have faced Cervera's fleet any day than these ramrod stiff Germans.

I had barely time to shift into Special Full Dress and hurry up on deck to see that the admiral's barge was ready when a German launch came alongside and an officer stepped out and came up the ladder. He introduced himself as Lieutenant Baron von Kottwitz and added, "I have orders direct from Prince Henry to report to your admiral for duty on his staff during your stay in Kiel."

This news came as a considerable relief as it was clear that the lieutenant baron knew a great deal more about protocol than I did. He wore at least a dozen medals, many of them gold and silver, but there was a bronze one with three bars that looked rather more businesslike than the others. I maneuvered until I had him in the proper light and then read on the bars, "Tientsin," "Peking" and "Seymour Expedition." He had been in the Boxer Rebellion in China and had been shot over after all—I had regarded him as nothing but an elaborately costumed lackey. We got to be good friends and I later asked him about the medals. Curiously, he was as proud of the medals that meant nothing as of the ones that represented really dangerous service. He positively beamed as he showed me a sunburst he had received for accompanying the emperor on a trip to Jerusalem, while the only medal of the whole lot that was worthwhile he passed over indifferently with the one word "Boxer."

When we saw that all the German officers on the *Frederick* had assembled and that their band and marine guard were paraded, Admiral Cotton, Flag Lieutenant Hussey and I left the *Kearsarge* in the admiral's barge. We ran along the German flagship and, as Admiral Cotton reached the quarterdeck, an honor guard of a hundred sailors brought their rifles to the present, then to the shoulder and then marched forward; every movement being like a piece of machinery. I had never seen anything like it, not even with our marines who, naturally, are far better drilled than our seamen.

We were presented to Vice Admiral Prince Henry of Prussia, who was most courteous and affable, and to the other flag officers and captains. They made a most impressive group in their gorgeous uniforms, and the two thin gold stripes on my sleeve were in pitiful contrast to the masses of gold lace, stars and crowns surrounding me. I met von Müller, Prince Henry's flag lieutenant, and he kindly asked me to dine with him at one of the open air gardens ashore that night. I accepted gratefully.

After conversing sufficiently to satisfy official etiquette, our barge was called alongside and we shoved clear of the gangway, standing at attention while the salute to our admiral was being fired. We then hurried back to the *Kearsarge* to be ready for the return visit.

We had only been on board for five minutes when Prince Henry and his staff arrived. They stayed only a few minutes, chatting with the admiral and captains on the quarterdeck, and when they left and the salutes had been fired, the guard, band, side boys and boatswains mate were allowed to go below for the first time that day. All forenoon they had been "standing by." I suspect that they were less impressed with German ceremony than we were.

While all this official business was being attended to, no visitors had been allowed to come on board, but now the ban was lifted and a party from the liner *Princessin Victoria Luise* came alongside. When they came on board I offered to show them the ship. There were three ladies and two men; the older of the two men introduced himself as Lieutenant General Baron Doppledorf; the other was Doctor Müller. The ladies were Baroness Franchetti from Vienna (little, dark, and lively), Baroness Hesse from Berlin (tall, blonde, and placid) and a very pretty girl, Countess Eulendorf, also from Berlin.

I took them over the upper decks and then down to the wardroom where we had wine; they were very jolly and spoke both English and French. A number of my messmates joined the party and our guests were very insistent that we visit the *Luise*, which we promised to do when the official functions were over. I made arrangements to meet Countess Eulendorf on shore later that evening and have her show me the town.

I should mention here that the German women are perfectly beautiful. They are magnificently built and by no means the clumsy creatures popular prejudice attributes to them. Quite the contrary, in fact. I found them most vivacious and delightful.

Shortly after they left, von Müller came alongside in the *Wittlesbach*'s launch and we went ashore together. Kiel, harbor and town, is a beautiful place; in fact, all of Schleswig-Holstein is beautiful. One can hardly blame the Danes for their bitter hatred of everything German when you remember that, fifty years ago, this entire region belonged to Denmark.

Ashore there was a large number of attractive outdoor cafés, each with its own band or orchestra. We went to the most pretentious and I had my first experience of what real beer is; the stuff we had been

drinking in the States was only a pale imitation. Von Müller had a
stein with a music box concealed in its bottom; every time he raised it
from the table it commenced playing a tune. He supplied me with a
similar stein which played a rousing march. There was a large orchestra on a stage which played selections from the lighter operas, songs,
and German waltzes with a great swing and dash. It was a positive
treat to watch the musicians; every man took the most intense interest
in his part, the bass violas and drums playing with the same vim and
enthusiasm as the first violin and solo cornet. Between the rich, strong
beer and the music I enjoyed myself greatly.

One selection I remember in particular was called, "March of
Heralds' Trumpets." A dozen men with long coach horns lined up in
front of the band proper and introduced trumpet calls through the
music. I was anxious to have this repeated and von Müller, observing
that I must begin to learn German, told me to ask the head waiter for
an encore. I didn't know a word of German except "Ich liebe dich"
which would hardly have done so when the waiter came over, I raised
my closed fist to my mouth and said sonorously, "Ta-ra-ta-ra" delighted at my ingenuity. The waiter, with a beaming smile, nodded
intelligently and said, "Ja, ja, bier!" and filled my musical stein to
overflowing.

The next morning Prince Henry's flag lieutenant brought on
board our ship a copy of a general signal that had been sent to the
German Fleet the evening before. As an example of the enormous
importance the Germans attached to form and ceremony as well as the
care with which they worked out every detail, I will include it here:

On the 24th instant in the forenoon his Majesty the Emperor will arrive
by way of the Kiel Canal. As soon as the ship nearest the canal sights the
Imperial Standard she will dress ship, followed down the line in succession
by each vessel, the National Ensign at the masthead, then will salute with 33
guns and man the rail. Bands to play the National Air. Ships' Companies to
give three cheers for the Emperor when the *Hohenzollern* passes.

We had received some time before unofficial information as to the
time of the Kaiser's arrival and also what we were expected to do
during the ceremonies. So we had had plenty of experience in firing
salutes and in "dressing ship" (running a line of signal flags from the
bow, over the mastheads, to the stern) but having to man the rails and
cheering in unison was something new.

With some help from von Müller, we worked out a system. All hands were assembled on deck, the only men below being those on watch in fire, engine, and dynamo rooms, whose presence at their posts was essential to the safety of the ship. Then the First Division was marched to the forecastle, the Fourth to the quarterdeck and the Second and Third to the superstructure. The Divisional Officers deployed their men along the rails as far outboard as possible, the proper interval being determined by each man extending his right arm and placing his hand on the left shoulder of the man on his right. Then the vacant places, or "holidays," were filled by members of the Engineer's and Powder Divisions. Thus we had a wall of men around the entire circumference of the upper deck, the tops of the turrets, the bridges and even the fighting tops, each man's arm extended and his hand on the shoulder of his neighbor.

After the men had learned their stations, came the "cheering drill." The Executive Officer, or "cheer leader" if you prefer, began by directing the bugler to sound the Assembly, whereupon the divisions fell in at their regular places for inspection. Then came the order "Man the rails!" the bugler sounded the Deploy and the men ran to their stations, extended their arms, and remained absolutely motionless. Then came the order, "Three cheers for the Kaiser!" every man of the eight hundred executed a half face to the right, removed his hat and dropped his right hand to his side, the left arm remaining extended. Then the order, "Hip!" at which each right arm was raised to its full length, and then again, "Hip!" at which the hats were waved in unison above the heads and then a "Hurrah!" At first the men regarded the whole business as nonsense and went through the drill reluctantly, but after awhile they got into the spirit of the thing and when the "Hurrah!" came you would have thought that William II was their dearest friend.

When von Müller was satisfied that we could go through the performance without disgracing ourselves—and him—he left, and we all shifted into our best clothes while the crew proceeded to brush each other until the carefully swept decks were littered with pieces of whisk broom and the long suffering sweepers had to be piped anew. All the officers put on their Special Full Dress uniforms with such medals as they possessed—mainly Spanish War, Philippine and China decorations—and then commenced struggling into new white kid gloves. As my Special Full Dress is so tight that I can't sit down in it, I went on deck to watch for the coming of royalty.

The signal flags had been broken out and bent to the dressing lines which were stretched along the decks, each individual flag being carefully spread out so it would fly clear when they were run aloft as "fouled" bunting is considered most slovenly and unnautical. All these long preparations were most nerve wracking, and I'm sure we could have gone into battle with far less trouble and anxiety.

The quartermasters were standing by the dressing lines and the chief was nervously watching the harbor entrance through his long glass. The executive officer had just returned after a run around the ship in the steam cutter to make sure her sides were clean and no "Irish pennants" visible anywhere when, away down the line we saw a puff of smoke followed by the boom of the first gun of the Royal Salute.

Immediately there was frantic activity; the guard and the band were paraded, the rails manned and the saluting guns' crews called to quarters. As ship after ship took up the salute, the roar of the guns was accompanied by the flutter and color of lines of dressing flags running aloft. We could see the *Hohenzollern* now; a yacht as big as a small liner, painted white with the Imperial Standard of Germany at her mainmast truck. Her rails were manned, her band and a guard of sailors under arms paraded on her quarterdeck and her bridge crowded with officers, both of the Army and Navy, glittering with decorations.

When her bow was abreast of our flagstaff the first gun of our salute was fired, the bugles sounded four flourishes, and the band struck up the German National Air. Just as our men gave the first cheer, I saw the emperor. I had been looking in vain for him among his officers; happening to cast my eyes aloft I saw a small flying bridge, just large enough to accommodate one person, and on this bridge was the emperor in the full dress uniform of an admiral of the Fleet, his sword by his side and his right hand raised in a rigid military salute. A most spectacular and impressive entrance. Whatever else he may have been, the Kaiser was a wonderful showman.

As soon as the *Hohenzollern* had moored to her buoy, our captains came on board, the barge was called away and we started for the Royal Yacht in company with launches from every flagship in the harbor. Here something happened which turned out rather unfortunately for me. As the barges ran alongside the German gangway our engines got "on center," failed to reverse, and we had the mortification of running by instead of stopping abreast the lower gangway platform. Very humiliating and before the eyes of the entire fleet. The admiral ordered me to stay in the barge to make sure that she came alongside properly when he left; so I never got a chance to go on board the Royal Yacht.

When we returned to the *Kearsarge*, we found cards from one of two German ships who were our sponsors—the *Kaiser Frederick II*—for a dance that afternoon from four to six. All the Wardroom Mess, except those on duty, put on their frock coats and went over at the hour specified. The quarterdeck of the *Frederick* had been cleared and waxed for dancing and on the superstructure were two long rows of booths and tents. Here I was able to renew my acquaintance with the pretty Countess Eulendorf who looked like an exquisite blue-eyed doll. She was so tiny that I had to take care not to step on her while we were dancing a German variety of the Lanciers.

The next afternoon I went ashore with Baron von Kottwitz who took me to the Yacht Club. As we crossed the threshold, he clicked his heels together and bowed to the room. Everyone there rose and bowed just as formally. Evidently Kottwitz is someone of importance.

During dinner, he told me some stories of the Boxer Rebellion. Two of his men had straggled and been cut off. Nothing was heard of them until the allies took Pekin several weeks later when the first sight that greeted him as he entered the gate was the bodies of his men crucified head downward. "Naturally, we took terrible vengeance," he remarked casually. I didn't know whom to be the most sorry for: the unhappy German captives or the wretched people of the city.

Also at our table was Lieutenant von Leffert of the Second Life Guards, Hussar Regiment of Queen Louise of Prussia. (Louise was the beautiful queen of the Napoleonic era.) I asked von Leffert how many regiments of hussars there were and he said ninety; then I asked him how many men in a regiment and he said a thousand. I thought of our own tiny army and how our newspapers and politicians were constantly complaining about German aggression and how we should put a stop to it. Yet whenever anyone suggested increasing our armed forces he was denounced as a militarist.

One of the guests was the celebrated Princess Daisy of Pless. I was always interested in "professional beauties" (nowadays they seem to have vanished like the dinosaurs) and was glad for the chance to see her. Princess Daisy wore a stiff-brimmed sailor hat and was decidedly

Junoesque proportioned. I wouldn't have cared to "get a little bit gay" with her. I was considered something of a boxer at Annapolis but Daisy could have laid me flat with one wallop of her lily white hand.

Later the Kaiser arrived with the Kaiserin; she looked much older than he and was dressed very quietly. They went from group to group chatting pleasantly and, as they moved, the entire company also changed front, for you must never turn your back on royalty. It was curious to me how he was able to combine a formal and yet friendly manner which, I suppose, was the result of long training.

While at Kiel, I noticed a German custom that seems strange to us. There is a regulation that prohibits an officer in uniform from carrying a parcel. Several times I saw men in brilliant uniforms with clinking swords striding along followed by their wives staggering under a huge bundle that looked like the week's wash. In Germany, the women know their place and a very humble place it is too.

We had been notified that the Kaiser was coming on board the *Kearsarge* for breakfast the next morning so elaborate preparations had to be made. A long horseshoe table was built on the quarterdeck, the awnings spread, and the ship decorated with flags and palms. When the Imperial Barge was reported heading our way the rails were manned, guard and band paraded, and the officers lined up on the starboard side of the quarterdeck with the left of the line abreast the gangway.

The emperor's barge had fourteen rowers; he steered it himself and made an excellent landing in coming alongside our gangway. I noticed that he had a special type of tiller on his boat. Instead of the ordinary tiller, which is moved left or right to make the boat turn to starboard or port, his steering gear was so arranged that it was pulled forward or pushed back and no lateral movement was necessary, making it far less awkward for an officer in dress uniform to handle.

He came over the side and, at the first note of the bugles sounding the flourishes, stood at attention, raised his hand to his vizor in return salute, and remained absolutely rigid until the last note of the National Anthem died away; then he walked down the line of officers, shaking hands with each in turn and speaking pleasantly in excellent English. He was about five feet ten inches tall, very well built, and apparently in fine physical condition.

In later years, when he became so bitterly hated, a lot was said about his "withered arm." I saw him every day for a week, was

presented to him and shook hands with him without noticing anything unusual about his left arm; it may have been a little shorter than
the right but he certainly had the full use of it. I will say that he usually
kept his left hand on his sword hilt which hid any defect there may
have been.

The emperor asked to be shown over the ship so the divisions
were ordered to quarters while he made an amazingly thorough
inspection of everything. He clearly knew what he was about, even
going down to the engine rooms and to the Armory. He took pains to
stop and chat with the men, as well as the officers. I remember his
stopping to converse with a gunners mate who had a large number of
service stripes on his sleeve and asking him numerous questions about
his life in the service. He also stopped a young apprentice (who had
been born in Germany and who looked it) to ask whether he was an
American citizen and then talked with him in German for some time.
Lastly, he checked the sick bay and went into great detail with the
senior medical officer about the X-ray outfit.

Rather to my surprise, he showed a sense of humor. We were
especially proud of our head, or toilet, which was very elegant with
shining brass and nickel and long rows of valves and pumps. Our flag
lieutenant Hussey eagerly exhibited it and then said, "Would you like
to see how it works, your Majesty?" The Kaiser replied politely,
"Why, certainly Mr. Hussey. Please sit right down."

Back on the quarterdeck, the emperor congratulated Captain
Hemphill, captain of the Kearsarge, on the fine condition of the ship
and said he intended to send a cable to "his friend Roosevelt" praising
the Kearsarge and Captain Hemphill's efficiency.

Before leaving, the emperor presented the ship with a beautiful
silver punch bowl over two feet long and foot and a half high and
wanted to give two medals to the orderlies who had attended him.
When he was told that regulations did not permit the acceptance of
decorations from a foreign power without permission of Congress, he
then offered to give ornamental pencils stamped with the royal arms to
all hands. When told that even this was impossible, he shrugged
and remarked, "At least, then, let the crew know that this was my
intention."

That evening I attended a ball at the Naval Academy with "my"
pretty little countess and met her mother who was almost as attractive
as she herself. I didn't meet her father because, as Eulendorf frankly

said, "Father doesn't like Americans," so I passed up the honor of seeing the old gentleman without regrets, being far more interested in his daughter.

All the German mounted officers wear spurs as a part of their uniform and in one "galop" (a "galop" being, as I understand it, a dance in which all the heaviest people in the room form a phalanx and dash down on the innocent spectators kicking right and left) I was spiked in a number of places, some of them so high up that they spoke well for the agility of the Emperor's Cavalry. Several of the ladies had their dresses almost cut to ribbons.

One of the guests wore the uniform of a Highland regiment; kilts, sporran, dirk, bare legs, and all. He was a fine chap but the invigorating air, aided perhaps by his native "Scotch" was a combination too strong for him and after welcoming us as brothers in arms, he insisted on seeing us safely back to our ship. As all the ship's launches had secured for the night, we had to hire a shore boat to get us back to the *Kearsarge*.

Why a soldier should have felt it necessary to row three sailors home is beyond me but, after carefully depositing us in the stern sheets, he manned the oars and gave way boldly. The boat darted from the landing and then stopped with a violent jerk that made our "crew" execute a clever back somersault. He had neglected to cast off the painter. We cast if off for him, put him back on the thwart, and started anew. At about the third stroke, he caught a "crab" and once more went over backwards into the bottom of the boat.

Now I yield to no man in my admiration for the Gordons or the Camerons when passing in review, but their uniforms were certainly never intended for sudden reversals. We lifted him tenderly and once more put him back on his thwart, and, eventually, after colliding with everything in the harbor, he succeeded in ramming the *Kearsarge*'s gangway bows on. We explained the situation to the officer of the deck who, not wishing to create a vacancy in a gallant British regiment, had the anchor watch turned out, the dinghy lowered and the last we saw of our devoted friend was a rear view of his martial figure lying in the bottom of the boat being towed shoreward while he shouted, "Scotland forever!" at the top of his voice.

The next afternoon we gave a reception in return for all the courtesies that Kiel had shown us. The quarterdeck was cleared and several squads set to whittling wax candles over every square inch;

then the band call was sounded and the word passed: "Lay aft to the quarterdeck all hands." Everybody came aft and the band played while the men "broke in the floor" by sliding up and down on it to make it smooth and slippery. Meanwhile the quartermasters and signalmen spread flags under the awnings and draped them around the stanchions. The mess boys arranged the tables for refreshments around the after barbette while, midway between the turret guns, was the Kaiser's punch bowl.

We were rather fearful of the success of the affair as we had had no experience in such formal entertainment. Fortunately, we were a novelty and the guests came in crowds. Among them was Prince Henry and his lovely mistress, a young American girl named Geraldine Farrar, who had a wonderful soprano voice. A few years later I heard her sing the role of Juliette at the Metroplitan Opera House in *Roméo et Juliette*. At first the guests were rather stiff and restrained but I had the happy inspiration of having the Kaiser's punch bowl filled with brandy smashes. American cocktails were unknown in Germany and they were a brilliant success! Soon the punch bowl was surrounded by an ever increasing throng frantically waving their glasses. Our dance floor was not as successful—we found that we had used too much wax and the couples kept falling down and sliding into the waterways—and we had to sprinkle sand on it. Our cards had read, "From Four to Six" but it was eight o'clock before the last boatload left cheering America in general and the *Kearsarge* in particular.

Just when everything looked so prosperous, an incident occurred that nearly turned our goodwill tour into a major disaster.

In the United States, in time of peace, we had never worn our uniforms ashore, and in Kiel no one had thought of changing this custom. In Germany it was understood that civilians got off the sidewalk and walked in the gutter when they saw a German officer in uniform approaching. One of the midshipmen on the *Kearsarge* who was, incidentally, a welterweight boxing champion, had gone ashore and was walking innocently along one of the main streets when he suddenly found himself shouldered into the gutter. At first he thought it was an accident but when he was jostled a second time, he realized it was intentional. This time he swung on the German officer and got home on his jaw. The Germans were not used to using their fists and besides the man never expected a humble civilian to strike an officer of the Kaiser. He went down for the count. By great good chance, there were some other American midshipmen present and they hustled their friend away to avoid trouble. However, in some way the Germans discovered that they were American officers from the *Kearsarge*.

I was just congratulating myself on my happy inspiration of putting cocktails in the punch bowl and thinking how well everything had gone, when the senior member of the Midshipmen's Mess came up to me and asked me to come down to their messroom. His face was as long as the proverbial maintopbowline and I knew at once that something was seriously wrong. He explained that he had come to me for two reasons: I was on the admiral's staff and I had, until recently, been a member of their mess myself.

When I got down to the steerage I found the entire mess assembled, all except the midshipman who had had the run-in with the German officer; they had wisely shut him up in his cabin. There were three young Prussian Army officers there, perfectly calm and perfectly courteous, in full dress uniform including the traditional spiked helmets. After having been formally presented to them, I was informed that they were the bearers of a challenge to fight a duel.

The European custom of dueling had long been considered a joke by most Americans. Mark Twain gives a humorous description of such a duel in which no one gets hurt and everybody kisses everybody else at the end. I would like to know what these wits would have done if actually challenged to fight one of these ridiculous duels. Would they have chosen swords or pistols? I am sure of one thing: the situation would have lost its humor.

In our case, the matter was even more serious. We were there on official business; on a goodwill tour. No matter how such a duel came out, it would have serious repercussions. Nor could our man have insisted on fighting with his fists. To the Germans, such an idea would have been grotesque—like two small boys kicking each other. Nor could our man refuse to fight without giving the impression that we were a nation of cowards, something that, with our strained relationship with Germany, we particularly wanted to avoid.

Suddenly I had what seemed to me a brilliant idea. Knowing the respect Germans had for military regulations, I said, "It is against our Articles of War for a naval officer to fight a duel. If our man does fight a duel, he will be courtmartialed." I thought that would settle the matter.

Instead, the Prussians looked at me in astonishment and replied:

"If our man DOESN'T fight a duel he will be courtmartialed."

This was a facer. I had no idea how to proceed.

Then I had a happy inspiration: one of the few that has ever come at the right moment. I explained that it was an American custom before fighting a duel to drink to one's adversary. The Germans looked rather surprised at this but concurred politely. I had our mess attendant make up a lot of especially potent cocktails called Earth-quakes, which were passed around. To my relief, our guests found them delightful. After we all had drunk to Germany, it was then obligatory on their part to drink to the United States. We then drank a toast to each of the Prussian officers individually. To return the compliment, they insisted on drinking individual toasts to the entire mess.

I am a little foggy about the rest of the afternoon. I seem to recall a chorus of "Ach, du lieber Augustine" being sung to the tune of "Oh Susannah" and a spirited polka danced by all hands, although looking back it might also have been a Tennessee hoe-down. At some point, the mess attendant brought in a bowl of fruit, including a number of apples, and it was unanimously decided that this called for another round of drinks.

Finally, when the proper moment seemed to have arrived, I asked the officer of the deck for the steam cutter to take our distinguished visitors ashore. When the boat was ready we escorted them to the gangway and saw them safely embarked. As the cutter cleared the ship's side, the three arose, gave a snappy salute and a resounding "HOCH!" I was just congratulating myself on the happy termination of the affair and admiring the Germans' martial bearing when to my horror I noticed that impaled on each helmet spike was a large, red apple.

We never heard anything more about the duel but the next day our admiral received a formal request from the German authorities suggesting that in the future all American officers wear their uniforms when on shore.

The last day we were in Kiel, it was announced that instead of sailing directly for home, we were to go to Portsmouth, England, by special invitation of King Edward VII. President Loubet of France would be in London, and we were invited to take part in the functions that were to be given in his honor, including a state ball at Buckingham Palace.

Our admiral took luncheon with Admiral von Koester and later went to the *Hohenzollern* to say good-bye to the emperor and to thank him for all the courtesies we had received. I took advantage of his absence to slip away for a last rendezvous with my countess. We had supper in an inn on the waterfront and later retired to a room overlooking the harbor. We were late getting to sleep and I lost all track of time.

I was awakened by the door being smashed open and in burst Lieutenant Baron von Kottwitz. But what a different individual from the affable, quiet young officer I had known! The baron's spiked mustache was bristling, his formerly impassive features were transformed into a mask of fierce emotion and he rushed toward the bed in a frenzy. I flung back the covers and sprang to my feet despite the countess' shrieks, determined to put up the best defense I could against this man who had obviously been driven into a berserk rage at the desecration of his countrywoman. So greatly moved was the baron that his English deserted him and he could only stand there gibbering German at me. Then realizing that I could not understand him, he rushed to the window and tearing away the curtains, pointed to the harbor shouting "Schau!"

There I beheld a sight far more terrifying than all the lieutenant barons in Germany. The *Kearsarge* was underway! Her anchor was clear of the water and there was a stream from the deck hose playing over the bow to clear the chain from the harbor mud. Even as I looked she began to gather headway and I had a vision of being left in a foreign country in dress uniform and without a penny in my pockets.

Von Kottwitz recovered his English. "Come with me at once!" he shouted. I tried to say good-bye to the countess but she could only sob while holding the sheets around her, "Nein, liebster, you must go with your ship!" I hustled on my clothes while the impatient von Kottwitz dragged me downstairs. On the wharf, he bundled me into a shore boat with a hearty slap on the back while informing the coxswain in choice German polysyllables what would happen to him if he didn't catch the *Kearsarge* before she reached the harbor entrance. We ran alongside the port sea ladder (the gangway ladders had both been unshipped and stowed for sea) and, with a flying leap, I made it and clambered on deck, getting wet to the waist in the process.

Flag Lieutenant Hussey was about to report me for dereliction of duty but Captain Hemphill stopped him. "The admiral's orders were that we were to consort with the locals," he explained. "Lieutenant

Mannix was only complying with his instructions."

I have always believed in obeying orders to the letter.

*   *   *

It seems so strange that a few years later we were fighting Germany. We had done everything we could in our goodwill tour and, I am sure, had created a feeling of friendship for ourselves and our country but beyond that we could not go. Perhaps in the North Sea fighting of 1918, I may even have killed von Kottwitz, and von Müller if they had submarine duty. If so, it was the fortunes of war. They were brave men and I admire them far more than some of the loud-mouthed American patriots who screamed about the "Huns" and wanted to hang the Kaiser but took care not to fight themselves.

Looking through an old scrapbook, I have come across a yellowed letter from my countess which reached me long after leaving Germany. In part it reads: "It is strange you should be reading this so far away in America which I will never see. Nor will I ever see you again I know. *Farewell.* I hope you will find happiness. I have a picture of your ship on my table while I write and no matter what happens, it will always remain there. I wish I had a picture of you also but that was not to be."

I have often wondered what happened to her; if she married, had children, and is happy. Oh well, it was all a long, long time ago.

CHAPTER SIX

Edwardian England (1903)

Oh, I love Society
High Society, Strict Propriety
I would be called an attractive girl
If my Papa had been born an Earl.

—From a musical show of the
period

THE ENGLISH GIRLS possess a special charm which no other women have. I have always been interested in studying the characteristics of other nations so I especially enjoyed our visit to England.

We cast anchor in Portsmouth, England, on the morning of July 7th, 1903, occupying the place of honor reserved for us alongside the railroad jetty, a berth generally kept sacred for the use of the Royal Yacht and the reception of royal visitors. We fired a salute of twenty-one guns to the British flag which was returned by a shore battery gun for gun. Then we fired a salute of seventeen guns to the flag of Admiral Sir Charles Hotham, commandant of the Dock Yard, which was returned—of all things—by Nelson's old flagship the *Victory* that fired thirteen guns to Rear Admiral Cotton. Imagine receiving a salute from the *Victory*! It made me feel as though I were among the immortals.

It was in truth a historic occasion. For the first time a foreign squadron was lying in Portsmouth Harbor. Many captured vessels had lain there since the time of the Spanish Armada but never before had the flag of any foreign power been borne past Southsea Castle by peaceful warships. We were the first.

Our salute was also answered by the British Channel Fleet, looking very grim and efficient in their battle color: six battleships and four cruisers. It is this fleet that has guarded the narrow passage between England and the Continent for four hundred years. I remember one of the cruisers was the *Hogue*. Eleven years later she, together with two other cruisers, the *Cressy* and the *Aboukir* would be torpedoed and sunk in the space of a few minutes by one German submarine, the U-9, commanded by the submarine ace, Weddigen. The loss of life was appalling. Who could then have foreseen the damage one small submarine could do? Well, at least the British got their revenge— such as it was. Later the U-9 was rammed by a British battleship, and Weddigen and all his men went down with her.

We received two communications which, as flag secretary, I opened. One was from King Edward VII and read: "Admiral Cotton, USS *Kearsarge*. The King welcomes you and your squadron to England and is looking forward to greeting you and your officers in London." The other warned us to be careful not to have our heads turned by the perfidious English, to remember our heritage of freedom and democracy, etc. It was signed E. H. Harriman. The name meant nothing to me, but I later learned that he was an American financier who had managed to acquire both the Union Pacific and the Southern Pacific by methods which caused him to be denounced by President Roosevelt. I turned the letter over to Admiral Cotton who after glancing at it, threw it away. I mention the matter only to show how strong the feeling against Great Britain was among a certain type of American.

We received formal visits from the ranking officers of the British Fleet in Portsmouth. Later, I got the chance to meet and chat with them. One was Lord Charles Beresford who had been with the Nile expedition at Abu Klea where the Fuzzy-Wuzzies armed only with swords and spears, broke the British square which had held out against the best of Napoleon's crack regiments. Lord Charles remarked that not only was he in the square but was in the corner that cracked and through which the Fuzzies poured.

"I had a rough go of it because the enemy used me as a 'point d'appui' from which to make flying leaps into the middle of the square," he explained. "Actually, I didn't mind that so much but when they were repulsed, they galloped back over me followed by the British Infantry and those swine, unlike the Fuzzies, wore boots."

Another of our guests, Commodore Sir Archibald Berkeley Milne, didn't appear to be too keen about Americans but after being on board for awhile, he thawed and explained his prejudice. "I was ADC to the King at the time of the William Waldorf Astor affair," he remarked. Astor, the father-in-law of Lady Nancy Astor, was an enormously rich American who moved to England explaining that "no gentleman could possible live in the United States." He was determined to break into English society and purchased Cliveden, one of the show places, where he gave elaborate parties. As he knew nothing about the English, anyone who could afford to rent evening clothes used to attend his dinners, calling themselves, "Lord This" or "The Honorable That," devour his food and wine, and then depart taking as much of the silver with them as their pockets could hold. Astor finally caught on to this practice and determined to stop it.

In an effort to lure the Prince of Wales (later King Edward VII) to his house, he gave large sums to any charity the prince happened to fancy. At last, His Highness felt forced to acknowledge the gifts and although he himself refused to attend this "Yankee blighter's galas" as he put it, he sent Sir Berkeley as his representative. Sir Berkeley explained:

"When I was announced, Astor shouted, 'Who is Sir Berkeley Milne? I never invited him!' and rushing up to me, ordered me out of the house. You may rest assured that I left immediately. While I was getting in my carriage, someone told Astor that I was the Prince of Wales' personal representative and insulting me was equivalent to insulting the prince himself. Astor chased my carriage down the drive, pleading with me to come back and crying out that it was all a terrible mistake. It was a wet night and he was splashed from head to foot with mud. Naturally, I did not return and the prince never asked me to go again."

No wonder Sir Berkeley didn't think much of Americans.

After the official visits were over, the ships were open to visitors and a number came on board, mostly young girls. There are an amazing number of women in England. I think they outnumber the men six to one; in the United States it is the other way around. This is probably the reason why American women are so much more independent. They are a scarce commodity and know it. I was especially struck by the English women's lovely "peaches and cream" complexions. I remember especially one extremely attractive girl who was shown around the ship by a group of enthusiastic young midshipmen. When she returned, I overheard a conversation between her and some of her friends.

A friend (eagerly): Tell me, dear, what is the principal difference between Englishmen and Americans, in your opinion?

Girl (disgustedly): There isn't any. Men are all alike.

No, the lady wasn't referring to me. As the admiral's aide I was on my good behavior. Besides, I have never forced myself on any woman. I never have had to.

All afternoon the harbor presented a brilliant picture; I never tired of watching it. Launches flying the Stars and Stripes were running back and forth, as well as gigs and whaleboats manned by sturdy young British sailors. Big gray picket boats, like miniature destroyers, plied between the dockyards and the fleet at Spithead, and a line of small steamers kept bringing excursionists to view the American ships. It was like a regatta.

We were granted leave and together with twenty-five other officers, I went up to London. We took a Negro mess attendant who was supposed to act as our valet, but he vanished shortly after we reached the city. His black face created a veritable sensation and he was constantly surrounded by crowds who had obviously never seen a Negro before. I remember one little boy gravely asking his mother, "Mummy, is that a proper blackamoor?" I don't know why it seems so amusing that English children talk with an English accent—oh, pardon me, I forgot. It is we who have the accent; they speak correct English. At all events, our valet was so overwhelmed with attention he disappeared to be lionized while we, supposedly his betters, were ignored.

We were given quarters at the Metropole, a splendid hotel that no longer exists. As we were were guests of the nation, we had no expenses except tips. A Lieutenant Forbes of the Royal Navy was given the duty of acting as our "chaperone." If anything, he was too conscientious. He could not believe that anyone could enjoy wandering around London on foot, but that was one of the things I enjoyed the most. Before we left I knew the West End of London almost as well as I did New York, although I was reduced to taking off my shoes and tiptoeing past Lieutenant Forbes' room when I returned late at night to avoid upsetting him.

The London streets were full of "ladies of the evening" as was New York. This did not surprise me; but I was taken aback to see a number of women smoking. In the smoking room of the Metropole there were smartly gowned women, obviously ladies, puffing away with their escorts. I must admit I was shocked. There was an opera in New York when we left called *The Secret of Suzanne*. Her shameful secret was that she smoked. I even saw some women smoking pipes. If they had been corncob pipes such as farm women smoked in the American South, I would not have been so surprised but these were smart little briars, not unlike Chinese opium pipes. I noticed that some of the other young American officers after one horrified glance, turned their heads away when passing the smoking room.

From an American point of view, the English seemed to vacillate between ultra elegance and extreme coarseness. One evening there was a state ball at Buckingham Palace, which we were asked to attend. En route I witnessed what, to my Yankee eyes, was an extraordinary spectacle. It was before the days of automobiles and all the feminine guests arrived in open carriages. There was a tremendously long line of them advancing at a snail's pace frequently being halted to permit the unloading of the carriages at the head of the line. In the carriages, in plain view, were the ladies in all the glory of their jewels and ball dresses. These dresses were incredibly elaborate with long trains that dragged behind them when they walked and which they lifted by means of a loop suspended from their right wrists when they danced.

The sidewalks were jammed by an enormous crowd. The carriages, when they stopped as they frequently did, could easily have been touched by the front rank of the crowd. Each time the carriages halted people in the crowd proceeded to make audible comments concerning the dresses, morals, and probably private lives of the ladies. All of these comments were coarse and many were extremely vulgar. Listening to these foul-mouthed ruffians, I was strongly tempted to interfere on the part of the ladies even though I realized the futility of such behavior.

To my surprise, the ladies paid absolutely no attention to this abuse. They sat bolt upright (I never saw an English woman slump in her seat) looking straight ahead and occasionally exchanging some remark with their carriage companions. They did not seem even conscious that the toughs existed. Amazing.

In the palace, we were presented first to the King and then to the Queen. The presentations were quite informal. We simply lined up in order of rank and, as each man's name and rank were announced, he entered the room where the King was receiving, bowed, shook hands and passed on.

Unlike the Kaiser, King Edward didn't put on a bit of swank. He greeted us pleasantly, simply, just as any host might have done. Cal O'Laughlin, a newspaper man who was present, gave the following report of my presentation: "When Lieutenant Mannix was presented His Majesty looked closely at the decorations on the breast of this gallant young officer who is well known as trainer of the gun crew on the *Kearsarge* which made a world's record (thank you, Cal!) and asked several questions about them."

Immediately afterwards we were presented to the Queen; we didn't shake hands with her, simply had our names announced, bowed, and passed on. Although her children were far older than any of us junior officers, there wasn't one of us who did not promptly fall in love with her. Not only was she beautiful but she seemed surrounded by an aura of goodness. One couldn't conceive of her doing anything mean or spiteful or anything that could possibly hurt anyone's feeling. I wish some of these alleged "social leaders" who enjoy snubbing people could have seen how a real lady behaves. There is all the difference in the world between cheap imitations and the genuine article.

There was one small contretemps. I have said the ladies wore long trains that dragged on the floor. Many were stunningly lovely and one of the midshipmen was so smitten by a fair young peeress that he stood goggling at her, unconscious of the fact that he was standing on her train. The lady tried to move, found it impossible, and said with a rising inflection, "I beg your pahdon." The middy continued his rapt gaze without moving. Once more she repeated, "I beg your pahdon!" with increasing emphasis. As the middy still remained hypnotized, the lady, taking a firm grip with both hands on her train, gave it a quick jerk. Luckily the wall was near; otherwise the middy would have executed as neat a back handspring as he ever did in the Academy gym. The lady, calm as ever, and still with that rising inflection, said, "Thank you," and swept away.

Shortly afterward, a gentleman wearing a field marshal's uniform and an impressive row of medals, on the right of which was the Victoria Cross, spoke to me and inquired pleasantly if I was an American. One look at his face and I knew who he was: it was Lord Roberts of Kandahar, the famous Bobs of the British Army. He had won the Cross during the Sepoy Rebellion in India. He and Kitchener together put an end to the Boer War, the graveyard of so many military reputations. He was not very tall and slightly bow-legged; a typical cavalryman. There was nothing blustering or "hard boiled" about him; "gentle" would be a better description. I often remember him when I see some high-ranking officer who thinks he has to adopt a bullying, aggressive manner to show how "tough" he is. Bobs was a genuine hero yet he could not have been more gracious.

Several of the high-ranking British officers put themselves out to make sure our visit was pleasant. I have mentioned Sir Berkeley

Milne, the King's ADC who had been thrown out of Cliveden by my fellow countryman, Mr. William Astor. On hearing that I was interested in military memorabilia, Sir Berkeley kindly offered to show me around the Royal United Service Museum in Whitehall. It is a fascinating place, once the Banqueting House of Old Whitehall Palace. In January 1649, King Charles stepped out of a window there onto a scaffold where he was beheaded.

There were all sorts of things in the museum; many Nelson relics, the trumpet that sounded the Charge of the Light Brigade, medals and uniforms. I was astonished to see an American flag in one case. I went over to examine it and read on a card, "Flag of the USS *Chesapeake*."

Every American school boy knows the story of that flag. During the War of 1812, Capt. James Lawrence of the *Chesapeake* was challenged to a frigate duel by Captain Broke of the British ship *Shannon*. Lawrence had newly been put in command of the *Chesapeake*, had never seen her under sail, and had a raw crew, many of them merchant sailors who had never seen a gun fired. However, he felt compelled to accept Broke's challenge. After a desperate encounter, Lawrence was mortally wounded and carried below shouting, "Don't give up the ship!" After his death, the crew were forced to strike and the *Chesapeake* was captured.

Seeing my interest, Sir Berkeley said, "Some time ago, the flag was sold at auction. A number of us planned to purchase it and return it to your country as a tribute to a brave man and a brave crew. Unfortunately, we were outbid."

I wondered who had been determined to keep this heroic and pitiful relic from coming home. I went closer and read the name of the donor. In small letters on a card was, "Presented by William Waldorf Astor, Esq."

Later, Sir Berkeley told me that the incident was greatly resented in England. He asked me how Americans felt about it. I told him no one had heard about it. "I am glad of that," he remarked.

The next afternoon I attended (by official request) a large luncheon given by a group named "The Pilgrims," which was devoted to the laudable purpose of cultivating good feeling between England and America. There were a number of young British officers there who, quite obviously, had also been "requested" to grace the occasion. There were a long series of speeches almost identically worded:

"Hands across the sea; blood thicker than water," etc. Sitting next to me was a British lieutenant of about my age. At the end of each speech we both applauded loudly as was our duty until finally my English counterpart remarked to me casually while clapping, "What rot! As everyone knows, what we'd really like to be doing is fighting each other. Here's to a sudden plague, a bloody war, and quick promotion! Let's get out of here." This we proceeded to do, crawling on our hands and knees so we wouldn't be seen from the speaker's table.

After a few drinks at the Junior Naval and Military Club in Piccadilly, we went to the Gaiety. A musical comedy was playing which was typical of several I later saw. The hero was almost invariably a naval officer with a comic sailor orderly who was certain to be referred to as a "disorderly." From there we went to the Empire, a popular music hall. In addition to tumblers, dancers, a magician, and a singer, there were two really excellent ballets. There were certain features of the Empire that were quite as interesting as the performance. One was the Promenade, a wide space back of the seats where the ladies of what someone has called the "demi john" strolled back and forth exhibiting their costumes and charms. At one end of the Promenade was a long bar presided over by a typical British barmaid, the first I had ever seen. She wore a semi-uniform black dress, very high in the neck, that fitted like the "paper on the wall;" her figure was, well, it was the kind you see in the illustrations of Physical Culture magazines; she may have been thirty and was blonde; dazzling blonde.

However, I wasn't so dazzled that I couldn't see the lady was able not only to look out for herself but was also quite capable of "looking out" for anything that took place at the bar. Any gentleman who had had "enough" was eased out in a fascinating and affectionate manner that left him charmed and also left him with the cold night air blowing on his face.

There have been several instances of barmaids becoming peeresses and, I believe, they made very good peeresses indeed.

Another interesting feature of the Empire was the ushers; they wore uniforms and must have averaged about seven feet tall. In addition to being ushers they were also "bowlers out" (the English for bouncers). They performed their bowler out duties with a suavity utterly unknown to our New York bouncers. For example, while throwing a gentleman through the door, they never failed to call him "sir." It is little touches like this that make the British such a cultivated people.

That evening, a group of young fellows, for no particular reason, insisted on sitting on the backs of their chairs with their feet on the seats. A uniformed Goliath of horrific proportions approached them and suavely observed: "I am afraid, gentlemen, that those seats are a little weak." Everybody got down except one man. Goliath waited a moment and then lifted him in his arms as though he were a baby, carried him, in his seated posture, out the door and deposited him, still in his seated position, on the curb. Then straightening up and daintily dusting his hands (as they do in the comic strips) he said: "Now, sir, you're hout. STAY HOUT!"

After the last show, my new-found friend suggested we visit an establishment with which he was familiar where, he assured me, the ladies were of the very highest type; in fact, a number of them had been recruited from the nobility. I suppose this may have been true as at the time it was almost impossible for an upper-class woman to find employment, except possibly as an old lady's companion or a governess, if she had the misfortune to have no money and no male relative who would give her a home. There was even a saying that the only two careers open to a lady were those of a wife or a prostitute. "The last time I went to this house, it was with a friend," said my fellow lieutenant. "The madam said she would pick out two nice girls for us so we went upstairs to our separate rooms. My girl arrived and we were about to settle down to business when there was a knock on the door. My friend called, 'I say, old chap, would you mind exchanging whores with me? I seem to have run into an aunt of mine.' "

Not wishing to encounter anyone's aunt, I declined his kind invitation and we parted on the best of terms. He was an extremely nice fellow and I was delighted to have made his acquaintance. Unlike Mr. Harriman, I have never had any prejudice against the English except for their arrogant assumption that their navy is as good as ours. My lieutenant friend, by a coincidence, was in command of a turret gun crew as I was and very proud of his men. I am sure they were an excellent lot but I would have been interested to see what they could do against my crew who established the world record with our 8-inch guns. It has always been one of my greatest regrets, as I think it is with all Regular Navy men, that in 1918 we did not go to war with Great Britain instead of Germany; there was some talk of it due to the

British blockade of the Continent and their stopping American ships. The Germans were brave men and good sailors but the English Navy after all was—to use their own phrase—"the First Fifteen" against which all other navies were measured. It would have been a great feather in our cap if we could have beaten them.

The following day we attended a luncheon given by the Lord Mayor of London at his official residence, The Mansion House. To those who may be interested in such things, I give the guest list as such affairs no longer exist:

Sir R. Awdry, K.C.B.; Mr. Henry White, United States Embassy; Admiral the Honorable Sir Edmund Freemantly; Right Honorable Sir Joseph Dimsdale, Bart., K.C.V.O., M.P.; Alderman Sir Joseph Savory, Bart.; Admiral Sir Henry Stephenson, G.C.B.; Admiral of the Fleet the Honorable Sir Henry Keppel, G.C.B., O.M.; Honorable Chauncey M. Depew; Lord Rothschild, G.C.V.O.; the Lady Mary Howard; the United States Ambassador and Mrs. Choate; The Lord Mayor and the Lady Mayoress; Admiral Cotton; Captain Prince Louis of Battenberg, G.C.B.; Mrs. Walter H. Levy; The Duke of Norfolk, K.G., G.C.V.O. (Earl Marshall, and a Knight of the Garter, no less); Right Honorable James Bryce, M.P. (Former Ambassador to the United States and author of *The American Commonwealth*;) Senator Gorman; Alderman Sir Henry Knight; Mr. Arnold-Forster, M.P., Secretary to the Admiralty; Admiral Markham, Commanding at the Nore; Captain Sir George Vyvyan, K.C.M.G., Deputy Master of the Trinity House; Colonel Sir H. Hozier, K.C.B.; Mr. J. Pierpont Morgan, Junior; Sir Henry Irving, the famous actor; Sheriff Sir Thomas and Lady Brooke-Hitching; Captain the Honorable Hugh Tyrwhitt (in the World War he distinguished himself as a cruiser and destroyer commander); Commander Godfrey Faussett, Equerry to Vice Admiral His Royal Highness the Prince of Wales.

In offering the various toasts the Lord Mayor would rise to his feet and say: "Your Serene Highness, Your Highness, Your Grace, Lords, Ladies and Gentlemen." After he had repeated this several times, Ensign George Steele, who sat near me, began pretending to listen intently and each time the Lord Mayor reached the "Gentlemen" part of it, George would whisper loudly, "Hurrah! He remembered me!"

The "Serene Highness" present was Prince Louis of Battenberg, father of the present Lord Louis Mountbatten, who is a rear admiral and commanded the "commandoes" in World War II. I don't remember who the "Highness" was; "Your Grace" referred to the Duke of Norfolk.

To my astonishment, most of the junior officers with our fleet were reluctant to attend the luncheon and would far rather have spent their time playing cards together or chatting in the wardroom mess. I simply cannot understand how anyone would want to pass up such an occasion. To me, meeting representatives of foreign nations and seeing new sights is one of the great attractions of a naval career yet I have seen officers who have traveled around the world and never bothered to look out a porthole at the wonders around them. When I reached command rank, I had often to order junior officers to attend important functions and meet foreign people.

It may be felt that I am a snob. I freely admit that I was interested in meeting at this luncheon several officers of the First Life Guards, the most "swagger" regiment in the British Army. At that time a second lieutenant in the Guards, to maintain his position, was obliged to have a private income of at least three thousand dollars a year to pay for his gorgeous uniforms and gold lace. Kipling contemptuously referred to them as the "fatted flunkies of the Army." Virtually everyone had a title besides his military one; "Major the Earl of So and So, Captain Sir Something, Bart., Lieutenant the Honorable This and That."

Twenty years later I was in Constantinople and the Household Brigade of the British Army was stationed there. I looked over the list to see if I could recognize any old acquaintances. Among all those names there were only two or three who had titles.

Where were all those young earls and baronets and honorables? They were dead. Most of them had died in August 1914 during the terrible retreat from Mons when the old British Regular Army virtually ceased to exist. They were not "fatted flunkies" there. Outnumbered a hundred to one they had recoiled step by step, taking a terrific toll on the enemy and giving the Allied troops behind them a chance to organize and prepare for what was coming. I am proud to have met them.

There were a few American girls at the luncheon and a large number of English women, many of them most attractive. My fellow officers paid no attention to the English girls and spent all their time with the Americans who were pleasant enough but no different from the girls we had all known at home. I concentrated on the English girls and had a delightful afternoon.

There was a minor but annoying incident. I have spoken of the
Sampson-Schley controversy that developed after the Battle of Santiago as to which commanding officer deserved the credit for the
victory. During the course of the meal, an English officer rose and
politely proposed a toast to Admiral Sampson "the victor of Santiago."
It was drunk and the officer sat down, whereupon a young American
lieutenant rose and said in a loud voice, "I demand that this officer
now proposes a second toast to Captain Schley!"

This lieutenant had served on Schley's ship and was a devoted
partisan. There was a dead silence and then Admiral Cotton said
sharply, "Sit down!" Some of the other junior officers pulled the man
down and conversation quickly began again. Of course, the English
had no idea what it was all about; one army officer told me later that
he thought the young fellow was attempting to voice a personal
grievance.

To show how insular many even high-ranking officers were at this
time, I was ordered to report to the admiral the morning after the
luncheon where I received an "admonition in the course of duty," in
other words, an official reproof for spending so much time with
"foreign women." When I was finally dismissed, the admiral called
after me as I left his cabin, "and this time, Mannix, don't miss the ship
when we sail"—a remark I considered totally unnecessary.

The next day I received something more pleasant: an invitation to
spend the week-end at a country house about twenty miles outside
London. It was from one of the girls I hadn't been supposed to dance
with, naturally one of the prettiest at the party.

I made the trip in a hansom cab and we must have seemed
incongruous trotting through the Hampshire lanes. It was expensive
but I was rich then, like all bachelor junior officers, much richer than I
have ever been again; while in England we were paid in gold sover-
eigns and nobody had ever heard of such a thing as an income tax.

The house I visited was very ancient, nearly two hundred years
old but in an excellent state of preservation. The grounds were magnificent and I noticed for the first time how much greener the English
countryside is than ours; due, I suppose, to the prevalence of rain and
fog. We certainly have them beat when it comes to sunshine.

To my great disappointment, I found I was never to be left alone
with my charmer. Wherever we went there was a chaperone. At last I
said, rather pompously to the girl's mother, "In America we feel that a

girl can go anywhere with a GENTLEMAN." She dryly replied, "In England, we DON'T." Although I found the English girls charming, when they grow older they tend to develop nasty, suspicious minds especially if they have daughters. Anyhow, it was a delightful week-end.

I got back to Portsmouth barely in time for the official visit of the Prince of Wales (later King George V) to the *Kearsarge*. All the ships in the harbor and the Channel Fleet at Spithead dressed ship rainbow fashion and fired a Royal Salute as the prince came on board.

The drums and bugles sounded four ruffles and flourishes and all the American ships hoisted the Royal Standard at the main and fired a salute of twenty-one guns. After lunch, the prince inspected the ship. When he left, the word was passed "Three cheers for his Royal Highness the Prince of Wales." Then our band played "God Save the King." Out of courtesy, Admiral Beresford ordered his band to play "The Star Spangled Banner." They made an awful hash of it (it is far more difficult to play than "God Save the King").

We sailed from England on July 12th. All we knew was that we were headed for the Mediterranean where we were to pay some more goodwill visits to Portugal, Greece, and Austria. We were not informed that part of our duties would be to rescue an American from a sheik high in the hills of North Africa.

CHAPTER SEVEN

The Mediterranean and Cuba (1904–1906)

Perdicaris alive or Raisuli dead!

—Theodore Roosevelt

WHAT had happened was this:

Perdicaris, an American citizen of Greek ancestry, had been living in Tangier, the main port of Morocco, when he was kidnapped by the sheik of a small hill tribe, named Raisuli, and held for ransom. The sheik had also kidnapped a British citizen named Varley at the same time. President Roosevelt decided it was necessary to show the world that no American citizen could be mistreated with impunity, so he delivered his famous order, "Perdicaris alive or Raisuli dead!" Our squadron was coaling at Tenerife in the Canaries when we received our orders to proceed to Morocco immediately.

To show how American feeling was aroused by the Perdicaris incident, I quote the *New York Herald* of May 29, 1904, page one; the following headlines were displayed in enormous type:

AMERICAN SHIPS TO JOIN SULTAN IN WAR ON MOROCCAN BANDITS
TWO FLEETS NOW RACING ON TO TANGIER
AUDACIOUSLY ASKS US TO GUARANTEE RANSOM

Three Admirals and ten warships have been ordered to break the power of the brigand who holds Perdicaris captive. The following warships have been ordered to proceed at once to Tangier: South Atlantic Fleet, consisting of Brooklyn (Flagship of Rear Admiral Chadwick), Atlanta, Castine, Marietta. European Squadron, consisting of Olympia (Flagship of Rear Admiral Jewell), Baltimore, Cleveland. The following ships are now at the Azores and may also be sent: Kearsarge (Flagship of Rear Admiral Barker), Alabama and Maine.

The State Department today received from Consul Gummers at Tangier the terms demanded by Raisuli, the brigand, for the release of Ion Perdicaris, American, and Cromwell Varley, Englishman. They are: (1) the payment of an enormous sum of money as ransom (the exact amount not specified by the Consul) by the Governors of Fez and Tangier who are personal enemies of Raisuli, (2) the guarantee of the payment by the United States and Britain,

(3) immunity for the brigands in a wide district where they may ravish and pillage as they will.

Secretary Hay and the President, after conferring over the proposals, concurred in the opinion that they were too absurd and impossible to think of granting. They particularly objected to the stipulation that the bandits shall be unmolested in law breaking.

On the *Kearsarge,* we are told the admiral has ordered us to capture Raisuli and liberate his captives. This plan has its difficulties, chief among them being the danger that the brigands, if attacked, may take the lives of Perdicaris and Varley, and the problem of how warships can fight bandits entrenched in mountain strongholds.

The South Atlantic Squadron has already departed. The European Squadron (to which I am attached) arrived at Horta this morning. After coaling we will proceed immediately for Tangier.

The United States, during its early days, had once before been involved with the countries of North Africa. These nations existed by piracy and our merchant ships were frequently attacked along the Barbary Coast, the cargoes seized and the crews sold as slaves. Then in 1801, President Jefferson sent a squadron to blockade the harbor of Tripoli. One of our frigates, the *Philadelphia*, ran aground and was captured by the Tripolitans. The *Philadelphia* was boarded and burned by Lt. Stephen Decatur in what Lord Nelson called "the most daring act of the age." Later, a small vessel, the *Intrepid*, was overcome by a large number of the pirates and her commanding officer, Lieutenant Somers, blew her up. All Americans on board were killed, as well as many of the pirates. The war was finally concluded when William Eaton with a force of United States Marines marched on Tripoli and scattered the Bashaw's forces.

I admit that I had dreams of emulating Decatur, although I was less eager to duplicate Somers' feat. But when we arrived in the harbor of Tangier, it quickly became evident that there was nothing we could do. Raisuli was a chief of the Rif tribe and safely hidden away in the Atlas Mountains, a range so high that the ancient Greeks thought they held up the sky. Admiral Chadwick sent the bandit chieftain several furious messages, suggesting that he come down to the shore where we could capture him. Surprisingly enough, he declined to oblige, sending us in turn a brief answer in flowing Arabic script. It was a single sentence and a classic: "Does the lion of the mountains go in swimming in order to fight sharks?"

He was a picturesque old scoundrel and had a sense of humor as his reply showed.

The situation was complicated by the fact that the French, who had already taken over Algeria, were now trying to occupy Morocco and didn't want any trouble with the tribes.

They were opposed by the Spaniards and the Germans, both of whom had designs on the country themselves while the English supported the French. The Sultan of Morocco was a young man, the son of a Circassian slave girl, and completely in the hands of his Grand Wazir who was prepared to sell out the country to anyone who offered him the biggest bribe. To make matters even more confused, it turned out that Perdicaris wasn't an American citizen after all; he had been born in the United States but at the time of the Civil War he had repudiated his citizenship and become a Greek national, I suppose to avoid being drafted. He had lived abroad ever since.

In spite of Roosevelt's order and the popular outcry, the Navy was helpless. At last a secret arrangement was worked out between us and the French. In return for having the United States recognize France's "special rights" in Morocco, the French agreed to pay the ransom (using Spanish silver coins as Spain was also involved in the deal). The two prisoners were then promptly released. Of course, the affair was hailed as a "famous victory" for us, the public being allowed to think that Raisuli had surrendered to our threat of force and nothing being said about the ransom having been paid. Naturally, we reimbursed the French afterward.

The whole business impressed me as being a farce, but it had curiously important repercussions. Germany was furious at having the French established in Morocco and the Kaiser, with his usual flair for the dramatic, sailed for Morocco and made an impressive landing in Tangier. The French minister who had been involved in the transaction was forced to resign. Germany's action strengthened the Franco-British entente and Germany built up the Triple Alliance. The stage for World War I was set.

Unconscious of the great events we had helped precipitate, the *Kearsarge* sailed for Lisbon, Portugal, on another "goodwill" mission. Here we entertained the king, Carlos I, the queen, Marie Amelie, and the queen mother. By now we were able to dress ship, man the rails, and go through the other routine greetings to royalty in our sleep. The king was a big man, perhaps six feet and very fat. Alongside the queen, however, he looked small and insignificant. She must have been at least seven feet tall. She was a good head and shoulders taller than any man present. Afterwards, we had a dance but although the king danced, the queen very wisely didn't. She would have looked as though she were bouncing a child on her knee.

King Carlos was obviously a good fellow and so was the crown prince, Louis, duke of Bregana, a plump, cheerful boy. The queen was a gentle and pleasant giantess. Less than five years later, she was to see her husband and son murdered before her eyes by anarchists. I cannot imagine what motivated these people except a desire to achieve fame by killing harmless prominent figures. They also blew the legs off Alexander II, who had just liberated all the serfs in Russia, and they murdered the beautiful Empress Elizabeth of Austria who had never in her whole unhappy life injured anyone. There was an epidemic of these senseless murders for a time. Thank heaven the madness has run its course and we see no more cases of terrorism now.

In return, the following day we were invited to attend a royal ball at the palace. In addition to the elegant invitation to the ball, we also received an invitation signed by "Rosalina" whose address was "Rua do Ferregial de Baixo 19" in case anyone is interested, although I doubt that the lady still maintains her establishment. In fact, Rosalina sent us five invitations addressed to the Admiral, the Captain, the Wardroom Mess, the Junior Officers' Mess and the Warrant Officers' Mess, thereby showing an intimate knowledge of the interior organization of a naval vessel. On each card was printed, "J'ai des bonnes femmes." I really think Rosalina might have omitted sending one of her cards to the admiral because of his high puritanical principles which had caused me so much trouble.

At the ball I met a beautiful blonde girl who was the Contessina Luisette di Bruno. The next day I invited her to be my guest on the *Kearsarge*. She assured me that she had been so carefully brought up that she had never been on a ship before but even so she knew her way around with remarkable skill; for example, in stepping through the watertight bulkhead doors, she never hit either her head or her shins. These doors have very high sills and in stepping through them it is necessary simultaneously to raise the feet and lower the head. It takes practice. I have an idea that the contessina had met every ship in the harbor for some years. Lovely as she was, I preferred a little brunette with the remarkable name of Sophia O'Donnell Pacheco. I asked her how she ever got such a name and she frankly replied, "One of my ancestors was in Wellington's Army during the Peninsular Campaign."

She was a remarkable linguist and not only spoke perfect English and all the Western European languages but amused the group doing "take-offs" of visitors speaking English with a Portuguese accent, Portuguese with an English accent, French with a German accent, and so on. I entirely agreed with an impressionable young midshipman who called her "the most delightful little thing in the world."

We went to the opera nearly every evening: *Tosca, Rigoletto, Traviata,* and one called *Os Pescadores de Napoles* which I did not know. They were sung in Portuguese and once Sophia rather took me aback by announcing cheerfully "she says she is going to have a baby." I was glad no one around us spoke English to be shocked by such frankness.

On the evening of our departure, we were all very sad; we always used to be sad on the eve of every departure. To make matters worse, Sophia and I were trying to get away together but our admiral had seen proper to include a number of old women to act as chaperones. For a time I thought I had solved the difficulty. There was a large open place called "The Drunken Man's Square" owing to an extraordinary mosaic design built into the paving: zig-zag, rays, curves and Heaven knows what. In the center was an enormous fountain or some such architectural monstrosity. It suddenly dawned on me that if Sophia and I could get on the other side of it, the fountain would hide us so we could slip away. By walking fast, we almost managed to get around it when Bobby Henderson, who had had plenty of the Portuguese wine, noticed us and shouted, "Run, Mannix, run! The chaperones are gaining on you!" This, of course, attracted everyone's attention and the admiral ordered me back. Otherwise, it was a delightful two weeks.

Our next stop was Athens, Greece. The great trouble with Athens is that the town is quite a distance from the port, called Piraeus, so you have to take a train back to your ship. Athens is built around a mesa (a flat-topped hill) called the Acropolis which was originally used for defense and is some distance inland. The Parthenon, the Porch of Maidens, and some other famous buildings are there. The Parthenon is missing its famous carved marble frescoes because an Englishman, Lord Elgin, went off with them. They are now in the British Museum. The Greeks have never forgiven him and our hosts spoke of him as a robber.

We had the usual official calls. King George came on board and we were all presented to him. We didn't see the queen who, before her marriage, was a Russian grand duchess.

After a stop at Corfu, we went on to Trieste in the Adriatic for a stay of nearly a month. Not finding Trieste too interesting, I put in an application for two weeks' leave, intending to go to Vienna, then down the Danube to Budapest, then to Venice and back to Trieste.

I made an initial mistake: I went to Vienna first and as a result never went anywhere else. I believe it is generally admitted that the Viennese girls are the most beautiful in the world. Looking back after a lapse of nearly fifty years, I sometimes wonder if the girls I saw driving in the Prater and the Ringstrasse were really as ravishing as they seemed to be. Of course, I wasn't very old but I know one thing. I didn't only see those girls "through the bottom of a champagne glass" as our grouchy old admiral later claimed.

I was handicapped at first during my stay in Vienna because I didn't know anybody and couldn't speak the language. In fact, I had been warned against anybody who could speak English, especially if the person were of the feminine gender. It meant either that she rated a sleeve full of service stripes or else was a small-time Mata Hari, ready to pick up any "military information" that was floating around loose. Luckily, I ran into several Austrian officers who had come on board the *Kearsarge* at Trieste to welcome us in the name of the emperor Francis Joseph and they took me around.

Long afterward, several people have asked me, "Was Vienna really as wonderful as they say?" I can answer unhesitatingly, "It was, only more so." I suppose some people worked there but I never saw them; everybody seemed intent on having a good time. Years later I heard an expression applied to the Paris cafés: Chacun à sa chacunne. (every fellow has his girl). That applied even more to Vienna; it might have been the city's motto.

There was an enormous open-air establishment on the Ringstrasse that was called the Volksgarten; the great Johann Strauss, both of them, used to play there in years gone by. Over the entrance was written, in German, naturally:

> Who loves not woman, wine and song
> Will be a fool his whole life long.

The Strauss tradition was maintained; the big orchestra played nothing but waltzes, with an occasional operetta. After your girl and you (I met several girls who could understand my French or at least pretended to) had a bottle or two of champagne not only were you waltzing but the chairs and tables were waltzing too. There were waitresses in smart uniforms, evidently selected for their good looks, each with her name on a little metal badge pinned on her shoulder. They all seemed to end in "zi:" Mitzi, Fritzi, etc. As for the feminine patrons, I hesitate to attempt a description of them; they looked wonderful even before the chairs and tables started waltzing.

These officers were very proud of their city and of the great art galleries for which it is famous. They insisted on taking me on a tour of the galleries and explaining each picture. There were a number of ladies in the galleries whom I found far more interesting. At last, one officer remarked unhappily, "I show you all de baintings und you look at de frauleins." Fortunately the galleries closed at five so we could then repair to the cafés.

The patrons used to go there either in the tram or in carriages, "low-necked hacks." If you had a girl you took a carriage; if you went stag you travelled on the tram. I remember one night we sighted ahead of us an open carriage with a man and a girl in it. The man put his arm around the girl and kissed her, whereupon the coxswain of our tram put on full speed and ran up alongside. Then the tram passengers leaned out, waved their hats and shouted, "Bravo, Bis!"

Many of the cafés had girl orchestras, all the musicians wearing dresses that were exactly alike, white usually, and curiously I noticed the same thing in the city; frequently you would see two girls, and sometimes three or four, all dressed exactly alike. Whether it was for economy or was a passing fad I don't know but its unusualness made it attractive.

The Austrians got tipsy more pleasantly than any people I have ever seen. Many people the moment they get a little too much become quarrelsome. If there is one duty that I have always detested it is taking care of drunks; it has more than once almost made me a prohibitionist. The Austrians, when they began to feel lively, didn't insult other people. They sang. And they COULD sing. It was like being in the midst of an operetta.

Once while away from my Austrian friends, I made the acquaintance of an attractive girl named Margo who took me out to see the famous hunting lodge at Mayerling. Here a few years before the Crown Prince Rudolph, heir to the Austro-Hungarian throne, took his seventeen-year-old sweetheart Baroness Marie Vetsera. The next morning Rudolph and Marie were found dead. No one knows what happened. Some said they had a suicide pact. Another was that Rudolph told his teenage sweetheart that he was breaking off the affair so she shot him and then herself. A third was that Marie had a lover who killed them both. If you cared to ask around, you could undoubtedly have picked up a dozen more theories. Anyhow, it is a romantic and tragic story.

The next morning, Margo left before I was awake and when I got up, I found that all my money was gone. As my leave was expiring, I was obliged to catch a train to Trieste that day. My Austrian officer friends dropped in to see me and when they heard what had happened, assured me they could recover my money. They did, a few hours later, less ten percent. As one explained to me, "That is all she is entitled to. That girl is a bum." I wondered where he got his colloquial American English. They put me on board the train to make sure "you do not get involved with any other women" and we all said goodbye after one of the most enjoyable leaves I have ever had.

Shortly afterwards, we sailed for the United States. It had been a highly successful goodwill tour.

When we arrived in Newport, Rhode Island, I learned that there was trouble in Cuba. A revolution had taken place and President Tomas Estrada Palma had issued a warning that he could no longer protect American lives or property. I heard that the *Brooklyn*, Schley's flagship at Santiago, was fitting out at Philadelphia for "special temporary duty" at the scene of the disturbances. I applied for duty on board her and was lucky enough to be accepted; I had served under her commanding officer, Captain Heilner before and he remembered me. When we sailed we took five hundred marines with us as well as the regular ship's complement of bluejackets. I was very excited and sure I'd see some action.

On the way, we ran into a storm during which our chief boatswains mate, Sonneman, was swept overboard. The ship was making twenty knots at the time with a stern wind adding to our speed. In attempting to launch the starboard lifeboat the detaching apparatus failed to function; the crew was in the boat seated on the thwarts ready to man the oars but the fall blocks didn't detach simultaneously; the stern one stuck, and the bow of the boat dropped sharply, dumping the crew into the wild sea. I could see them, some below, some above the surface, gripping the grab ropes while they were being towed through the water by the forward motion of the ship, for our backing engines had not as yet checked our headway.

Instead of being rescuers, they now had to be rescued themselves. There were a number of men of my division nearby, and I called for volunteers to man the port lifeboat. We were lowered safely, but in the rough sea, it was impossible to find all the men, and I had to go over the side after them. Fortunately, I am a good swimmer so we were able to save them all. Afterward, we spent an hour searching for poor Sonneman but without success. He was probably killed when he struck the water.

Captain Heilner was kind enough to make an entry on my record: "As usual, always the first to volunteer for dangerous duty." This did something to counterbalance the unkind comments I'd acquired on the European cruise.

We headed directly for Havana passing Morro Castle (there are two Morro castles: one in Santiago and one here) and anchored not far from the wreck of the *Maine*, the American flag flying from her mainmast which still showed above the water. There was great excitement with troops and ships arriving from every direction. The troops were commanded by Funston, the celebrated captor of Aguinaldo, who had led the Philippine insurrection. Unfortunately, by the time we arrived, the uprising was virtually over. It had been put down almost entirely by the efforts of one man: Captain Colwell of the cruiser *Denver*, which had been rushed to the city some days before.

What had happened was this: The rebel forces (or the Liberals as they preferred to call themselves) had taken over most of the island and then marched on the capital under such leaders as General Guerra, General Loynay del Castillo, and so on. Everyone seemed to be a general. The loyal army had been commanded by General Rodriguez, who marched out to meet them as they approached Havana. He had been defeated and fled leaving his silk embroidered rain coat and 170 men on the field. The rebel forces were said to number 7,000 men, and the remains of the governmental forces was approximately 3,000. It was obvious that the rebels could take Havana whenever they wished.

At this point, the *Denver* arrived in the harbor. Captain Colwell landed 109 armed sailors who took up a position in front of the presidential palace. Immediately both sides stopped fighting. The bluejackets had rifles and machine guns (the Cubans were mainly armed with revolvers and machetes), were disciplined, and clearly knew what they were doing. Also, the *Denver* had anchored close to the wharf and her rapid fire 6-pounders were pointed up O'Reilly St.

(I never did find out how the main street in Havana came to be named after an Irishman).

Secretary Taft had accompanied the fleet, and he now went ashore with a guard of several hundred bluejackets and marines. I commanded one landing party. There had been a lot of indiscriminate killing and looting. All the stores and most of the more prosperous houses had been broken into and we passed a number of corpses, several of them little children, but we encountered no resistance. Later I learned that the rebels had offered to surrender to Captain Colwell but he had refused, not being authorized to accept it. Of course, the rebels had no intention of surrendering to President Palma and his followers. They knew well what their fate would be.

Havana was more like Vienna than a captured city. Everywhere there were bands playing, the theaters were full, and the cafés crowded; patrons eating their tortonis and sipping their ices often with a dead body only a few yards away. They were clearly used to violence.

Secretary Taft and his staff occupied the home of our minister, Morgan, in the suburbs. It was a magnificent estate with palm trees, spacious verandas, and an enormous drawing room. I was in command of the Naval Guard stationed to protect our officials. Here Secretary Taft listened to the complaints of President Palma concerning the fiendish brutality of the rebels. When the president had run out of atrocity stories, Taft told him, "Now I want to hear what the rebel leaders have to say."

Palma was outraged. "We have called you in to protect us. Why listen to rebels?" he demanded. Taft insisted and finally Palma yielded with no good grace. Taft sent out messengers to the rebel army with a promise of safe conduct, and soon half a dozen of them arrived. I was greatly impressed by the fact that the Cubans trusted us to keep our word, although they would never have trusted another Cuban.

The rebel leaders were quite as indignant as the government representatives. They claimed that a recent election in which the government had been returned to office was blatantly fraudulent, government troops even keeping liberals away from the polling booths by force. Taft asked Palma if this was so. "Of course it is," replied the indignant president. "But we did it for the sake of Cuba. Anyhow, if the Liberals had been in power, they would have done the same thing." "Would you have?" Taft asked General Castillo, one of the rebel leaders. "Naturally, why not?" Castillo asked in surprise.

I had the feeling that Secretary Taft was going to have some trouble making the Cubans understand the basic principles of democracy. One of our greatest mistakes is the belief that all countries want to become democracies when most of them are used to living under an absolute ruler and can conceive of no other system of government. Also, except for a small elite class, the people are illiterate and cannot vote intelligently on national questions. Trying to explain democracy to them is like trying to explain what red looks like to a blind man.

Taft then called for a new election under the auspices of the Cuban Congress, to be supervised by the United States. Both sides angrily refused.

Palma declared, "We could have put down this revolution ourselves without your help. Did you Americans come here only to help our enemies?" This was nonsense. The government could not possibly have put down the uprising; the rebels had easily defeated the army. The rebels, on the other hand, pointed out that they were the conquerors and we were robbing them of the fruits of victory.

Taft remained firm. The congressmen had fled, expecting to be murdered by one side or the other, and had to be rounded up. While they were preparing to appoint an interim government, it was discovered that Palma and his followers had moved up 1,500 soldiers of the Regular Army to wipe out the congressmen if they did not return him to office. In appealing for help, one of the congressmen pleaded, "Without your protection there will be nothing left of us but fragments." Captain Cowden, the fleet commander, promptly moved in 2,000 marines and sailors who surrounded the capitol building. Thus shielded, the congress was able to appoint a body of moderates to take over the government. Our mission accomplished, we returned to our ships.

We didn't see any fighting in Cuba, except for the verbal kind. We remained in Havana all that winter and as the presence of our ships and troops gradually exerted a soothing effect on the local turbulance, were able to establish social contacts with the Cuban leaders and their families. The Cuban women are charming; it is a pity that they are so difficult to meet. The conventions of Old Spain are still in force down there. Still, I was able to meet Miss Estrada, the daughter of the president, Miss de la Torre, and a number of others.

I knew a little Spanish and rapidly brushed up on it. I don't know of a pleasanter or easier way to learn a language than with the help of a pretty girl. Not surprisingly, I made mistakes. Once after being introduced to some distinguished visitors I said with true Castilian courtesy: "Buenos Dios, caballos." I thought the visitors looked surprised and afterward the embarrassed Miss de la Torre asked me what I was trying to say. I explained, "I said 'Good day, gentlemen.' " "No, you didn't," my teacher replied unhappily. "You should have said 'Buenas dias, caballeros.' What you did say was, 'Good God, horses!' "

We did have some excitement in Cuba. It took the form of a hurricane, the first I had ever seen and I sincerely hope the last. It not only blew down most of the trees and lamp posts in Havana but also blew the *Brooklyn* ashore on the Catalina side. It came so quickly and with so little warning that we didn't even have time to furl the quarterdeck awning, but the hurricane did that for us, getting under the awning and blowing it away. It disappeared to leeward like a great bird carrying a number of the steel stanchions with it and twisting and bending those that remained; these stanchions were of hardened steel and three inches in diameter. Some wind!

When the *Brooklyn* struck the bottom she took a list of about twenty degrees and we spent the night that way. We got afloat again the next morning without trouble; luckily the bottom was soft mud so, except for clogging our condensers, no damage was done.

We returned to Philadelphia and put the old *Brooklyn* out of commission. I hated to see her go. It was like saying goodbye to a beloved home. I received another decoration, the Cuban Pacification Medal, conferred upon me for my duties in Havana during the uprising. I hadn't done much to earn it, but if I ever returned to the courts of Europe, my chest would look a little less bare.

I was not inactive for long. Fresh trouble had broken out in the Philippines. Early in 1907, Rear Admiral Joseph N. Hemphill (formerly captain of the *Kearsarge*, under whom I had served at Kiel), had been ordered to command the Philippine Squadron of the Pacific Fleet. He asked me if I would go with him to China as his flag lieutenant. Naturally I jumped at the chance, and we left Washington in May, via the Canadian Pacific, enroute to Vancouver where we were to take the *Empress of China* for Yokohama. I was looking forward to seeing some action, but frankly I saw more of it than I had bargained on.

CHAPTER EIGHT

The Bamboo Fleet (1907–1908)

Oh, I've been havin'
A hell of a time
Out in the Philippines.

—The "Governor
General's Song"

FOR SEVERAL WEEKS before leaving Washington I was on duty in the Office of Naval Intelligence studying plans for the defense of the Philippines. Even then, thirty-four years before Pearl Harbor, the Japanese were a menace and we anticipated an attack on Manila and North Luzon. When we left Washington I carried with me highly secret plans for the defense of the islands.

At Vancouver we went on board the *Empress of China*, one of the Empress Line belonging to the Canadian Pacific Railway. We took the Northern Great Circle on our way to Yokohama and three days after leaving port, land was sighted on the starboard bow. The captain said: "Take your last look at the United States." What we saw were the Aleutian Islands, so much in the news during World War II. I had never realized before how far they stick out in the Pacific and what a tremendous distance they are from the continental United States. Still, they were American, and it was to be many a long day before I saw American soil again.

As soon as we dropped anchor in Yokohama Harbor, the Japanese customs people swarmed on board. They didn't subject us to a personal search but they did everything else; they opened every piece of luggage; they opened every box and package, including our toilet cases; they searched our staterooms, even looking between the mattresses. They knew perfectly well that we were an American admiral and his personal staff. They also knew that in all probability we were carrying classified material and they intended to find it.

I had the confidential plans they were looking for. As they were quite bulky, I had put them in my suitcase. If the Japanese found them, as they surely would, I would be held responsible. The plans were far too large to be concealed on my person. They were covered with canvas and were weighted with lead so they could be thrown overboard and sunk if in danger of capture. I thought of tossing them over the side but the water of Yokohama Harbor isn't deep and a diver probably could have recovered them. I considered demanding "diplomatic immunity" but legally we had no such immunity, and I knew that the Japs would pay no attention to it even if we had. I think I was more frightened at this moment than I have ever been in my life. My position seemed hopeless.

The plans looked much like the Abandon Ship provisions in a lifeboat as these are also covered with canvas. This gave me an idea. While the Japanese were busy searching our staterooms, I slipped the plans under the tarpaulin cover of a nearby lifeboat. To my intense relief, the trick worked and the Japanese, obviously frustrated, had to depart empty handed. Had they found them, I might as well have resigned my commission. I would have been ruined for life.

Admiral Hemphill's flagship, the *Rainbow*, was at Yokohama waiting for us. After transferring on board, we proceeded for the Philippines. Three days later we arrived at Olongapo in Northern Luzon. Olongapo is situated on Subic Bay, a fine natural anchorage; at the entrance is a big island, Isla Grande. It and Cavite in Manila Bay were our two main Naval Stations. Besides the Naval Station, there was a local garrison of marines and batteries of ships' guns mounted ashore.

Perhaps here I should say something of the political situation. When we went to war with Spain, we did so, as far as I know, with no intention of acquiring colonies; we were merely interested in freeing the Cubans from what seemed to us an oppressive government. The Filipinos at the time were also in rebellion against Spain, and after Dewey's victory at Manila Bay, we had supported the insurrectos in their seizing Spanish shore installations. One of the leaders of the rebellion had been a brilliant young man named Aguinaldo. He was an exile at the time of Dewey's victory and our consul-general, Spencer Pratt, in Singapore, had assured him that we intended to grant the Philippines independence as we did Cuba. Pratt had no authorization from Washington to make this promise but he felt that he needed none; it could be taken for granted. We brought Aguinaldo back to the Philippines where he did a capable job of organizing and leading the insurrectos against the Spaniards. After Spain's defeat, he was regarded by many of the people as their liberator, much as we regard George Washington.

However, after the war we decided to keep the islands. I believe this was largely due to Germany's attempted seizure of them and the fact that Japan also clearly intended to take them over if possible. Then, too, we had become increasingly conscious of the value of bases in the Pacific. We had acquired Samoa and the Hawaiian Islands. It would be extremely useful to us to have bases closer to the mainland. The Philippines were such a base.

We have been severely criticized for having taken over the islands but under the conditions existing in the world in 1900, it was impossible for the Philippines to have been independent. The only question was whether they would belong to Spain, Germany, Japan, or us. I am sure the diplomats in Washington took it for granted that the Filipinos would be delighted to accept our kindly rule until such time as we could build them up so they could shift for themselves. Unfortunately, it turned out that the Filipinos had very different ideas. They no more wanted to be ruled by us than they wanted to be ruled by Spain. By this time we felt that we had committed ourselves and had to dominate the islands by force. It seemed simple; the modern, highly advanced United States against a handful of poorly equipped, uncivilized savages living in rice paddies and jungles. We had no idea how costly and frustrating guerrilla warfare can be. No one foresaw the years of fighting and mountains of expense that lay ahead. In Cuba, our battle casualties amounted to 379 men. Before we were through in the Philippines, 250,000 people had died.

By the time the *Rainbow* arrived in 1907, the war was officially over. Aguinaldo had been captured in 1901 by General Funston and the main body of insurrectos had surrendered. However, many others continued the struggle and lives were being lost daily although little was said about it in the American papers. As a professional fighting man, the rights and wrongs of the situation did not bother me greatly. I agreed with Kipling, "Why should I hate the man I'm paid to kill?" My primary interest was that there would be fighting, and I would have the opportunity to see a new kind of warfare.

Shortly after we arrived in Luzon, I learned of the death of my classmate, Loveman Noa. He was serving on a small gunboat and went ashore in Samar with a patrol of about a dozen men. While they were making their way through the jungle, Noa stepped off the trail for a moment to answer a call of nature. The absence of their officer was noticed by the men in a very few minutes and they turned back. They found him lying on his face with the back of his head crushed in. Nearby was a long flexible bamboo pole with a jagged rock lashed to the end. Apart from this there wasn't a sign of life anywhere in the vicinity and at no time did they see or hear anyone. Noa was an exceptionally powerful man but his physique did not do him any good. Nor had anything he had learned in four years at the Naval Academy prepare him for such an attack.

Although Olongapo is only fifty miles from Manila all communication between the two places was by water as an overland route not only lay through dense tropical jungle but involved climbing a chain of mountains. In addition to these difficulties, certain wild hill tribes frequented the region, and on several occasions during my tour of duty in the Philippines surveying parties were killed by headhunters.

Several of us were eager to see something of the country and some visiting marines told us of a Negrito village only a few miles inland. We decided to go ashore and visit it. We knew there were plenty of insurrectos about, but it never occurred to us that a party of able-bodied white men, armed with revolvers, would be in any danger. It was incredible how little the average American knew of tropical countries and tropical people. We took it for granted that we were immune to primitive weapons. Our only precaution was to take along some canned fruit and salmon as presents for the Negritos should we meet them. Our guide was Captain Swain of the Marines.

The trail led across a wide field and near a mud-and-water wallow in which half a dozen carabao lay submerged to the nostrils. This was the first time any of us had ever seen or heard of these big water buffalos that have long, straight horns and a hide not unlike that of a hippopotamus. They are used as beasts of burden, and their strength is so great that one can easily drag loads that would stagger a team of horses. Usually slow and deliberate in their movements, if angered or deprived of water for even a short period they can exhibit the most surprising activity and speed, so that even a man on horseback is by no means safe unless there are obstacles behind which he can dodge. One of their pet aversions is a stranger and particularly a white man.

None of this we knew at the time and passed about twenty feet from the wallow. As we came abreast of it, six great heads emerged simultaneously from the slime and, snorting angrily, the monsters burst out of the mud and charged us. I doubt if I have ever run so hard in all my life. We would almost certainly have been killed if the beasts' keeper had not appeared and headed them off, shouting to us in Tagalog. Surprisingly, I found that I understood Tagalog perfectly.

He was saying, "Get out of here, you damned fools!" We obeyed him.

A mile further on we reached the banks of the Bouton River, a small stream that flows into Subic Bay. Here we noticed a series of splashes which I thought might be some variety of frog but when I cautiously approached the bank, I saw they were not frogs but fish, about six inches long. Some had even climbed up the trunks of low trees that overhung the stream and were roosting in the branches! Their eyes protruded and they could move them back and forth at will.

When I returned to America, I told several people about these curious fish and was invariably greeted with derisive laughter, and the suggestion to go easy on the hard stuff. Finally I wrote to Captain Swain and asked him if I had imagined the tree climbing fish. He wrote back, "We certainly did see those fish." They are now quite well known and their scientific name, if you're interested, is *Periopthalmus hoelreuteri*. Some fifteen years later, my son, Daniel P. Mannix 4th, who has a passion for animals bought one at Wanamakers in Philadelphia. It used to stroll around our place in Rosemont, in the Philadelphia suburbs, until it unwisely ventured on the driveway and was run over by a motor car.

I mention this minor matter because the average American was positive that he knew all about the flora and fauna of Asia—as well as the people—and anyone who challenged his beliefs was either a fool or a liar. Actually, Americans were abysmally ignorant about everything foreign. I might add that my son wrote an article on some fish he owned that gave birth to living young rather than laying eggs. The article appeared in *The Saturday Evening Post* and was attacked by a man who claimed to be an expert on fish. So prominent was this man and so violent was his letter that for years the *Post* refused to print any more contributions by Dan, considering him a nature faker. The fish in question were called guppies.

Leaving our amphibious friends we pushed through the jungle where, a mile further on, we met a native clad only in a breech clout with the bleeding carcass of a small deer slung over his shoulder. He was only about five feet high, black but without Negro features, and could have stepped out of the Stone Age. He had killed the deer with a bow and arrow, the arrow having a curious toggle arrangement which allowed the shaft to disengage as the head (carved from some hard wood) entered the body. He could speak neither English nor Spanish, but he showed us how the shaft, secured to the head by a strong vine, trailed behind and, catching in trees and vines, served to impede the flight of the wounded game through the brush. As far as I know, the American Indians and the European bowmen had never thought of this device. Under the circumstances, his bow was probably more efficient than a rifle.

While we were examining the deer we were joined by a second native who had a weapon not unlike the harpoon gun used by whalers. It was an old smooth bore musket of very large caliber, the missile being a long arrow, the butt end of which was enlarged to nearly the inside diameter of the gun making a tight fit. The gun was a muzzle loader, and the arrow rammed down on top of the charge performing the double function of bullet and ramrod. Although this man looked, if possible, even more animal-like than his comrade, it must have taken considerable ingenuity to reason out this adaptation of a firearm.

We left the natives and continued along the trail until we arrived at the place where Captain Swain said the Negrito village was reported to be, but never a sign of it did we see. We were wandering on aimlessly without the slightest suspicion that there was anyone within a mile of us when, suddenly at my very elbow, I heard a voice say, "Amigo." I must have jumped a foot. Starting back, I saw for the first time a hole about four feet deep that had been dug on one side of the trail and skillfully covered with underbrush. In this hole was a black dwarf, a good foot shorter than the other natives, a bow in his hand and a quiver of what turned out to be poisoned arrows hanging from one shoulder. He had been waiting there for some game animal to pass along the trail and could have easily killed every member of our party without one of us knowing from whence were coming the arrows.

We hurriedly answered, "Amigo!" and, crawling out of his hole, he conducted us to the village which, though but a dozen feet from the trail, we had passed without knowing of its presence.

It consisted of a few low shacks of nipa about the size of the ordinary dog tent. Our host crawled into one of these and shortly emerged clad in a filthy white blouse which he evidently kept for state occasions. We presented him with one of our cans of salmon but after endeavoring to take a bite out of the tin he promptly returned it to us. We then opened it for him but he took one taste of the contents and then threw it into the bushes to the intense indignation of the caterer of the Wardroom Mess who was a member of the party. As the

Negritos are said to eat anything, including fat grubs they find under stones, we never let our caterer hear the last of this episode.

We then presented him with the canned fruit, which was accorded a better reception than the salmon, and took the trail back to the ship as we wished to be well clear of the brush before dark. We found our boat waiting for us and were back on board in time for dinner. We were all rather quiet for the next few days, thinking over our experience. For the first time we realized the terrific task our unthinking government had inflicted on our unfortunate troops, expecting them to hunt down and subdue people living in these impenetrable jungles armed with primitive yet deadly efficient weapons. The three people we had met proved to be friendly, otherwise not one of us would have returned alive, in spite of our modern revolvers and years of costly education. Being back on shipboard seemed like heaven. I could not imagine how the soldiers endured the long months in rain, mud, dense underbrush, and disease, never knowing when a bullet or an arrow of a poisoned blow dart would leap out of the jungle and take their lives.

From Olongapo we went to Cavite on Manila Bay about thirty miles from the city. There was no land communication between Cavite and Manila because of the insurrectos so we always went by water. Manila was very gay in those days. The central part was the ancient "Walled City," the Intramuros Section, surrounded by high and very thick walls. This section was also surrounded by an ancient moat spanned by what were once draw bridges but the bridges had long ago become stationary. In the Intramuros Section was the old Army and Navy Club, a meeting place for all arms of the Service. There were tables under the trees, Japanese lanterns, and pretty girls. It was an attractive place to dine and decide what to do later in the evening.

Most of the girls were of mixed blood of the sort called Eurasians in China and Japan. In Manila they were called Mestizos and were perfectly beautiful. I don't know why it is, but a mixture of Oriental and European blood seems to produce stunningly lovely women. Many had been in Paris and Madrid and were extremely well educated. They dressed exquisitely. There was a considerable amount of prejudice against them but not on the part of the American men. The American women attended to the Prejudice Department, although I did not see a single American woman who had anything like the looks, intelligence, and good breeding of these "half-cast niggers" as the American ladies contemptuously called the Mestizos.

Later on I met one of the Paris-educated Mestizos and we became very good friends. To say that she was a dream was to understate it scandalously. Then, one afternoon in the Luneta—the big open park outside the walls—we happened to meet her mother. Mama wore flat slippers and was, well, Mama was DARK. Several of our men married Mestizos but afterward left the islands taking their wives with them. If they had stayed on in Manila, I should imagine there would have been complications with the ladies' families.

Shortly after our arrival the Army gave what they called a Wild West Show. It was one of the most interesting spectacles, amateur or professional, that I have ever seen. It was a combined military spectacle and circus with races, lariat throwing, sharp shooting, dismantling guns and loading them on mules, then unloading them, assembling them and seeing who could fire the first shot, and many other demonstrations. The Roman Race, performed by men each riding two horses in a standing position, was executed by the Tenth Cavalry, an all-Negro regiment. They were remarkably skillful although I heard a dusky-looking Roman say to another who was crowding him: "Column right, Pete."

A number of these Negro regiments were outstanding for their skill and pluck. It was a Negro regiment that had distinguished itself at San Juan Hill, bravely charging the Spanish position when the white troops refused to advance. When one of these black regiments was in Texas they were attacked by a white crowd for having broken a local taboo, such as entering a restaurant reserved for whites or some such thing. In my opinion, those troopers would have been perfectly justified in taking their rifles and firing a volley into that mob of crackers and tarheels. My family were slaveholders and not even my worst enemy could have called me a "nigger-lover," but those troopers were in their country's uniform, had distinguished themselves in battle, and no civilians had any justification in molesting them.

The climax of the show was a drama described as "The Philippine Constabulary passing through a narrow jungle trail are ambushed by Wild Men from the Hills. They repulse them and drive them back to their caves."

All the actors in this part of the show, except the officers, were native Filipino troops, the part of the Wild Men being taken by

Constabulary soldiers who had doffed their uniforms, arrayed themselves in breech clouts and painted their bodies like Red Indians on
the war path as did the insurrectos. The Filipinos are most theatrical
and throw themselves in their parts with everything they have.

We watched while the Constabulary advanced cautiously through
the "jungle;" we could also see the Wild Men crawling like snakes in
the underbrush prepared to ambush the advancing soldiers. There
was a most convincing burst of rifle fire and the two forces met; with
an inspiring cheer the Constabulary dashed at the savages with fixed
bayonets and, simultaneously, the stage manager gave the signal for
the Wild Men to fly to their caves. They didn't fly; instead they flew at
the Constabulary and in a moment a free-for-all was in progress that
would have done credit to the Roman Coliseum. The Wild Men and
the Constabulary had to be dragged apart by American soldiers.

We remained in Manila until November. Summer is the most
disagreeable period in the Philippines; not only is the heat terrific but
it is the rainy season, and regularly every afternoon there is a torrential
downpour; anyone caught in it has but one thing to do, go back on
board ship and change his clothes; he could not be wetter if he fell
overboard.

Fortunately on the *Rainbow* we had Chinese mess attendants and,
in consequence, perfect service. Every officer had his own "boy" and
in addition there were a number of "makee learn" boys in training
who received no pay, only rations and a straw mat on which to sleep.
We always wore white uniforms and used to change them several
times a day; these uniforms, perfectly tailored and fitted, cost three
dollars each. Our boys kept our buttons polished brightly and always
had a clean uniform laid out with buttons, shoulder marks, and
campaign ribbons secured properly.

Wonderful as they were, our mess attendants weren't quite perfect. One officer ordered his boy to have a dozen pairs of white trousers
made for him by a Chinese tailor. He gave the boy an old pair as a
sample that had a patched seat. When the new trousers were delivered
the fit and workmanship were perfect but every pair had a patch on
the seat.

I had a somewhat similar experience at Emergency Drill. Part of
the Fire Drill was the formation of a bucket line. In order not to mess
up the deck I directed the last man in the line to empty the buckets
overboard. One day there was a real fire on the ship. Rushing aft to the

scene of the blaze I found the bucket line all present and efficiently passing the full buckets along as I had trained them. However, the last man, instead of putting out the fire, was pouring the water over the side. His not to reason why!

Our greatest regret in leaving the Orient was not being able to take our Chinese boys with us; the Chinese Exclusion Act made this impossible. Even our steward, a most superior and self-respecting man who wore the Dewey Medal for his participation in the Battle of Manila Bay and who had served in our Navy for many years was not permitted to put his foot on sacred American soil. We regretted losing him many times after returning to the indifferent service and frequently poor meals provided by the American attendants.

On several occasions, the Army was required to make landings along the coast in the hopes of cutting off bodies of the insurrectos before they could escape to the jungle. We were to supply the boats. These men were supposed to swim in full field equipment carrying their rifles above their heads. None of them could have swum the required distance naked. As soon as they got into the boats and looked at the water something like panic overtook them. Even after they had lowered themselves over the side they refused to let go of the gunwales. I saw one man who let go and immediately sank. He went down screaming and came up still screaming; he didn't even shut his mouth when he sank. We dragged him into the boat and pumped the water out of him while one of our men dove for and recovered his rifle. Nearly all these soldiers came from the West and most of them had never seen a body of water larger than a horse trough.

On the other hand, we Navy men did a lot of swimming during the typhoon season, or at least some of us did. We would hang from the rope ladders attached to the *Rainbow*'s boat booms and, when the big waves hit us, they would set us swinging like monkeys in a cage. Then we would dive overboard and when we came to the surface, if in the trough of the sea, we wouldn't be able to see the ship, not even her topmasts. All we could see were walls of water. Then up we would go and in a moment would be level with the spar deck. It was great fun and, as long as we avoided being thrown against the side of the ship or being caught under the lower gangway grating, there was no danger.*

---

*There was a brief notice in the *Philadelphia Inquirer* that I was working on a book telling the story of my father's life. A few days later I received the following letter from a Mr. H. Hertach. Part of the letter read:

Although the Philippine Insurrection ended "officially" on July 1st, 1902, the insurrectos didn't know about it. The heart of the trouble lay in Mindanao, an island in the Malay Archipelago. This island was almost completely unexplored. However, a few heroic Jesuit missionaries had been there, and they reported that there were twenty-four distinct nations dwelling in this beautiful, mysterious spot. Seventeen of these tribes were placid pagan people who were content to live at peace with their neighbors, even tolerating one community of Visayan Christians, who clung fearfully to a precarious foothold on the northern coast.

But shortly after Spain had discovered the islands in 1521, there had come a horde of warlike Moros, little brown men from Borneo with pipestem legs and arms and apparently frail physiques which entirely belied their really extraordinary strength and stamina. They landed first at Basilan and spread rapidly over the land to establish themselves near the great rivers and inland lakes and to force the supremacy of Allah and his fierce prophet on this new country.

As they grew and prospered, not content with local conquests, they organized piratical forays against the people of the Central and Northern Islands. When the southeast monsoon began to blow they would assemble in their war praus in some sheltered bay, hoist their lateen sails colored with brilliant tropic dyes and, with outriggers nicely set to balance their frail craft through the deep ocean swells, they would dash out to sea.

Like a flock of stormy petrels they skimmed before the gale, swooping on their single wings to deal death and destruction to peaceful Filipino farmer and haughty Spanish don alike.

Then sensing, as the sea birds they resembled do, the first veering of the wind to the north, they would swing south again ladened with

"We were anchored in Manila Bay at Cavite. I was a seaman aboard the USS *Wilmington* when on or about Oct. 27, 1907, a terrific typhoon blew up. We got orders from the flagship to let out all chain to the bitter end which was 105 fathoms. Winds of 70 to 80 miles per hour, sea running waves four to five feet high, storm course from east to west. At about 8:30 A.M. I was on the forecastle battening down hatches when on our port bow I saw the *Rainbow* steamer and a man swimming along side. My thoughts were 'Man overboard.' I went aft to the Off. Deck and reported to the lieutenant. The answer I got was, 'Oh, that's Mannix at his morning exercise.' He rounded our stern, then swam 600 yards against the storm back to the *Rainbow*. I watched him go up to the starboard gangway, not believing any man could have performed such a feat.

"The report the next day was he bet a fellow officer $20 he could swim around the *Wilmington* and back in the middle of the typhoon. He won the bet. He was a great athlete and an incomparable, powerful swimmer. I've heard that later he was the first American to swim the Hellespont. Well, that's the story of your father and another of his exploits."

gold, silver, arms, women for their harems, and children to be raised as slaves in their villages, immeasurably strengthened by each wild flight in their belief that, with Allah's power to back them, they stood invincible against the world.

To force these warring alien peoples to live at peace with each other was the tremendous problem that America had to solve when our war with Spain ended and we took over these fertile isles. Our Army officers, appointed governors of the far-flung provinces, had had no experience in such an undertaking.

Up to at least 1910, there was almost constant fighting on the southern islands, sometimes in one place and sometimes in another. Few of these fights were recorded in the American press, indeed there was seldom any mention of them in the Manila papers, but they went on just the same and people were killed in them quite as conclusively as people were killed at Belleau Wood or Pearl Harbor. As Kipling said: "It doesn't make any difference to a dead man whether he was killed in a border skirmish or at Waterloo."

A lot of this irregular warfare was amphibious; Navy gunboats took part in it and Navy personnel served ashore. Also the Navy frequently transported troops and maintained lines of communication.

In February 1908, rumors having reached Manila of goings on in the south, Admiral Hemphill decided to make a tour of inspection in the old Spanish gunboat *General Alava*; the *Rainbow* drew too much water to enter the smaller harbors.

We left Manila on January 9th and arrived at Camp Overton on the northern coast of Mindanao February 4th. Here the *Alava* left us and proceeded to Malabang on the southern coast where we were to join her after visiting the inland garrisons.

Overton lay between the ocean and the great jungle, a small Army post where officers and men were quartered in nipa shacks. Nipa is a kind of dried grass through which any sharp object, such as a spear head, can easily be thrust. Our first lesson in jungle etiquette was an admonition never to lean against the walls while occupying these frail huts but to sit as near the middle of the room as possible.

The local regiment lived in an eternal unrest ready to move on any foe in any direction at any moment, for here the famous "trail" began that wound gradually upwards through mountain passes to Camp Keithley on the shores of Lake Lanao and descended again to Malabang. For forty miles it cut through the heart of the jungle, this narrow path that formed the white man's sole means of communication in the enemy's country.

While we were at Overton, the Army received a message from an American who was living with a Moro wife in the interior. He had always considered himself quite safe, but now he had sent a runner through to Overton asking for help. An expedition was formed to bring him out. Five of us Navy men asked to go along. It was decided that we would continue on along the trail and rejoin our ship at Malabang.

At six o'clock on the morning of February 5th, we started out. There were a hundred troopers of the Sixth Cavalry commanded by Lt. Archie Miller who, several years later, was to become an aviator and be killed in a plane crash. Our cavalrymen were all young fellows in their early twenties whose rough campaigning had not left an ounce of superfluous flesh on them. They were not big men, about five feet seven or so, and they were so trained down that they looked positively gaunt.

In ten minutes after leaving Overton the sea had disappeared and we rode through a primeval and apparently impenetrable jungle. On either side were dense tangled masses of green interspersed with vividly colored orchids and other gorgeous masses of tropic bloom. In many places the high trees met overhead reducing the light to a semblance of dusk. Riding through these twilight alleys we would be suddenly blinded by the full glare of the morning sun pouring through a rift in the branches.

Once, as we were passing under a great tree whose huge branches stretched over the trail, the trooper next to me pointed out a long line of gray monkeys who were seated just above our heads. They squatted with their backs to us, arms around each other, tails hanging down in parallel lines, deep in weighty confab.

As we advanced they turned simultaneously looking over their shoulders. Then they began to scream and chatter. Our Navy doctor was particularly annoyed by their behavior and, drawing his pistol, aimed it at the bobbing gray mass but, before he could pull the trigger, Miller had him by the wrist. "Don't shoot," he said. "The noise of it will bring down every hostile Moro within hearing."

We waited silently for a while to make sure the monkeys had not betrayed us. Then we continued on to a little clearing where stood the American's nipa cabin.

Not more than an hour before our arrival (so our Filipino scouts believed) the Moro tribesmen had crept out of the brush and, surrounding the little building, fired cross volleys through the nipa walls. Then, in a swift rush, they had closed in completing their hideous work with a typical butchery.

I shall never forget that clearing. The deserted home, walls smashed in, door sagging open on its one remaining hinge and, across the gaping threshold, the shocking corpse of the white man lying in a pool of blood. We never found his Moro wife nor knew her fate. Had she betrayed her husband, or, remaining faithful, been dragged off to torture in the heart of the jungle?

A squad of troopers dismounted, hastily improvised a horse litter, placed the body on it and quickly swung back into their saddles. Miller issued a curt command against straggling and, putting spurs to the nervous horses, we plunged again into the somber forest. With the Moros "out" no loitering was possible; we had to reach Camp Keithley before sunset.

The trail was just wide enough to allow two men to ride abreast. We could touch the vegetation on either hand but it was so dense we couldn't see through it. A little further on, we heard the noise of some terrific battle in the brush.

"Dismount!" shouted Miller. In a second we were all on our feet, ready for the attack. Nothing happened. Moving cautiously through the underbrush we found a six-foot lizard with his head jammed in an abandoned meat tin. He was rolling around on his prehistoric back clawing frantically at the tin like a kitten with her head in a milk jug, a most undignified exhibition for a descendant of the dinosaurs.

We released the lizard and rode on. Only once did we see any humans. We passed a clearing where two Moros were at work. The soldiers hailed them and waved a greeting. The Moros, showing their pointed teeth, snarled like angry dogs. Evidently they were not a bit afraid of the soldiers in spite of our numbers and weapons. I don't believe they were afraid of anything.

Our way now began to slope gradually upward across the mountain chain that forms the backbone of this part of Mindanao. At times it became very narrow and excessively steep. As we approached these rises a shout would go down the line: "Remember the Maine" whereupon every man would lean forward, take a firm grip of his horse's mane and rise in the stirrups to relieve the saddle of as much weight as possible lest it slip and deposit him in some deep ravine.

The scenery grew indescribably wild and majestic; waterfalls dashed themselves into foam over the rocky sides of canyons whose massive walls were still covered by the relentless jungle. Just at sunset we had our first view of beautiful Lake Lanao lying like a blue cloud on the very top of the mountains. Keithley sprawled on its banks, the little nipa huts and frail barrios so dwarfed by the great lake and the isolation and menace of the trees it seemed impossible that for three long years they had maintained their foothold in this wilderness serving as a base for all the mounted troops.

We were to see another example of Moro warfare that night. We made quite a party at the colonel's table and among the guests was the newly appointed civil governor of Lanao Province. He was a Harvard graduate, a man with very positive ideas, well over six feet and weighing two hundred pounds. He had come to the Philippines a short time before with the fixed idea that justice and kindness were all that was needed in dealing with non-civilized peoples. He had evidently formed the habit of visiting outlying barrios and conferring with the natives without keeping the Military informed of his actions.

The Army officers spent most of the dinner hour urging him to restrict his visits to daylight hours but he received their advice in a stubborn silence that showed quite plainly he meant to ignore it, so no one was surprised when later on he started off alone on one of his nocturnal strolls.

It was a rainy night and he was tramping along a muddy trail with the jungle close on either hand, his only light a hand lantern when suddenly (as he afterwards told us) at the edge of the flickering yellow arc, he saw a shadow slip from behind a bush to crouch close to his path. Raising the lantern he saw a diminutive shape, completely enveloped in a dark cloak, huddled like a gnome at his feet.

Without a moment's hesitation he set his lantern on the ground, raised his right hand and calling, "Amigo!" took a step toward the eerie figure. The cloak swayed slightly, the bell-like muzzle of an old blunderbus appeared from beneath it, a flash illuminated the dim trail and with a roar the old weapon belched its charge of broken glass, stones, and rusty nails directly into his face at a range of ten feet.

The noise was heard by us back in the camp and a scouting party soon located the governor lying face downward in the mud and water. They carried him back to camp through the wind and rain, slipping and sliding under his weight in the ooze of the trail. Curiously he had not been struck in the body but both arms and his right leg received severe wounds, and it was found necessary to amputate the leg.

The following day was to be spent in rest before starting the long descent to Malabang on the south coast, but Keithley had one more thrill still in store for us.

That night a hostile Moro slipped into the camp and crawled under one of the buildings used as a barracks. Lying flat on his back he thrust a spear through a crack in the floor; the spear pierced the canvas bottom of a soldier's cot passing through the mattress into his body. The soldier screamed and his comrades woke to find him transfixed.

Rushing out into the dark they saw the Moro, apparently unarmed, creeping from beneath the barracks. Two men attempted to seize him but found that his body had been greased and he easily slipped through their hands. Before the soldiers could leap out of reach he snatched a barong from his breech clout and, with a single sweeping slash which began with the withdrawal of the heavy knife from its sheath, he cut off the left arm of the man nearest him as neatly as a surgeon could have done it.

The soldiers ran in every direction leaving a path clear to the jungle. Down it he fled followed by random shots, a wild black figure in the moonlight, only to fall within a few feet of the first trees dropped by a scattered volley from the hastily loaded rifles. He was immediately surrounded but, before anyone was allowed to approach him, a soldier with a long bamboo pole struck the barong out of his hand. He had received more than twenty wounds before he died.

We were all glad when we were finally off on the last leg of our journey to Malabang, our backs turned on the beauty and tragedy of the mountains and our hearts filled with admiration for the Army of Occupation. We had hardly left the post when a horse shied violently at something concealed by the underbrush. Slipping their stirrups the flanking troopers dismounted and, deploying warily, entered the jungle but instead of the Moros they expected to find, they stumbled over a python nearly forty feet long. It was lying on the ground as though asleep and half way down its length a prominent bulge showed that it had recently dined. The bulge proved to be a fifty pound wild hog swallowed whole.

As we looked I sensed that we were being watched by something or somebody in the jungle. Before I could put my thoughts into words there was a slight movement of the tall grass and, without the slightest sound, a group of men appeared.

They wore the uniform of American soldiers except, instead of the campaign hat, their heads were covered, Mohammedan fashion, with a red fez. They wore wrap puttees, then regulation in the Army, but right there the American uniform stopped. They were all barefooted, hence the absolute silence of their movements. Looking at their feet, I could understand why one of the Moros' deadliest weapons were sharpened bamboo spikes hidden under leaves along the trail although not even the heavy soled boots of the soldiers were much protection against the knife sharp, steel hard spikes.

These were the famous Moro Constabulary; Moros who had formerly fought for the Spaniards and had now transferred their allegiance to us. When, a few minutes later, they resumed their march they seemed to fade into the woods; there must have been fifty of them but they made no more noise than a hunting cat.

The soft tropic twilight was filling the woods with fantastic gray shadows and dimly glimpsed ghosts that flitted before and around us as we rode down the last slope to Malabang. Our horses were very restless, snorting and sweating as they picked their way out of the dense thickets into a partial clearing. Miller passed the word down the line, "There are Moros about. The horses can smell them. Prepare for an attack."

Suddenly my mount threw back his head in wild terror and bolted across the opening in a series of mad leaps. Miller yelled: "Fall off, fall off, don't let him get you among the trees!" Off I went and into the jungle raced the horse. A crash of breaking branches, a rapidly diminishing clatter of hoof beats and he was gone. We never saw him again.

"Keep close to us until we reach Malabang," Miller told me. "Even a gun isn't always a match for a barong. I saw a constabulary sergeant who was attacked by a Moro and tried to protect his head by executing the high parry with his rifle. The barong cut the steel barrel of the rifle in two and killed the sergeant. No, I wouldn't have believed it possible either if I hadn't seen it." I kept close.

Below us lay the sea and the twinkling lights of the little port; another hour of arduous scrambling down the steep trail and we were in her sleepy, dirty streets. A the end of a squalid alley we found the *Alava* anchored in the stream, her chain was at short stay, the gun covers off her 6-pounders, steam was up and she lay ready to slip out to sea the moment we reached her. The Moros were busy in more islands than one, the monsoon was moderating, and we were to depart at once for the ancient walled city of Jolo across the Sulu Sea.

Jolo is only five degrees above the equator and within easy sailing distance of Borneo. Borneo was the stronghold of the Moros, and at the time of our visit the only part of the island occupied by Americans was the town of Jolo. The walls were loop-holed for defense and had three gates which were kept open only during the daylight hours.

At each gate was a strong military guard, and when the country people entered the town to sell their fruit and vegetables they were carefully searched for weapons. This did not prevent certain fanatics from throwing their weapons over the wall before passing through the gates and afterwards recovering and concealing them. To prevent this, a considerable area had been cleared around the town and sentries were posted in watch towers but still some of the fanatics were able to elude them.

The local garrison had strict orders always to carry their sidearms. We saw a baseball game in which the umpire and all the players carried revolvers; there was very little sliding for bases in that game. At another place a group of soldiers were in swimming. No, they did not wear their weapons in the water but took turns in going overboard, those ashore guarding weapons and clothes. Even nurses wheeling baby carriages wore pistol holsters.

The very strict orders concerning arms were due not to fear of an attack by the Moros en masse but because certain religious fanatics know as Juramentados (from the Spanish "oath takers") made a practice of surreptitiously entering the town, either by mingling with the crowd bringing in farm produce or by slipping through some undiscovered breach in the walls. Once inside they "ran amok" killing indiscriminately until they themselves were killed. Very few of them survived one running amok; as a matter of fact they didn't want to survive. Their one object was to create as much damage as possible and then, having left a bloody trail behind them, to be killed; a spectacular way of committing suicide.

The more savage Moslems believed that it was a righteous act to kill an unbeliever and that a Son of the Prophet who died committing this laudable act was at once transported to paradise. I was also told that many believed the more Christians they killed the more houris they would have in heaven, but this may have been just a story.

The true believer who was a candidate for paradise went into the jungle with the native priests. Then various rites were held, one of which was the shaving of the Juramentado's eyebrows. Frequently his arms and legs were bound with strips of cloth to act as tourniquets and keep life in him as long as possible after he was shot or bayoneted. His weapon was either a krise (a long knife with a wavy blade), or a barong—the heavy, razor sharp cleaver.

When the gates of the city were opened in the morning he would slip in with the crowd, his weapon either concealed in a basket or having previously been thrown over the wall. Selecting the most crowded street he would start his headlong rush which ended only with his death. One shout of "Juramentado!" and all the shops and houses barred their doors and all the inhabitants, except the armed military, fled in every direction, just as they would have fled from a mad dog.

I talked to the daughter of an Army officer who was in a Chinese shop when a Juramentado attacked. She told me:

"I heard a commotion in the street and looking out of the window, I saw an Army wagon, driven by a Negro trooper, stop just in front of the shop door. A stout commissary sergeant stepped down from the wagon and, as his foot touched the ground, a wild-looking native whipped out a krise and made a vicious slash at him. The sergeant turned and started running around the wagon with the Moro bounding after him. The Negro driver, who must have been a newcomer, thought it was some sort of a game and roared with laughter, shouting, "Run, Sergeant!" In passing, the Moro made a side swipe at the driver which ripped his flannel shirt from wrist to shoulder and sent him tumbling backward. He stopped laughing then.

"Soldiers and constabulary came running from every direction, some in their undershirts, some without hats, some with one arm thrust in a coat sleeve, but all with their rifles. A scattered volley was fired and I was grabbed by the two Chinese who ran the shop and dragged backward to the rear while another Chinaman closed and barred the door. I didn't quite understand what was going on and thought that I was being kidnapped. I fought and screamed but after listening at the closed door for a few minutes, the shopkeepers opened it and politely bowed me out. There was the Juramentado lying dead in the street, the soldiers afraid to go near him as he still held his krise and they weren't sure he was stone dead."

At that time, the standard Army sidearm was the .38 caliber revolver, but a bullet from a .38 wouldn't stop a Juramentado. You could empty the gun into him and he'd keep on coming and kill you before he died. So the .45 was introduced. I was told that a bullet from it would knock a man down even if it only hit his hand. Fully loaded, the gun weighed three pounds. A standard joke by drill instructors was to tell a recruit, "Fire seven rounds and if the man keeps on coming, throw the gun at him."

It was well known that the Sultan of Jolo instigated many of the Juramentado attacks, but there was no way to prove it and he always denied it, claiming the fanatics went insane and he had no control over them. He lived in a palace some distance from the town, and finally Admiral Hemphill sent a gunboat to shell the palace. The furious sultan arrived the next day to protest this unwonted attack. The admiral listened to his tirade and then explained that he was very sorry but he had no control over the gunboat; it had gone Juramentado. The sultan got the idea and from then on the Juramentado attacks were greatly reduced.

What finally stopped the Juramentados was the custom of wrapping the dead man in a pig's skin and stuffing his mouth with pork. As the pig was an unclean animal, this was considered unspeakable defilement.

An English Army officer I met had another suggestion. "After the Sepoy Mutiny, we finally hit on the perfect punishment for anyone who had commited atrocities on British women and children," he told me. "We used to bind them to the muzzles of the field guns and then fire the guns. Moslems believe in the literal resurrection of the body. A man who has been hit by a 3-inch shell will look like it for all eternity."

I suggested this must have been rather sloppy. The Englishman smiled condescendingly. "After you Yanks have had some more experience in handling native peoples, you'll get over these scruples."

Some distance outside the city was a mountain called Bud Dajo. Here, in 1906, the last really big fight in the Philippines took place. The Moros had entrenched themselves at the very top of this hill, and when the fighting was over, it was found that their women had joined with the men in opposing the Americans and a number of them had been killed.

A photograph, taken of the dead, was afterward published in the American papers. In the picture a dead woman, her breasts bare, occupied a prominent place. This picture created a great outcry as an example of American atrocities and the government had it suppressed.

Of course, in a jungle fight at the top of an almost inaccessible mountain it was impossible for our men to tell whom they were fighting, but they did know that their comrades were being killed.

In this fight was a detachment of sailors from the gunboat *Pampanga* commanded by their captain, Lt. Henry Cooke. Henry received a very peculiar wound; he was shot through the sole of one foot. The Moro who did it was at the bottom of a hole and shot upward as Henry stepped over the hole.

The day we visited Bud Dajo we rode to within a short distance of the foot of the mountain, and then dismounting, we went on by foot as there were no trails and we had to force our way through the jungle. Our guide was a lieutenant of artillery who had taken part in the battle.

Although there were no Moros about, we had troubles enough with other enemies. The man next to me had the entire back of his thick flannel shirt torn away by a bayonet thorn. A little later, as we paused to get our breath, I noticed something hanging from the chin of one of the men. I told him about it and he attempted to brush it off. It wouldn't brush.

Going closer, I saw that it was an enormous tropical leech that was visibly swelling before our eyes. The bushes were full of them and we began to find them attached to our hands, the backs of our necks, every place where the flesh was exposed. It was impossible to pull them off; the body came away leaving the head embedded in the wound. The only way to get rid of them was to apply a lighted cigarette to their bodies. When that was done they would curl up and drop off.

It was not until we started the actual climb that we began to realize the really formidable feat that we had undertaken. How the soldiers, with their rifles and equipment, and the *Pampanga*'s men with machine guns had ever reached the top under enemy fire I cannot imagine. The sides of the mountain were almost perpendicular and were covered with dense jungle vegetation. The only way we ascended was by pulling ourselves up by the tree roots most of which were above ground. Our guide not only did this but he led the column and cleared a way for us with his bolo. I wish I could remember his name as it was an amazing exhibition of strength.

When we finally got to the top I was so utterly exhausted that, had any Moros appeared, I couldn't have raised a finger. We remained there for an hour and examined the trenches and rifle pits which had been dug and positioned with considerable skill. That the Army had been able to overcome such adversaries under such conditions greatly increased my admiration for them. It had always seemed incredible to me that soldiers could drown in a few feet of nice, warm, calm sea water without knowing enough to drop their rifles or grab a nearby boat's gunwales, and yet here were these same men able to perform feats utterly beyond me. Well, to each his own.

Going down was much easier. We simply sat on our sterns and slid. However, at least once we all slid in the wrong direction and were obliged to retrace our steps—or slides—for a hundred yards or so. I, for one, could hardly make it.

That evening in the Officers' Mess we received an honor, unofficial but valued nevertheless. We were created members of the Ancient and Honorable Order of Jolo Goats, a most exclusive society. To be eligible you must climb Bud Dajo.

In the autumn of 1907, the Honorable William H. Taft then secretary of war, visited the islands to discuss with native leader plans for the ultimate independence of the Philippines. The formal opening of the Assembly took place at the Ayuntamiento Palace. There were about three hundred delegates who had come from the outermost parts of the archipelago, in which there are more than a thousand islands, to assist in the making of the laws which were to govern them.

I was very much impressed by the earnestness of the members. They took themselves and their task very seriously and listened with rapt attention to long discourses in both Spanish and English. Many of them wore the most original costumes, one very popular combination being a pair of perfectly transparent gauze trousers worn over a breech clout while the upper garment or shirt fluttered gaily in the breeze. Others wore no shoes, and, judging from their spatulated toes, had never worn them.

Despite these idiosyncrasies of dress, they showed much natural courtesy and good breeding, certainly more than the American wit who hung a placard near the entrance to the Palace reading: "Please check your bolos at the door."

That same afternoon a reception was given the Assembly by the Chinese Merchants' Association of Manila. There was an orchestra and the music was so superior that I took the first opportunity to get a view of the musicians. They were playing a very difficult Chopin

The *Cleveland*'s landing troops with field gun.

Reception of nobles on ship in Japan.

Viceroy of China's Chili Province; Lieutenant Mannix in left-hand window, second from right.

Execution of Korean bandits in China.

Pekin.

Sunken Russian ships, Port Arthur.

Port Arthur.

Polly Perkins.

Polly and Pratt.

The Hedges, Rosemont, Pennsylvania. This was the picture *Distinctive Homes* used on its cover to illustrate the perfect country estate.

President Wilson decides to send warships to Vera Cruz.

NOW IN MEXICO CITY

HERALD BUREAU,
No. 1502 H STREET, N. W.,
WASHINGTON, D. C., Tuesday.

Eighty United States marines with general machine guns are secretly in Mexico City in plain clothes, prepared to lead in the defense of the American colony if the aggressive measures by the United States government should precipitate retaliatory measures.

The American colony was supplied with small arms under the Taft administration. While Henry Lane Wilson was there a programme for defence was mapped out. In the last few months, however, this programme has been greatly perfected. Several weeks ago an additional shipment of arms was sent into Mexico City with machine guns.

The other foreign colonies also have arms and marines of their navies in Mexico City. Concentration points have been agreed upon and a general outbreak in Mexico City would not take the foreign colony unawares.

Naval officers have counselled that marines be sent to Mexico City. They wanted them sent in uniform and in a larger force, but President Wilson feared the effect that this move might have upon the international situation.

As a compromise the smaller force in plain clothes and the machine guns were sent in.

Rear Admiral Badger, commander of chief of the Atlantic fleet, in reply to an order from the Navy Department to proceed to Tampico with all available ships:—

"Can sail from Hampton Roads to-morrow forenoon with Arkansas, Vermont and New Jersey. The New Hampshire may be delayed a few hours for coal and provision; will follow as soon as possible Louisiana and Michigan will be directed to follow and South Carolina ordered to await fleet at Key West."

This despatch was received from the Hancock at New Orleans in reply to an order to proceed to Tampico with a regiment of marines:—

"Receipt of order to proceed at once to Tampico with regiment of marines without advance base outfit acknowledged. Ship ready to sail since ten o'clock Monday night. Brigade commander believes marines and necessary field equipment can be re-embarked ready for sailing by Wednesday morning."

THE TIME FOR "WATCHING

The evacuation of
Tampico.

Newspaper announcing
attack on Tampico.

Model ships in the N
Academy in Vera Cru
after our shelling.

Destruction of Vera Cruz classroom.

American dead at Vera Cruz.

Snipers hanged in Vera Cruz.

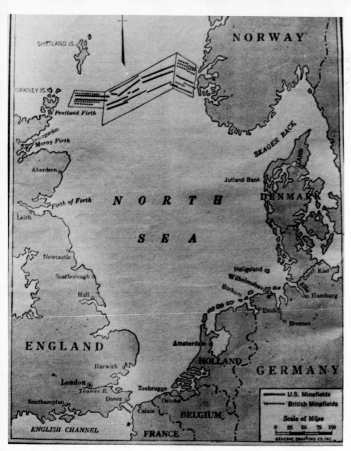

The location of the North Sea mine barrage. (*National Geographic Magazine*)

Squadron commanders of the mine-laying flotilla. Commander Mannix is standing on right end, arms folded. (*National Geographic Magazine*)

Premature mine explosion.

Trucking mine cases.
(*National Geographic Magazine*)

How a mine is anchored.
(*National Geographic Magazine*)

USS *Quinnebaug*, Commander Mannix's ship.

Submarine attack. The *Vampire* was the British destroyer escort leader.

Warships in Constantinople.

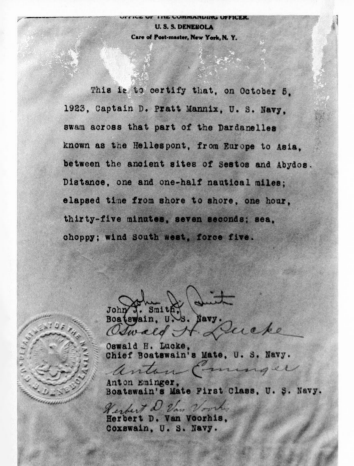

This is to certify that, on October 5, 1923, Captain D. Pratt Mannix, U. S. Navy, swam across that part of the Dardanelles known as the Hellespont, from Europe to Asia, between the ancient sites of Sestos and Abydos. Distance, one and one-half nautical miles; elapsed time from shore to shore, one hour, thirty-five minutes, seven seconds; sea, choppy; wind South west, force five.

John J. Smith,
Boatswain, U. S. Navy.

Oswald H. Lucke,
Chief Boatswain's Mate, U. S. Navy.

Anton Eminger,
Boatswain's Mate First Class, U. S. Navy.

Herbert D. Van Voorhis,
Coxswain, U. S. Navy.

Certificate of Hellespont swim, October 5, 1923.

The USS *Dendola* in the Bosphorus.

American destroyers off Constantinople.

The fire and rescue party.

waltz, the "Minute Waltz." There were probably fifty Filipinos in the orchestra; the leader wore an old slouch hat rammed over his eyes and was smoking a cigarette while the first violins, their legs crossed, beat time with bare toes. The other musicians looked like a congress of scarecrows, nearly all barefooted and nearly all with the inevitable cigarette in the corner of their mouths. Not a sheet of music was visible yet they were playing a difficult classical selection with an accuracy and feeling that was truly remarkable.

The next day there was a big parade with everyone in fancy costume. The band took part dressed as monkeys. There was something unreal about seeing a monkey marching down the street playing a slide trombone. Again, none of them had any music; they were all playing by ear.

When Mr. Taft left, he was so popular with all classes of natives that he was accompanied as far as Corregidor by a swarm of nondescript craft bearing serenaders and other well-wishers. I believe that with a little luck, he could have reconciled all the warring factions.

The soldiers didn't appreciate Mr. Taft's sympathy for the people who were killing them, especially when Taft referred to the Filipinos as our "little brown brothers." The troops made up a song part of which went like this:

> I'm only a common soldier in the blasted Philippines.
> They say I've got brown brothers here but I don't
>   know what that means.
> I like the word fraternity as sure as I can be,
> They *may* be a brother to William H. Taft,
> But they're no relation to me!

Apart from securing us bases, the Philippine affair had an even more important function. Never again, I am sure, will the United States allow herself to become embroiled in a war in the Orient against a primitive people using guerrilla tactics. No one who remembers the Philippine Campaign could make that mistake a second time.

Shortly after this, the *Rainbow* was dispatched on another goodwill tour to Japan, Vladivostok, and China. In Japan we saw the famous Yoshiwara (red-light district) and in Manchuria witnessed the beginnings of the Russian Revolution. I don't know which was more interesting.

CHAPTER NINE

Japan, China, and Vladivostok (1909)

Another foreign devil has just dropped dead!

—Li Lien-ying, the Empress Dowager's head
eunuch, gave this cry each time the
Empress repeated a magic formula
guaranteed to kill invaders.

THE FOLLOWING APRIL we arrived in Yokohama, where we had the unusual experience of having our ship coaled by women. Each one carried a small canvas bag on her head, and they came up the gangway like a swarm of ants. Without pausing each emptied her bag in turn and, leaving the ship by the forward gangway, got another load. They finished coaling us in far shorter time than it had ever been done before.

In spite of the heavy labor they perfomed, these coolie women were far from "tough." They were modesty and good breeding personified. I saw one of the Japanese men on the coal barge make some indecent gestures toward one of them; she seemed to be as embarrassed and annoyed as any other respectable young girl would have been and got away from him as quickly as possible.

The men coolies were a hardy lot. It is queeer that it was not until World War II that America made the astonishing discovery that the Japanese are rough, ruthless, and efficient. Most Americans seem to regard them as funny little people out of Gilbert and Sullivan's *The Mikado*. They should have seen those ricksha coolies trotting through the sleet and frozen slush of the streets with straw sandals on their bare feet clad in a costume very like a swimming suit. I have often seen those same coolies sleeping in open rickshas on nights when I was chilled to the bone. I can also remember Yokohama Harbor where barges carrying railroad cars were propelled not by tugs but by a few men sculling with incredibly long oars.

Many of these coolies enjoyed embarrassing white people, especially white women. While in Yokohama, I met a fellow countrywoman who looked like the personification of the New England School Marm: thin, very tall, and wearing glasses with a broad ribbon attached. We were doing some sightseeing and we both took rickshas; mine followed just behind hers. They always travel in single file.

Suddenly her ricksha coolie stopped and mine, perforce, stopped

171

also. The lady's coolie indicated the house that we were passing and said in English, "That is a whorehouse."

The lady replied absently, "Did you say Porterhouse?" Then she looked around and noticed for the first time the leer on the coolie's face. She leisurely adjusted her glasses, looked the building over carefully, calmly remarked, "Looks more like the Tenderloin to me," and imperiously motioned the human horse to continue. It was a very neat remark and I'm only sorry that the coolie didn't get the reference.

A few days later, the admiral and his staff (which included me) went on to Tokyo to make a round of official calls. I think we called on every naval and military chief of Japan. One of them was the famous Admiral Count Heihachiro Togo. It was Admiral Togo who had destroyed the Russian Fleet a few years before at Tsushima. He looked very amiable but said only one word during our visit. When we rose to go, he said, "Pleased."

While in Tokyo, as the admiral's flag lieutenant, I received the following letter:

"By order of His Majesty the Emperor, Count Mitsuaki Tanaka, Minister of the Imperial Household, requests the honor of the company of His Excellency Rear Admiral Hemphill, his Personal Staff and his Commanding Officers at luncheon at the Shiba Detached Palace on the 18th instant at 12:30 P.M. His Imperial Highness Prince Yosibito will honor the occasion with his presence.

"No answer is necessary.

"The officers of the Squadron will accompany the Ambassador to the Palace after the audience. The Commander of the Third Squadron, his Personal Staff and the Commanding Officers are the only officers who will attend the audience."

In case you didn't know, the words "No answer is necessary" meant that this kind of invitation is a command and cannot be declined. The notification of our presentation had the Royal Chrysanthemum engraved at the top.

We met at the embassy at the designated hour, everybody in Special Full Dress, a uniform that has since been abolished owing, I understand, to its expense. It seems rather a pity as, in that uniform, we were never ashamed to be in any company. The coat buttoned up to the neck with a high gold laced collar that had something of the eighteenth century about it. There were gold epaulettes, cocked hats, swords, a broad gold stripe down the trouser leg and the inside of the coattails were lined with white satin. Being aides, Walter Anderson and I also wore gold aiguillettes.

At the embassy we were instructed in what we were to do at the presentation. Our name being called we were to enter the Audience Chamber, pause, make a deep bow, advance half-way to the Mikado, pause again and make a second deep bow, then advance until directly in front of him where we were to pause for the third time and make a third deep bow. The Emperor would, presumably, offer his hand which we would take and then would back out (being careful not to trip over our swords), and make our exit by a second door. The same procedure was to be carried out when we later were presented to the Empress.

As we entered the palace we passed along a long corridor; the walls were of wood, unpainted, and exquisitely put together. I think the beauty of their workmanship made more impression on me than anything in the ceremony.

Outside the Audience Chamber we were halted and, as our names were called went in one by one. When my turn came I entered and had my first view of a Son of Heaven.

The Mikado was dressed in a uniform not unlike that of the old French Army: red trousers and a coat of darker material. His clothes were much too big for him. Later I heard that, as his person was sacred, tailors are not permitted to measure him but must look at him from a distance and make his uniforms by guesswork. I don't know how authentic this story is but his uniform was certainly too large. He did not look as though he was in good health; his face was pinched and his complexion was bad.

Everything passed smoothly. I made my pauses and bows, shook hands with him, and backed out without accident.

Next came our presentation to the Empress. She and her ladies-in-waiting were dressed in European clothes, which certainly was a mistake, from the picturesque point of view. There was nothing particularly striking about her appearance; she looked like any other Japanese lady.

I made my pauses and bows, eventually arriving directly in front of her where I waited for her to hold out her hand. For a moment she didn't do it and Admiral Hemphill, who, naturally was very anxious for everything to run smoothly, hissed at me, "Mannix, Mannix, hold out your hand!" I was sorry for the admiral's anxiety but I hadn't the slightest idea of offering my hand to her. I had done that once to the wife of the British governor of Grenada and she had refused to take it, "to put me in my place" I suppose. The Empress must have heard the admiral's hisses for she smiled faintly and offered me her hand. I fell on it like a hungry wolf.

A day or so later we attended a memorial service in honor of an event which, had it happened ten days earlier, might have involved us in a war with Japan.

The midshipmen's training ship *Matsushima* had paid a goodwill visit to Manila and had remained at anchor in Manila Bay for a week. The Japanese Navy was, and is, very aristocratic and among the midshipmen were sons of virtually every noble house in Japan; there was even a Royal Prince on board. Among them was the son of General Nogi. A few years later, when the Mikado died, Nogi and his wife committed hari-kari so as to accompany him into the Beyond.

A few days after the *Matsushima* left Manila Bay, she exploded, exactly like the *Maine* in Havana Harbor. Most of the midshipmen were killed. Had the accident occurred in Manila, the Japanese would most certainly have thought that we were responsible as relations between the two nations were as strained as ours had been with Spain. Just think of it; a war that would have meant the lives of thousands of men and have cost millions of dollars depending on a fluke. Why the ship exploded, I never found out.

This was shortly after the Russo-Japanese War and Japan had the entire Western world thoroughly bluffed because of her victory over Russia. The playing of Gilbert and Sullivan's operetta *The Mikado* had been banned in England for fear that the Japanese might consider it insulting.

Back in Yokohama, Admiral Hemphill gave a big dinner party which included all the naval and military chiefs and a number of other guests. We congratulated ourselves that everything had gone off so smoothly.

One of the main sights in all Japanese cities is the red-light district; known as the Yoshiwara. In Tokyo the Yoshiwara is enormous, a city in itself. However, both Yokohama and Nagasaki have very—I was about to say "respectable" but perhaps "considerable" is a better adjective—Yoshiwaras.

At the entrance to these districts one may hire, if one desires, a wicker helmet with a visor that effectually conceals the face; the

Japanese nobles frequently use these. Inside the Yoshiwara everything is wide open. Each establishment has a big show window like the shop windows along Fifth Avenue; the windows have no glass but there are wooden bars set rather close together running along the front of them. In the windows, in plain view of the passerby, are the young ladies of the establishment, seated on cushions and provided with their toilet articles, tea sets, etc.

From their demeanor these young ladies might easily have been mistaken for the pupils of a fashionable girls' school. they conversed politely with each other, absolutely ignoring the passing crowd looking at them through the bars. There was absolutely no "soliciting" on their part, not even by look; there was no "rough stuff" as in Chefoo where the women stationed themselves in the street and attempted to drag passing men into the houses; nothing like the appalling "cribs" which existed, certainly as late as 1909, in New Orleans where women, in all costumes and lack of costumes, used to lean out of the windows and endeavor to attract the passing males, seamen and landsmen alike.

What struck me most about these Japanese girls was the youth of some of them. Of course, it is difficult to tell the age of Orientals but many of the younger ones seemed to be mere children, ten or twelve years old. They had two insignia to indicate their profession: instead of tying their obis (sashes) behind, as is customary, they tied them in front and most of them wore a complete circle of ornamental hair pins. "Respectable" women in Japan didn't wear more than a certain number of these pins, I think it was four.

There was also a large number of devices offered for sale that were supposed to increase your sexual enjoyment, although they looked more like instruments of torture to me. Some of them had signs in several languages explaining their use. The wording was very striking, indeed.

One device that looked somewhat like a large mushroom came with the following instructions:

"Tortoise shaped. Especially made for convenience to carry in the pocket (comes with cloth bag). To use this you feel absolutely the same as you do touching to the human body or more better!"

Other instructions read:

"Ball shaped. This article is to use after filled with air (air pipe attached). You can use this when it is necessary in secret."

"Night Flower. The name Night Flower is hair on female or male organ or of secret parts and this made of artificial hair technically and you cannot find the difference between human hair and this. There are two colors prepared—Black and Brown. Prepared medicine glue with hair and after attached cannot come off even if you bathed but if you want to take off it is easy."

"Patent Blesser. After many times sexual union when man becomes weak use blesser then you can feel very young. Old man must use this without saying."

"For ladies. A lady who does not wish a man in bed use this after putting hot water inside then she will dream happy dream."

"Musical balls. If you are too short, put these inside a lady and wonderful music will ring inside her organ and both will feel very good."

I asked Walter Anderson, "What tune do you suppose they play?" After thinking for a moment he suggested, "Carry me back to old Vagina."

In addition there were numerous items such as Sexual Desirous Stimulant, Make Hot Cream, Happy Powder, Vacuum Vessel, Open Mystery, Night Cap, etc.

I heard that frequently Japanese girls enter the Yoshiwara in order to provide themselves with a dowry and had no difficulty in marrying afterward; this may not be true; I certainly cannot vouch for it. Be that as it may, Japanese psychology is difficult for us to understand.

I also heard a story about a Japanese noble who handed his wife over to a foreign naval officer in order to learn certain naval secrets and, when she returned having accomplished her mission, he then spurned her as being no longer fit to live with him. A foreigner arriving in Japan is astonished at how casually the differences between the sexes is ignored. If you are in the shower and call for a towel, it will often be brought to you by a pretty young girl. Once at a theater between the acts I went below for a necessary purpose and somebody lined up alongside of me. I looked around and saw it was a woman. She was a female wrestler, at least six feet tall and built like the hired man. In some mysterious fashion, she was using a wall urinal.

The famous Geishas are not prostitutes. They are professional entertainers. A famous resort in Yokohama was the Hundred and One Steps Tea House. It was necessary to climb that number of steps to get there. It was presided over by the dean of all the Geishas; she had known everybody as far back as Farragut and had just missed seeing

Perry land in Japan. This establishment was extremely pleasant and well run but not all Geisha houses were this outstanding. One evening several of us went out on the town and stopped at a pretentious looking tea house. First removing our shoes and leaving them in the entry we entered the main room and sat down on the cushions prepared for guests. All these places had straw matting on the floors and were spic and span clean. We ordered supper and the national drink, sake. Sake, incidentally, tastes rather like sherry and is deceptively mild. It is served in shallow cups without handles which hold only a thimbleful and it is quite easy to dispose of a dozen of these cups without realizing what you are doing, after which it begins to dawn on you that sake, like the lady of the song, isn't as mild or as young as it appears.

Our supper being served we also "ordered" Geishas to entertain us during the meal with their posture dancing and singing; to the Occidental ear the singing sounds very like caterwauling. After an hour or so of this we asked for our bill and, looking at it, realized that we had been charged about four times the legal rate for our entertainment.

We were in civilian clothes and evidently the mistress of the establishment thought we were American tourists. Paying no attention to the bill we carefully laid down the exact legal charge for our entertainment adding a generous tip, and, returning to the entrance, commenced putting on our shoes.

As we did so we noticed that the head Geisha had manned the telephone. Whom was she calling? We made one guess and decided it was the nearest police station. Grabbing our shoes, we fled in our stocking feet down the main thoroughfare and a tolerably scandalous spectacle we must have presented.

Incidentally, I have heard a number of stories of how Americans have made monkeys of the ridiculous foreign police. Speaking from considerable experience, I would say that if there is a class of people it is wise to avoid it is foreign police, any foreign police. I would much prefer attempting simian conversion of a New York traffic police officer—and that would be a big mistake. Americans who attempt games with police abroad are in for a lot of trouble.

We made several trips while we were in Japan. On one which lasted for three days, we went from Nagasaki to Karatsu, traveling by jinrickshas, boat, and train. We stayed at all the best hotels and saw everything. The cost came to $8 a man.

From Yokohama we sailed for Hong Kong, arriving on June 2nd.

Hong Kong, like Port Arthur, is surrounded by high hills forming a sort of amphitheater. Here we met with a curious experience.

After dropping anchor it was necessary for us to fire several salutes; first one of twenty-one guns to the Port and the British flag, which the British would answer gun for gun; then one of fifteen guns to the British vice admiral which they would answer with thirteen guns to our rear admiral; then the British commodore would fire thirteen guns to our admiral which we would answer with eleven.

All of this was punctiliously performed, but as the last of the eleven gun salute was fired by us our officer of the deck, a young ensign who was directing the firing, distinctly heard the British fire an additional salute; he naturally replied to it gun for gun.

Hardly had our guns ceased firing than the British fired still another salute. We could see the smoke of the black saluting powder coming from the muzzles of their guns. We, naturally, replied to this salute gun for gun. The moment we completed our salute the British fired STILL ANOTHER salute to which we commenced replying. A haze of incredulity commenced descending on us; it was like one of those bad dreams in which the dreamer runs at top speed and doesn't advance an inch.

Just as we started replying to their last salute we noticed a British picket boat speeding toward us; it came alongside and out jumped Vice Admiral Sir Hedworth Lambton, hero of Ladysmith, whom I had met in London. During the Boer War, Sir Hedworth had commanded the *Powerful* and when Ladysmith was about to be invested he took his men and guns ashore and helped defend the place during the long siege. Some years later an old lady, Lady Meux, took a liking to him (he was very good-looking) and offered him a great fortune if he would change his name to Meux, which he promptly did.

As Captain Sowerby of the British Navy remarked to me in London, "For that amount of money I would call myself anything." Sowerby, by the way, was later killed at Jutland.

Sir Hedworth ran up our gangway ladder, very like a midshipman, saluted the quarterdeck and inquired cheerfully, "What in the devil's name is going on? Let's stop and commence all over again."

It seems that the "extra" British salutes to which we replied was the echo of our own guns, bouncing off the enclosing hills. Naturally, after we fired a salute in reply to the echo, the British fired one in reply to ours and there we were, like two kittens chasing their own tails.

Admiral Hemphill was so annoyed that he ordered the officer of the deck placed under suspension for ten days. Sir Hedworth heard of it and paid us another call in which he persuaded our admiral to cancel the order of suspension and forget all about the affair, a very generous and kindly thing for an officer of his rank to do on behalf of a young ensign.

I always liked and admired him. Later, when he and his flag lieutenant, Molyneux, called officially, except for the uniforms we couldn't tell which was the lieutenant and which the vice admiral. No wonder Lady Meux left him all that money.

Our next port of call was Canton. The streets here are so narrow that litters and sedan chairs have trouble rounding corners. It is far more "native" than most Chinese coast cities. Not infrequently the people we passed showed their disapproval of "foreign devils" by scowling and making what were evidently insulting remarks. I listened hoping that the Chinese in my subconscious mind might come to life again, but the chatter around us remained a chatter and nothing more. Of course, Cantonese and Mandarin are utterly different languages, and it is not unusual to hear Chinese from different provinces speaking to each other in Pidgin English.

We went on to Woosung, at the entrance to the Yangtse River. Our first stop was at Nanking, site of the Ming Tombs. We hired donkeys and rode out to the Tombs, a long double row of stone animals ranging in size from elephants down. We carried our lunch in haversacks, and here I was reminded how difficult it was to eat out in the open in China. We were surrounded, at a respectful distance, by a crowd of Chinese who watched every mouthful we took with an anxious expectancy that quickly took away our appetites. When we rose and left the "table" they rushed in and fought over what remained.

Wherever we went in China, we witnessed examples of the appalling poverty. When our ship was anchored in a Chinese port, we would be surrounded by sampans with beggars in them who would pick up any remnants of food that were thrown overboard. Sometimes they would come alongside and put a bag under the botton of our slop chute to catch anything that was discarded. In order to drive them away from the side of the ship it was sometimes necessary to turn the fire hose on them. That seemed cruel but the danger of their infecting our crew with some terrible contagion was too real to be trifled with. I have seen diseases in the Orient that simply don't exist in the Western world or, if they do, they certainly don't walk around the streets.

This misery carried inevitable lawlessness in its wake. We were warned by the old-timers to avoid using sampans or other "shore boats" in the evening if we were alone, and if we did use them always to sit facing the man who was skulling the boat. These boats had little enclosed cabins in the stern with low doors opening outward. We were advised to sit with our feet braced against these doors so they couldn't be opened from the inside; sometimes there was another man hidden in there. The last bit of advice was to make our bargain with the waterman before getting in his boat. This didn't always work for sometimes, half-way to the ship, he would rest on his oars and demand double fare. The only thing to do then was to fight fire with fire, agree to his demands and when you were alongside your ship with the anchor watch at your back give him the amount originally agreed on and tell him to go to hell.

We went on to Kiukiang. Here I got into an argument with a ricksha coolie, and a passing missionary, seeing that I was a fellow American, came over and said, "Let me show you how to handle these fellows." He pretended great solicitude for the man and asked how much I had given him. The coolie, who was screaming for more money, held out the hand in which he had the coins. The missionary carefully inspected the hand and remarking, "You paid him too much," grabbed the coins and then spit in the man's face. The coolie subsided at once. What struck me especially about the business was that the missionary kept the coins!

Our last stop on the Yangtse was at Hankow, six hundred miles from the mouth of the river. Here I had a curious experience. We were presented to the viceroy who had a most resplendent staff. They didn't look like Chinese; they looked more like Tartars or, perhaps, Mongols. They were all big men, well over six feet, and wore gorgeous trappings.

One of them, a splendid-looking fellow, sat quietly, his yellow, slant-eyed face utterly impassive; apparently he didn't understand a word of what was being said. Just then one of our officers entered and the Manchu jumped up and exclaimed in perfect American-English, "Why, hullo Bill! Do you ever get back to Cleveland? What ever became of Susie Smith? That was a girl for you!" We discovered that he had gone to school in Cleveland with our shipmate. His English was so fluent and colloquial that he seemed more like a disguised American than what he actually was.

From Woosung we got underway for Chin Wang Tao in North China, one of the ports of Pekin and Tientsin, arriving after a four-days' cruise. A group of us went on to Pekin. This was not too long after the Boxer Rebellion and we saw East Indian, Japanese soldiers, Cameron Highlanders, and various other foreign troops. I remembered the city vaguely.

The Boxer Rebellion broke out in 1900. For a long time before the Chinese had grown increasingly restless with the constant demands of the great powers for more land, more mining privileges, the right to collect taxes in their "spheres of influence" and the right to build railroads and run telegraph lines across rice paddies. Also, the steamers on the rivers took work away from the coolies who had previously hauled the barges by hand as I remembered as a child. In addition to these genuine grievances, there were many superstitions which may well have bulked larger with the people than their real problems. It was believed that the missionaries took in children in order to kill them and make magic potions from their bodies, that the railroads prevented the crops from growing and the telegraph lines poisoned the air. The Boxers (their real name was the Righteous Harmony Fists) claimed that they could expel all foreigners from China through magical powers. To prove it, they allowed themselves to be shot and then rose from the dead (they used blank cartridges). The old Empress Dowager, Tzu Hsi, who was still alive, supported them. She believed in their powers and used to sit in her palace repeating a magical charm they had guaranteed would kill foreigners. Every time she repeated it, her old eunuch Li Lien-ying would shout excitedly, "Another foreign devil has just dropped dead!"

In June 1900, the Boxers occupied Pekin with the empress's consent. The foreign legations barricaded their doors and sent for help. A relief force from the coast under the British admiral Seymour was turned back while the Boxers burned churches and looted stores that had dealt with the hated foreigners.

The German minister Baron von Ketteler was killed and a Professor Jones beheaded after being tortured and his head exhibited in a cage. Scores of Chinese converts to Christianity were murdered and the Boxers opened fire on the legations with a light cannon. The excited Tzu Hsi declared war against the world.

An international force seized the Taku forts that guarded the approaches to Pekin and advanced inland. They met a Chinese army and easily defeated it. Tzu Hsi put the elderly Li Hung-chang (who was known for his sympathy with foreigners) in charge of the city and then fled northward, disguised as a peasant woman, cutting off her six-inch nails, the mark of a lady of quality. The allies took Pekin, looting and burning great sections of it. The Russian took Manchuria and the other powers seized whatever they wished.

I talked to a number of soldiers who had been in at the loot of Pekin. Having no idea of the value of jade, carvings, embroidery, precious stones, and paintings, most of them had taken virtually worthless junk while ignoring a king's ransom in priceless artifacts. I have always felt that it is a great mistake not to give the military at least a basic course in how to distinguish fine workmanship. I have tried to learn something about objects d'art so as not to make this error.

The allies were determined to dispose of Tzu Hsi for good, rightly considering her the sources of the trouble. This old woman who thought she could kill by magic and back in father's day had refused to believe that guns could kill people, returned to Pekin and met the raging leaders of her combined enemies. She presented them with hand-carved ivory back-scratchers or some such thing, charmed them completely, and they ended by restoring her to power and sending their friend Li Hung-chang into exile. As Li himself had told father many years before, the empress didn't know many things but she certainly knew how to handle men.

We went on to Port Arthur and anchored off Golden Hill. The shores of the harbor were literally lined with the wrecks of both men of war and merchant vessels, the results of the Russo-Japanese War of 1905. In a drydock was a big Russian cruiser lying on her side and riddled with shell holes; evidently the Japs had caught her while she was undergoing repairs. The hills surrounding the harbor were covered with human bones. No attempt had been made to bury the bodies; at least, not the Russians.

The Russo-Japanese War is nearly forgotten now, which is a pity as we could have learned some interesting lessons from it. We would have been prepared for the sneak attack on Pearl Harobr. On the night of February 8, 1904, the Japs attacked the Russian Fleet in the outer harbor of Port Arthur before any declaration of war. The only difference was that against the Russians they used destroyers; against us they used planes.

The Russo-Japanese War was a curious mixture of tactics out of the eighteenth century combined with modern technology. One was the case of the Russian destroyer *Ryshitelni*. She ran into Chefoo Harbor where she was followed by a Japanese destroyer whose officers and men boarded her as in the days of Nelson and during a rough-and-tumble fight on her decks, the two captains rolled overboard clasped in each other's arms and continued fighting in the water. The Russians were defeated and the *Ryshitelni* was towed out of the harbor by the victorious Japanese in absolute defiance of the fact that China was a neutral country.

I talked to some officers on the USS *Wisconsin* who told me of a sight none of them would ever forget. They were lying at anchor off Shanghai one summer's day in 1905 when a great armored cruiser came dashing in at full speed from seaward. Four of her five stacks were standing; where the fifth had been was a gaping hole in her decks from which smoke and flames rose masthead high, a veritable floating volcano. Close at her heels, like hounds after a stag, sped two Japanese destroyers. She was the *Askold* escaping from the Battle of Tsushima. The Chinese authorities, whose duty it was to protect the ships in their harbor, hovered on the outskirts wringing their hands. They did not dare take any action in the face of a Japanse squadron that was just outside the harbor entrance. And yet many people think a nation can protect its sovereignty without a powerful navy!

We received orders to proceed to Vladivostok in Manchuria, Russia's principal port in the Pacific. There were rumors that affairs there were in a turbulent state owing to mutinies in the Russian Army and Navy. We had heard some talk of "Bloody Sunday" in Moscow back in 1905 when the Cossacks sabered some thousands of demonstrators in front of the Winter Palace for asking for a constitution, but most of us attributed these current reports to that famous disseminator of news the paper the *Shanghai Liar*. As we were soon to learn, events were taking place in that city which sounded more like the Dark Ages than the happenings of the twentieth century.

On the morning of November 17th, the *Rainbow* entered Vladivostok Harbor. We passed the wreck of a destoyer partially submerged and riddled with shot holes which we innocently supposed

dated back to the 1905 war. We anchored off the fortress and exchanged salutes with the shore batteries.

The weather was bitterly cold, a long residence in the tropics
having thinned our blood to such an extent that the mere sight of the
bleak snow-covered hills was sufficient to chill us to the bone. Already
there was a film of ice on the harbor water which the *Rainbow* cracked
as she swung at her anchor. The temperature was about five degrees
Fahrenheit during the warmest part of the day.

As soon as our gangway ladder was lowered the high officials came
on board to pay their respects. The first was General Irman, commanding the forces. When he arrived the Marine Guard and the band
were paraded in his honor. The band tried to play the Russian
National Anthem but their valve instruments had frozen solid. A
Russian band on shore had better luck playing "The Star Spangled
Banner." I couldn't imagine how they did it and then noticed that
even when not playing, the men kept the valves of their instruments
constantly moving up and down.

There was a pleasant-looking young officer, part of the general's
staff. He was wearing a very handsome Astrakhan hat and the jovial
Clarence Edwards advised him, "Take that old muff off your head."
One of the other Russian officers told Edwards quietly, "You are
addressing Prince Bariatinsky." Fortunately the prince's English was
so limited that Edward's suggestion made no impression.

Having been at sea for nearly a week we were all anxious to dine
ashore and left the ship as soon as we were off duty, accompanied by
several of the Russian officers. It was shortly after seven o'clock and
the night was clear as a bell and so cold that as soon as we landed we
ran at full speed in the direction of a café, swinging our arms to keep
the blood circulating.

Inside all was gaiety, the large dining room being crowded to the
doors. It was very like the restaurants in Vienna with transoms or
sofas extending along the walls on which the guests sat with small
tables in front of them. The music was furnished by a ladies' orchestra
and, in a a moment of ill-advised generosity, I asked the orchestra
what it would have, instead of ordering the wine and sending it to
them myself. Needless to say the "artistes" took the most expensive
beverage on the menu.

The Russian officers looked particularly well in their tight-fitting
overcoats of Confederate gray. They all carried heavy swords, which

were more like cutlasses than swords proper, suspended from highly ornamental shoulder belts. I discovered later that these swords were ground to a razor edge unlike ours which are intended only for show.

After dinner we went to a circus, and although it was excellent the audience interested me more than the performance. The frigid temperature in the tent can be imagined; the place was crowded and every spectator wore a fur cap and his coat collar rolled up until only the tip of his nose was visible. From the aperture between collar and cap clouds of frosty breath arose. The little Russian children, bundled up in their furs, looked like animated teddy bears. The performers, on the other hand, were clad as scantily as is customary in circuses but didn't seem to mind the arctic temperature in the slightest. I have never seen finer physiques, particularly among the women.

The next afternoon the admiral and his staff went ashore to return the official calls. We were given an escort of eight Cossacks, their carbines strapped to their backs. Perfect horsemen they were with faces flint in their severity.

The town had the appearance of a besieged camp, soldiers everywhere. I was told later that there were a hundred thousand troops in and about Vladivostok. The place was certainly swarming with them; every block had about four sentry posts and each of these posts was occupied, not by a single sentry, but by a squad of infantry. The men themselves were splendid athletic fellows, but unless their faces belied them, the standard of intelligence was very low. Everywhere bayonets were fixed; one of the peculiarities of the Russian soldier is that he never unfixes his bayonet. I could not imagine why all these elaborate precautions were necessary, but I was soon to learn the reason.

We made a tour of the town in troikas, or three-horse droshkies, the third horse being hitched to an outrigger which enabled it to pull at right angles to the others in rounding sharp corners suddenly. The vehicles traveled at a dead-run up hill and down and the seats had no backs. We kept passing men and girls in other troikas and invariably the man had his arm around the girl not, apparently from affection but to keep her from turning a back somersault in case the troika stopped suddenly.

Crowds of people were on the streets pursuing the regular round of shopping and visiting, but everywhere there seemed to be a latent anticipation and uncertainty in the atmosphere. The reason for this universal uneasiness we did not learn until the last evening of our stay as the Russian officers were singularly uncommunicative about it.

Prince Bariatinsky took us to the officers' club and proved to be an interesting raconteur (of course through a translator). He had won the St. Andrew's Cross for bravery at Liao Yan in the Russo-Japanese War and said the Japanese were good soldiers but whenever his men resorted to the bayonet, the Japs would invariably fall back and commence shooting. Considering the size of his men and the excellent targets they must have presented we could hardly blame the Japs. He also said that the Russians were always outnumbered at least four to one.

An armistice between the two combatants was arranged largely by President Theodore Roosevelt and the peace treaty signed in Portsmouth, New Hampshire. It was highly favorable to Japan and started Japan on her rise to being a world power. It makes one cynical to remember how warmly Americans sympathized with the Japanese at the time. Our people actually thought that Japan was a "little fellow" being jumped on by a big bully. I remember a joke very popular at the time which went, "We have learned that 'Banzai' is the Japanese for 'Hurrah.' We haven't yet learned what the Russian for 'Hurrah' is."

None of the Russian officers we met showed any resentment of the attitude of our country although Prince Bariatinsky did say that without the American interference the war would have had a very different outcome. Reinforcements were pouring into Manchuria from Russia daily, and the Japanese were getting further and further from their bases and finding it more and more difficult to get supplies and men to the front. He said the armistice was so unpopular with the officers of the Russian Army that a "round robin" was circulated protesting the cessation of hostilities. I don't know about the Russian Army but the Russian Navy certainly didn't show up well in that war. One of the amazing examples of their inefficiency was their permitting the Japanese scout destroyers that were trailing them to report their movements to Togo and the fleet at will without mixing up their messages by using their own wireless, a basic precaution. As a result, Admiral Togo was able to trap and destroy the Russian Fleet in the Sea of Japan.

I believe our interference in the war was a mistake. We did it with the idea that we were protecting a weak nation from a strong one, but we didn't know the circumstances. Neither our government nor our people really understand international politics, so we permitted Japan to start her upward climb. In 1941 at Pearl Harbor we were to pay a terrible price for that error.

I met only one person who did show resentment. A very lovely Russian girl (many of the Russian women were really stunners) said to me, "Why were you against us and for those creatures? Are we not white, are we not Christians?" I had no answer.

At our reception in the Military Club, we were decidedly puzzled by the number of dishes that greeted us on a table in the first room we entered. Several of us thought that this was the dinner itself but, fortunately before we had indulged too heartily we discovered that these dishes were merely appetizers. The Russians are as good trenchermen as they are hosts. I must admit that I was disappointed in their national drink, vodka. I had heard a great deal of its potency and how even a small glass would make you drunk. It turned out to be a clear liquid not unlike gin and certainly no stronger. It was completely tasteless.

There were a number of ladies at the party, many of whom showed Tartar or other Oriental blood by the very pronounced slant of their eyes, which, combined with perfect pink and white complexions, proved as attractive as it was unusual. We had such a good time that we had to be told to go home when the party was over.

The vodka loosened the tongues of our hosts so before we left, we at last heard the story that accounted for the sunken destroyer in the harbor and the general uneasiness in Vladivostok.

There had indeed been a mutinous outbreak instigated by professional agitators or anarchists. They had come from Petersburg for the purpose. Their chief was a young girl. She met the captain of one of the Russian destroyers and by her beauty and charm completely fascinated him. He invited her to his cabin on board ship.

As soon as they had descended the ladder leading to the officers' quarters she drew a revolver and killed her host who was in the act of assisting her down the narrow companionway. Then she found her way to the room of the only other officer on board, who was lying ill in his bunk, and shot him also. Her mission successfully accomplished she went on deck and hoisted the red flag of the revolutionists.

This was to have been the signal for a general uprising both on the ships and among the garrisons of the harbor fort but, at the critical moment, the majority of the mutineers lost their nerve. The crew of the destroyer on which the girl had raised the flag joined her as did one other vessel, the crew killing their officers. The two mutinous ships then began to bombard the town but the loyal destroyers fired on them, sinking one and forcing the other to escape to sea. This vessel was still at large in the Pacific, a veritable pirate under irresponsible command.

The girl chief of the revolutionists was on the ship that sank. She managed to reach shore in a dinghy with several members of the crew but, as the officer who told me the story related, "The soldiers in the fort were very angry; I have never seen them so angry. They came running down to the water and fired volley after volley into her and her companions."

The incipient revolt in the Fleet and Army was quelled with an iron hand. The day before we entered the harbor, the authorities executed one hundred and twenty of the mutineers. A great military funeral with many hundred-rubles-worth of flowers was given the murdered officers.

It had been our original intention to remain several weeks in Vladivostok but, lest our presence be taken advantage of by the revolutionists to involve Russia with a friendly power, it was wisely decided to curtail our visit so at daylight the next morning we put to sea again.

On the way back to the United States, we stopped at Guam. Guam is beautiful with a natural coral breakwater that protects the anchorage and the swimming is wonderful, but it is the most isolated and lonely spot I have ever seen. A man on duty in Guam who wrote a letter to the United States was lucky to receive a reply in six months.

I didn't meet anyone in Guam who had applied for duty there and who wasn't eager to escape from the place. All of them had offended some superior who had sent them there much as a nobleman who had offended the king in seventeenth century France ended up in the Bastille with a "lettre de cachet." I talked to one man, a second lieutenant of Marines, who had served under a martinet of a colonel who had made his life miserable. There was a fancy dress ball and the colonel attended in a domino that made him look much like a clown. The second lieutenant also attended dressed as an out-and-out clown and armed with a slap stick. He encountered the colonel and the opportunity was too good to miss. The following dialogue ensued:

Lieutenant: "Why, hello, clown!" (WHACK!)

Colonel (through gritted teeth): "You know perfectly well who I am."

Lieutenant: "Oh, no, I don't clown. (WHACK!) You don't mind my calling you a clown, do you, clown?" (WHACK!)

The next day the lieutenant received his orders for Guam for an indefinite tour of duty. Also, he was given such a murderous fitness report that his chance of promotion was ruined. These fitness reports put a power almost of life and death in the hands of a superior officer. At the end of a tour of duty, your commanding officer must submit a report on each officer under him to the Navy Department. These reports are intended to weed out the incompetent and unfit but virtually no decent officer will give a man a bad fitness report for it is enough to ruin him. When I reached command rank, I never gave a man under me an unfavorable report even if I was convinced of his inadequacy. I could have misjudged him and perhaps the poor fellow had had a run of bad luck. A fitness report can easily be used by a vindictive officer to destroy any younger man to whom he had taken a personal dislike as he needs give no reason for his opinion.

I did not foresee it, but a few years later I was to be the victim of such an attack for a matter over which I had absolutely no control.

CHAPTER TEN

Destroyer Service (1910–1914)

The Light Cavalry of the Seas

AFTER returning to the United States, I received my first regular command, the destroyer *Jarvis*. For my remaining years of active duty all of the sea service, except that performed during World War I, was with destroyers; first in command of single ships, then in command of a division of five ships, and finally in command of a destroyer "mother ship" at Constantinople, commanding a destroyer squadron of twenty-two ships, nearly three thousand officers and men. I think that I can call myself a "destroyer man."

The *Jarvis* was built by the New York Ship Building Company, and I saw her keel laid and inspected her every day until she was completed. I felt that in more than one way she was my ship. She was one of the first of the new oil-burning destroyers and her trial runs were witnessed by a number of high-ranking officers who were interested in such an innovation. These old-timers had never been on such a small vessel, and we encountered some heavy seas. When we returned to port, I heard the following conversation between two mess attendants:

"Yah, you was seasick!"

"I has a right to be seasick. All them captains was seasick!"

He was right. Destroyer duty is a young man's job.

As their name suggests, destroyers were developed to destroy the torpedo-boats, which had become a serious menace to the battleships and large cruisers. The torpedo-boats were so small, fast, and maneuverable that they could dash in under the fire of the larger vessels, launch their deadly torpedoes and escape in spite of the searchlights and rapid-fire guns of their big victims. Soon, however, the duties of the destroyers greatly broadened. Their duties became almost precisely the same as those of the light cavalry of a land army. They were "the eyes of the fleet."

Each ship carried four officers and a hundred men. Their armament consisted of three double torpedo tubes and five semi-automatic

3-inch guns. They had no armor protection for that would slow them down. They were capable of doing thirty knots (about thirty-four miles an hour). Modern destroyers are four times the size of these early ships and much more seaworthy. The Navy had twenty-five of these new crafts and they were generally referred to as "floating coffins" by the rest of the fleet.

Even so, the destroyers were perhaps the most versatile of all warships. They could be used for scouting, protecting larger ships from night attacks, attacking enemy ships with torpedoes, and because they drew only ten feet of water, they could patrol the enemy's coast, run up rivers, capture merchant vessels and fire on troops and field batteries ashore. I saw all of these actions.

Without question, service on a destroyer involves more hardship than any other kind of naval work except perhaps submarine duty. Many officers, including myself, have gone to sea for years in the larger vessels without ever feeling even slightly uncomfortable yet, after joining the Destroyer Flotilla, they have on frequent occasions been violently and unblushingly seasick. It is a common saying that a man doesn't know what "seagoing" really is until he has tried it on a destroyer. It makes one appreciate the tremendous hardships that Columbus, Cabot, and the other early navigators must have endured when they crossed the Atlantic in their cockleshells.

Let me give you one example. The entire Atlantic Fleet cruised from Guantanamo, Cuba, to the Isthmus of Panama while the canal was being constructed. The usual cruising speed of the destroyers was twenty knots, but as it was advisable for all units of the fleet to arrive at the same time, we were obliged to steam at the same speed as the battleships: twelve knots. All the way across the Gulf of Mexico we rolled between thirty and forty degrees on a side and there was not a moment's cessation of this rolling. We could see the people on the nearby battleships standing on their perfectly steady decks gazing at us in awed amazement and evidently thanking what gods there may be that they had been intelligent enough to get duty on the big ships. We anchored in Colon Harbor and all that night, even with our anchors down, the rolling continued as there was a heavy swell coming in from the gulf. Early the next morning we were able to run up the old French canal and all hands from captain to cabin boy turned in and had their first sleep in four days.

On our return, the *Jarvis* had to come north before the other vessels in order to hold certain steaming trials. Course was set for Cape Maysi on the eastern end of Cuba and orders given to make twenty knots speed.

As everything was running smoothly I went below to get a few hours sleep. About two o'clock in the morning I awoke to find that the ship was rolling and pitching very heavily. She would go flying up in the air, pause for an instant, and then descend with dizzy suddenness, landing on top of a wave with a crash that made her quiver from stem to stern. It wasn't unlike coming down in an express elevator and being stopped too quickly. Realizing that we were no longer in the lee of Cuba I jumped out of my bunk, but hardly had my feet touched the deck, when I was thrown the entire length of the room flat on my face and the next instant the heavy swivel desk chair came down on top of me cutting a gash six inches long in one shin. Struggling to my feet with violent seasickness, I managed to get my clothes on and climbed up on the bridge.

Here I found that after passing Maysi our change of course to the north had brought wind and sea directly ahead and the ship was receiving tremendous blows from the high waves as she forced her way through them. Speed was reduced to fifteen knots, but just as the change was made an enormous green sea came over the bridge drenching us to the skin and smashing the glass in the binnacle and the top of the chart board.

All day we labored through it and late in the afternoon sighted Watling's Island (which, by the way, was the first land seen by Columbus in 1492) and, passing through the Crooked Island Passage, set course for Cape Hatteras. The weather kept getting worse all the time and seas constantly swept the forecastle; several of the hatch covers were forced open and water came in to such an extent that the ship had to be headed off (turned away from the wind) and volunteers sent to close and secure the hatches.

Galley fires were kept alight with the greatest difficulty; we subsisted mainly on hardtack and coffee, drinking the coffee from the spout of the pot; it was impossible to use a cup as the wind would blow the hot coffee into our faces. Anyone attempting to use the toilet did so at his peril. The ship would poise herself on the crest of a wave and then make a Lucifer-like descent and simultaneously a water spout very like Old Faithful, except it was icy cold, would fly upward from the toilet bowl and woe to the unhappy one who happened to be in the line of fire. There was a flap on the outboard discharge but we discovered later that the violence of the sea had knocked it off. As a natural sequence there was about two feet of water swishing around the floor of the toilet room with—well, I won't gild the lily by entering into any further descriptions.

For three days neither sun nor stars had been visible; hence we were by no means certain of where we were as no observations could be taken. Finally our dead reckoning showed that we should be within fifty miles of the Diamond Shoals Light Vessel, which is just off Cape Hatteras. From the appearance of the water we could tell that it was rapidly getting shallower and, as there are some very dangerous shoals off Hatteras with only a few feet of water on them, we were very anxious to know our exact position.

There is only one way of ascertaining a ship's position in thick weather at sea and that is by taking soundings. Orders were given to start the sounding machine. This machine is a large steel reel on which is wound about five hundred fathoms of strong wire with a heavy lead on the end. The men sent aft returned and reported that the sounding machine had been washed overboard. Its steel legs, riveted to the deck, were still there but were broken off short by the force of the waves. The ship was then hove to and an effort made to find the depth of water by lowering a long line with several leads on the end. We kept drifting to leeward so fast that the line stood out straight from the ship's side and no sounding could be taken.

Meanwhile darkness was rapidly approaching and our position was becoming more and more dangerous. Just then the sun showed itself for about three seconds and, snatching a sextant, I managed to take a very doubtful altitude which placed us FIFTY MILES beyond our dead-reckoning position. Hardly had this discovery been made when a sharp-eyed quartermaster pointed to a dim object well on the port hand and, heading for it, we discovered, to our extreme relief, that it was Diamond Shoals Light Vessel.

This fixed our position absolutely and we headed up the coast for the entrance to Chesapeake Bay. Hardly had we dropped the light vessel astern when a terrific downpour of rain commenced drenching us to the skin and entirely obliterated all the shore lights and other aids to navigation. It was bitterly cold and I had to decide between wearing a sweater drenched with ice water or wearing no sweater at all. I decided on the ice water. All around us we could hear whistles and fog bells getting louder and louder as we approached the entrance to the bay. Finally I decided that further progress would be foolhardy and we let go the anchor, veered to sixty fathoms, and rolled out the night, bitterly cold and drenched to the skin. With the rising sun we discovered that we were directly in the entrance to Chesapeake Bay and at six o'clock got underway and proceeded to the Norfolk Navy Yard. For five days we had not taken off our clothes or sat down to a meal.

There was no report ever made of this trip for there was nothing to report. It was all in the day's work.

I recall one other incident of destroyer duty where we were saved from disaster by a miraculous piece of luck. We were at Guantanamo, Cuba, when we received orders to report to San Juan immediately. We made a night run at thirty knots and at dawn saw ahead two long, low islands with a narrow passage between them. We had a navigator on board who had a very good opinion of himself and he told me that we were to proceed through the passage at full-speed. "It is marked on the chart and there is plenty of water," he explained.

I demurred but he said, in the wearily, condescending tone one uses with a petulent child, "I assure you, sir, the passage is well marked, I have carefully checked our position, and there is no possibility that I am mistaken." He was so sure of himself and as time was important, we continued at thirty knots.

As we drew closer, I noticed a curious-looking bird that was swimming back and forth across the passage, catching fish. As I have always been interested in natural history and as I had never seen a bird quite like it, I called for a telescope so I could examine the unique specimen more closely. As soon as I had the glass on him, I realized that the bird was not swimming; he was WALKING to and fro on the bottom! I must have broken all records for ringing full speed astern. As it was, we barely hove to in time.

I then spotted an old fisherman leisurely rowing along the shore off one island. I shouted and held up some bills, whereupon he just as leisurely rowed alongside. In my best Spanish I asked him where we were. He gave us the names of the islands. We were some twenty miles from where we should have been. There were two other islands identical to the ones before us, with a deep passage between them at the other position. I gave him fifty dollars and we departed with the fisherman calling down the blessings of all the saints in heaven on us.

Later, my navigator sent me fifty dollars in an envelope. I was so relieved at our narrow escape that I returned it to him. We never mentioned the matter again. I did not record the incident in his fitness report although I was tempted.

In 1910 I was stationed at the Philadelphia Navy Yard. I had applied for duty at the New York Yard but it was refused. At first, I was greatly disappointed as I had always regarded Philadelphia as a "dead" town but I soon changed my mind. The Philadelphia girls are delightful. I don't think I have ever seen such charming girls. Also, there is an air to the old city which reminded me of Europe. There was a true society such as I had never encountered anywhere else in America, many of the families tracing their ancestry back before the Revolution and often living in houses that were old before Benjamin Franklin and Washington visited what is now called Independence Hall. As a commissioned officer, I naturally had the entrée everywhere.

After my duties at the Yard were over for the day, I would generally drop in at the Bellevue-Stratford for tea and nearly always one or two young ladies whom I had met could be found there. Afterward, we would have supper and then attend an opera, usually at the Academy of Music. I remember that season I saw *Thaïs, Pagliacci, Traviata, Rigoletto, Faust, La Bohème, Tales of Hoffman,* and Samson and Delilah. I especially remember Mary Garden in *Griseldi.* On the lighter side, we saw *The Dollar Princess* and *Fra Diavolo.* As I have always loved music, it was a wonderful time.

Some of the girls were lemons, but most were true queens. Even among the society debutantes there were a number of warm bodies and I was very seldom queered. Looking through the diary which I kept at the time (and which I still have) I note that on January 25th I attended a tea at the home of Anna Gilpins. It was a tea that was to have important results for me. There were a number of attractive girls there, including a Miss Mary Perkins (who was called Polly). I see by consulting my diary that I marked her name with an X as she was the most charming.

A few days later I went to call on Polly at her home 2005 DeLancey Place. The house, like all the houses on the block, was a brownstone building, very old, that breathed quiet elegance. The whole block seemed indeed to belong to another age; red brick pavements and old trees every few yards, the street so narrow two carriages had trouble passing. I met her parents. Her father was a slender, elegant old gentleman, almost stone deaf; her mother a large woman of great dignity. Polly's grandfather on her mother's side had been John Armstrong Wright, who had made a fortune in the iron and coal business at the time of the Civil War. Freedom Forge, which he built near Altoona, was regarded as a show place. Charles Penrose Perkins, her father, was prominent in Philadelphia society. He showed me a deed, written on parchmen, and dated 1710 in which the Penroses were granted a tract of land along the Schuylkill River. The Perkins had one other child: Rowan Perkins, a big, blond, good-natured young man, slightly older than Polly, who was twenty.

Polly was the most striking girl I had ever seen. Tall (she was only an inch shorter than I and I am six feet), and magnificently proportioned with lovely blue eyes and brown hair. She had a great sense of humor and was fond of telling amusing stories, often purely the products of her lively imagination, which delighted people. Wherever we appeared together, heads would turn for we made a handsome couple. As she had never wanted for anything in her life, she was inclined to be somewhat headstrong and spoiled but in such a pretty, gay girl I found these traits made her even more attractive.

Although many houses were lighted by electricity, the Perkins were conservative and still used gas. In each room there was an L-shaped gas bracket which threw up a fan-shaped flame, yellow at the top and dark green below. Under each bracket hung a lighter, consisting of two long wires held together by a spring. When the spring was squeezed, the wires rubbed against each other and produced a spark. In the evening, maids brought in kerosene lamps with colorful Tiffany shades.

Once a week Mrs. Perkins, accompanied by Polly and a maid, went shopping at Wanamakers. I was allowed to accompany them on some of these trips. As there was no telephone, Bounds, the houseman, was dispatched to the stable to call the coachman. Once when Bounds was otherwise employed, I performed this task myself. The stable was two blocks away and smelt of leather, tobacco smoke, horses, and manure. A number of families kept their horses there. There were single stalls for the horses running down one side of the building and racks to hold the harness along the other. The grooms and coachmen sat around a table before the potbellied stove playing endless games of cards. When summoned, the old Irish coachman would make a careful note of his gains or losses, and with the help of a groom, tack up the team of big grays. In a little time, they would come trotting down DeLancey Place to stop before the house. The ladies, swathed in furs, would emerge and a maid would open the carriage door.

Inside the coach, in addition to the main seat where the ladies sat, there were two small "jump" seats that folded up when not in use. The maid and I sat on these. I recall that there were cutglass vases held in brackets on the sides which always contained fresh flowers. By each lady's seat were containers holding rectangular, cutglass jars with smelling salts, sal volatile, hyssop-and-water, and other remedies in case one of the ladies had an attack of the vapors or some other feminine disorder.

It always seemed to be snowing on these expeditions. We would jog over the cobbles on Juniper Street flanked by castiron tubes standing erect and filled with concrete intended to keep the carriages from running up on the narrow sidewalk. At the end of Juniper, the coachman turned into the covered carriage sweep before Wanamakers entrance. Here a doorman sprang forward to open the coach's door while a footman held the horses' heads. The coachman took advantage of this to jump down from his box and cover the horses with waterproof slickers. As soon as the ladies had entered Wanamakers he would drive across the street to City Hall where the team could be tied to a hitching post and he could chat with other coachmen until the doorman shouted through a megaphone that "Mrs. Perkins' carriage is wanted."

Women's shopping took hours. Afterward, we would have lunch on the balcony overlooking Wanamakers main hall while a huge organ played classical selections, and we could look down on the teeming crowd below us in the center part of the store, where stood a gigantic black eagle. Always the ladies met friends at lunch, also come to shop. They all went to the Assembly (the great midwinter ball that dates back before the Revolution), all lived in the same part of town, all had summer places in the country. Their husbands all belonged to the Union League, the Racquet Club, and were or had been members of the City Troop, America's oldest cavalry unit.

It was a pleasant way of life that I had never seen before. It is all gone now; part of another age.

When spring came, the Perkins family moved to their summer home in Rosemont, on the Philadelphia Main Line. Most Philadelphia families maintained two establishments: one in the city for winter so they could be near the theaters, the balls, and parties, and one in the country for summer where it was cool and they could enjoy strolling in the gardens, taking tea on the terraces, and playing tennis or croquet under the great shade trees. The Perkins' country place was called The Hedges as the various gardens, arbors, and lawns were surrounded by tall privet hedges, carefully clipped and maintained by the head gardener and his staff. The Hedges was one of the show places of the Main Line. It was featured on the cover of *House Beautiful* and in *Distinctive Homes*, the most important house-and-garden book; a picture of the estate was used to advertise the volume.

In order to see Polly and take her out, I purchased one of the new automobiles, a Peerless, and learned to drive. My diary shows that I at first came to grief in a collision with a lamp post but after a few weeks I learned to navigate the car reasonably well. The Perkins, being conservative, had no car. There was a newly installed train line called the Paoli Local, but as far as I could see, none of the old families used it.

Polly had a personal maid, as did most young ladies of the time, an Irish woman named Mary Clark, who had been Polly's nurse when she was a child and continued to regard her as personal property. It was almost impossible to lose the old woman, but fortunately the Peerless was only a two-seater so when I took Polly out for a spin, there was no place for Miss Clark unless she chose to roost on the rear tire, which I sometimes thought she was capable of doing. Mary Clark did not approve of me as I was neither a Philadelphian nor wealthy. She seemed unable to realize that an officer in the United States Navy was at least the equal of anyone no matter what his position of wealth. Mary was to stay with us until my wife's death, and I could never make up my mind whether she was more of a blessing or a curse.

My diary shows that I proposed to Polly on April 5th, 1910. She accepted me. Although her family never said anything, I suspect they were rather put out. Her mother told me, "I am afraid Polly will have trouble adjusting to life as a naval officer's wife. She has never been anywhere except Philadelphia and accustoming herself to such a different way of living will be hard on her." I assured Mrs. Perkins that I foresaw no difficulty. A household should be run like a ship. I would be captain and my orders obeyed without question. My wife would be in the position of an executive officer, subject to me but in complete command over any others in the household. Mary Clark, who Polly insisted on taking with her, would be a chief petty officer.

To my surprise, and somewhat to my alarm, Polly envisioned a household with a minimum of four servants: Mary Clark, a cook, a waitress, and a maid. It required two maids to lace up Polly's corsets for her. I had had no idea how complicated women's clothing is. When we had children there would also be a nurse. None of my married friends maintained such an elaborate household, and I doubted if on a lieutenant's pay I could support so many people. The Perkins relieved my mind on this score by saying that, of course, Polly would continue to receive her regular allowance so all seemed smooth sailing.

We were married at Holy Trinity Church on Rittenhouse Square October 6, 1910. According to the Society Editor of the *Evening Bulletin*, it was the "wedding of the year." For those interested in such matters—and to illustrate how things were done in those days—I will quote from the full page account that appeared in the papers at the time:

The chancel was transformed into a flower bank with blossoms of pale yellow chrysanthemums shaded to deep red, with a row of soft white blossoms along the top. Inside the chancel the decorations were all of white. Bride roses, lilies of the valley, and numerous orchids massed about and above the altar. The only greens used as a background for the blossoms were dwarf bay trees, all about the chancel, and tiny ones in pots, marking the pews for members of the families.

The bride's gown was an imported one of heavy ivory satin, veiled with old family lace studded with brilliants. The bodice was of rare old Dutch lace. Her veil of tulle was held with a coronet of orange blossoms. Her only ornament among the great number of superb jewels she received as gifts was the bridegroom's gift of a necklace of aquamarines and pearls.

It was a military wedding and the couple left the church under a canopy of drawn swords, held by Lieutenant Mannix's fellow officers. The breakfast and reception followed in the Perkins' home on DeLancey Place. The bride and bridegroom stood under a canopy of white orchids while they received their friends' congratulations. The house was a mass of flowers and a marquee was erected in the garden behind the house where small tables were set.

I had managed to obtain two months' leave, and we sailed the next day for Europe. On board the vessel were another young couple, the lady being the daughter of a prominent bishop of the Episcopal Church. Her husband's name, I recall, was Harold.

Polly had never been to sea before and hardly had the ship stuck her nose beyond Ambrose Channel than she and Harold collapsed as though struck by a sledgehammer. They were seasick and remained sick during the entire crossing. The bishop's daughter and I were unaffected.

One sunny morning, as my wife and Harold, extended in deck chairs, were hoping fervently that the ship would sink, the bishop's daughter and I conversed over their prostrate remains:

Me: "The last time I went abroad I wasn't a mere tourist; I was PERSONAL AIDE to the ADMIRAL; we were GUESTS of the NATION and were PRESENTED to the KING and QUEEN and . . . ."

The bishop's daughter (breaking in at the first possible moment): "When I was abroad the last time I was with my FATHER, the BISHOP. We were HOUSE GUESTS of the ARCHBISHOP of CANTERBURY and . . . ."

Harold had just enought strength to turn his head and gasp: "Oh God damn it!" Polly muttered, "Thank you! That's just how I feel!" I had a suspicion that marriage was going to be a more complicated affair than I had envisioned.

We traveled to France, Germany, Switzerland, and Italy before returning to Philadelphia. Polly was pregnant and stayed with her family while I resumed my naval duties. The child was a boy, and, of course, he was named Daniel Pratt Mannix 4th. We called him Dan, just as I had always been called Pratt to avoid confusion. His son, in turn, would be called Pratt. I hoped to see something of him before he entered the Naval Academy when he was sixteen, the earliest possible age for acceptance. After that, of course, he would be on his own.

I had been assigned to the destroyer *Warrington* when trouble broke out in Mexico. President Madero, who had been elected by popular vote, was deposed by a military leader named Huerta before he had been two years in office. After keeping him in prison for awhile, Huerta had him shot for no particular reason. Madero had been a gentle man, called with a combination of affection and pity "the Christ fool" because of his trusting nature. Huerta seized the presidency but President Woodrow Wilson, an idealist who believed that he could force the rest of the world to live according to his own standards, refused to recognize him. Warships were sent to Vera Cruz, Mexico's main port, on a "goodwill" mission. As usual, this goodwill mission was meant to remind Mexico of the power of the United States, as well as for diplomatic reasons.

The Torpedo Flotilla, of which the *Warrington* was a part, was at anchor in Pensacola Harbor fitting out when we received a radio message to proceed to Vera Cruz immediately. We were underway within a few hours with no idea of what was happening but looking forward to any excitement.

All that day we cruised and all the next without hearing anything, but early on the second evening the radio began to crackle and message after mesage was intercepted, most of them badly garbled. The most important and unfortunately the most unintelligible ran "dead, twenty wounded, fire from streets and housetops." Evidently fighting had broken out.

A few minutes before midnight the messenger came down from the bridge and reported, "Course has been changed forty-five degrees to the right without signal." This meant that our destination had ceased to be Vera Cruz and had become Tampico. What was happening at Tampico? We were still wondering when a second message came from the flagship. "Increase speed to twenty-five knots." This could only mean there was a major emergency. We began to draw ahead of the flag and just before getting out of signal distance came a third message, "Clear ships for action." So it was war.

All the stanchions were taken down, the awnings furled, guns cast loose, ammunition broken out from the magazines, and every possible preparation made. In the wardroom, rifles, pistols, and thousands of rounds of ammunition were laid ready to hand. The landing force shifted into improvised khaki (by boiling a suit of whites in coffee an excellent substitute for khaki may be made; we learned that in the Philippines) and wore their belts and bayonets, the belts filled with ball cartridges.

About five o'clock we intercepted a radio: "Rush destroyers to Tampico; situation critical." Nobody waited for special orders; the dense smoke incident to the lighting of cold boilers appeared almost simultaneously above each of the fourteen vessels, and we gained speed in such leaps and bounds that in ten minutes the engine room reported we were making the turns for twenty-eight knots and that the speed was constantly increasing.

By six o'clock we could make out the Mexican coast ahead and the senior ship sent a radio asking if we should turn up the Panuco River to the town; to our disappointment we were told to anchor outside the bar.

We arrived at seven and all that day witnessed a spectacle which was rare indeed in those days, although it has unfortunately become increasingly common. It seemed as though the migration of an entire people was underway; men, women and children, hundreds of them, some carrying large bundles, some smaller ones wrapped up in handkerchiefs, some nothing at all. It reminded me of the flight of the people from the provinces before Lars Porsena in "Lays of Ancient Rome."

What had happened was this. The USS *Dolphin* had arrived at Tampico and a work party of eight sailors under a paymaster had been sent ashore to purchase gasoline for the ship's boats. They had been arrested by the local authorities who were suspicious of all foreigners and their boat confiscated. They were soon released but as the boat had been flying the American flag this was a breech of international law. Rd. Admiral Henry T. Mayo, in command of the American squadron, demanded an apology and also insisted that a salute be fired to our flag. President Huerta refused to do this, arguing that as we refused to acknowledge him as president, it was inconsistent for us to demand that he salute the flag.

Meanwhile, there had been more trouble at Vera Cruz, some 250 miles farther down the coast. Here a mail orderly who had gone ashore had been arrested and, more serious, a German cargo vessel named the *Ypiranga* loaded with arms for Huerta was due to arrive in the harbor. With such a supply of arms, Huerta would have been able to establish himself firmly. We had another squadron at Vera Cruz under Rear Admiral Frank F. Fletcher. Fletcher was ordered by President Woodrow Wilson to occupy the custom house buildings to prevent the landing of the arms. The Mexicans attacked the American shore parties and fighting had broken out.

When word of this reached Tampico, mobs yelling "Death to Americans!" raged through the streets. The Americans in Tampico, mostly business men with their families, took refuge in the Southern Hotel which they fortified. A number of men risked their lives to ride to outlying districts to warn their fellow citizens of the danger and bring them to the hotel. The mob was armed and far outnumbered the Americans, who amounted to some two thousand people. They would almost certainly have all been killed had not the commanding officers of a German and English warship in the harbor come to their help. Landing their armed crews, these men rescued the Americans and brought them down to the docks where the ships' guns could protect them.

All the small boats of the fleet were requisitioned to transport the fugitives to our vessels. Soon the decks became so crowded that it was necessary to spread nets to keep the people from falling overboard. Most of the men were typical South Westerners, many wore spurs and some carried their saddles. Of the women, some were in rags, some wore fashionable hats and gowns, many had small children. One carried a baby three hours old, born prematurely. She was carried up the ship's gangway on a stretcher, clutching her baby. The sailors formed lines down the ladder and passed the children from hand to hand.

Sir Christopher Craddock from the English Squadron and Count von Spee from the German had risked the lives not only of their men but of themselves to save the citizens of a foreign nation. Gallant gentlemen, they had worked side by side in perfect accord to protect the helpless. A few months later, in World War I, these two fine men met in battle and Craddock and all his crew perished. Still later, von Spee, in turn, was cornered by battle cruisers and he, his sons, and every member of his ship's company were either killed in battle or drowned.

Rumors and counterrumors kept coming from the city culminating in a cheerful threat from somebody, presumably in authority, that if we didn't go away and leave our fellow countrymen to be murdered, he would set fire to all the oil wells in the vicinity and send a sea of burning oil floating down the river that would consume us utterly.

Meanwhile, another military gentleman named Carranza had decided to start a revolution against Huerta. The next morning the rebels made a general assault on the city. All that day, from daylight until dark, we could hear the booming of artillery and see great clouds of smoke rising from the burning buildings and oil tanks. God have mercy on any Americans left in Tampico then—or Mexicans either.

That evening we received orders to take the refugees to Galveston, Texas, and return immediately. With every square foot of deck space jammed, we got underway. Half-way to Galveston we received a radio from the Board of Health that no one would be permitted to land unless everyone on board had been vaccinated. We thanked heaven that we had the necessary equipment on board and our chief pharmacist's mate started the vaccination. He was progressing splendidly until he ran into a boy of about twenty who said it was against his religious principles to be vaccinated and refused to submit to it.

Here was a poser. I couldn't very well have him thrown down and vaccinated, although I'll admit I was tempted. I am all for religious liberty—unless, of course, it interferes with the efficient working of a ship—but it did seem rather unreasonable to me that this young man's scruples should be allowed to endanger the lives of several hundred people, many of whom were ill or wounded and desperately needed medical help in Galveston. Well, if I couldn't vaccinate him I could lock him up which I promptly did, using as a brig a paint locker located in the bow of the ship where, incidentally, the pitching was the most pronounced. I then sent for the leader of the refugees. This man was a husky executive of one of the Tampico oil companies. I explained the situation to him and stressed that if the "objector" wasn't vaccinated none of them would be allowed to land. He thought this over and then suggested, "Suppose you let me talk to this fellow."

I cheerfully gave him permission. He went up on the forecastle, climbed down the vertical iron ladder into the paint locker and remained there with the objector for about fifteen minutes. When he emerged he assured me, "That kid wants to be vaccinated now. In fact, he insists on it." I gave the necessary orders, and we were able to land our passengers in Galveston without trouble.

Returning to Tampico, while yet a good way away, we could see the flotilla of destroyers, twenty of them, in the open roadstead. The town was still burning, and we could hear shots and cries coming from it. There were heavy swells so we were pitching and rolling constantly. Apart from its effect on our constitutions, it was impossible to take on fuel oil as any attempt to go alongside a tanker would have smashed the lighter vessel. This necessitated another base and Lobos Island was selected. Lobos Island is sixty miles down the coast. A slight protection is given here by a short reef and after several anxious moments, we were able to get alongside a tanker and start taking fuel.

Before returning to the pitching agony of Tampico roadstead, we decided to have a swim. Luckily, we launched a dinghy to watch over the swimmers although as the sea was dead calm, this seemed an unnecessary precaution.

I was swimming about fifty feet from the ship and with me was one of the young officers, Ensign Jeans. Jeans left me to swim to a circular life buoy which had been tossed overboard. He grabbed it and rested while talking to some members of the crew on the *Warrington*'s deck.

Suddenly I heard a petty officer call to Jeans in a quiet, conversational tone: "Mr. Jeans, there is a great big shark sniffing at your legs." I had seen a shadow flickering back and forth in the water around Jeans but had thought it was the shadow of a cloud.

Jeans splashed with his hands and kicked at the shark and it backed away. Then it returned. Jeans splashed still more vigorously and again the shark retreated but not so far this time. Then it came in a third time and looked as though it meant business, but now the dinghy ran alongside the buoy and Jeans was hauled on board. One of the men on deck threw a baited line over the side and at once the shark, obviously excited by the smell of meat, seized it and was hauled on board. He was about twenty feet long.

There were all sorts of strange creatures in the waters around Lobos. We secured the dinghy by a line astern and shortly afterward, for no apparent reason, a great manta ray—a fish like a gigantic skate—broke water and landed with a crash on the dinghy, smashing it to bits and scattering the oars, boathooks, and other equipment in every direction. The thing was so big that it completely enveloped the boat. That was the last time any of us went swimming near Lobos.

We were still trying to retrieve our gear from the wrecked dinghy when the radio operator came running aft to tell me, "Captain, the *Henley* is receiving orders to go to Vera Cruz and to take one other destroyer with her."

The *Henley* was our flagship and Vera Cruz was where the fighting was reported to be going on. I ran up on the bridge and told the quartermaster of the watch to call the *Henley* and send the message, "*Warrington* volunteers to accompany you to Vera Cruz." I could see the *Drayton,* another destroyer in our flotilla, was also making frantic efforts to signal the *Henley*. By a curious coincidence, just then we started to swing so we blocked her signalman and he couldn't get his message through before ours had been completed and acknowledged. As a result, the *Henley* sent us orders to get underway and follow her.

We made Vera Cruz Harbor before sunrise and at dawn went into the outer harbor which was crowded with an immense fleet, fourteen battleships and a great number of smaller vessels. The battleships were moored in a semicircle and, had the necessity arisen, could have directed a converging fire on the city that would have razed it.

As soon as we had reported to the commander in chief on board the *Arkansas* we went ashore. There were corpses everywhere and plenty of signs of destruction. Particularly hard hit was the Mexican Naval Academy, which occupied a commanding position above the town, which is built on the slope of a hill.

A landing party under Capt. E. A. Anderson had gone ashore and been caught in a murderous fire from the cadets in the Naval Academy. Capt. Anderson's party was brought to a halt and he and his men were forced to lie down in the street to escape the storm of bullets. Anderson sent back word of his predicament and one of our scout cruisers, the *Chester*, moved in to his support. The water is very deep here and the *Chester* was able to come almost alongside the wharfs. As the street was straight, she could train her guns right up to it. She fired a number of five inch shells into the windows of the Academy while Anderson led a bayonet charge, the men forcing their way into the lower rooms as the shells were still exploding in the upper stories. After that, the occupation of the city was comparatively easy.

We saw the famous old fortress of San Juan de Ullos which our forces had captured. The castle had been used as a political prison for many years and all those confined within were released. The doors, when thrown open disclosed many insane and blind prisoners who had been in the place for years, they themselves could not say how many. Some of the lower dungeons could be reached only through tunnels leading out under the harbor. Many of these cells were half-filled with water, and scattered through the place were instruments of torture such as "the iron maiden," racks, and so on. It reminded me of Dumas' description of the Chateau d'If.

All the Americans we met carried arms. Fighting was still going on in parts of the town. Practically every house roof was surrounded by a thick stone or brick wall about four feet high forming a natural barricade and making each housetop a little fortress. It is here that the people go in the cool of the evening and it was from here that most of our losses were inflicted, not always by soldiers in uniform but frequently by civilians who dropped their arms and fled the moment their positions were rushed, appearing later as "friendlies," an old trick practiced hundreds of times in the Philippines. In the first three days of fighting we had lost seventeen men killed and seventy-three wounded.

We heard a story about one Mexican who was especially friendly with our men, often being invited to take meals on board the ships, and inviting officers and men to his home in return. One afternoon during an outburst of sniping, our Mexican friend was seen on the porch of his house reading a newspaper, indifferent to the turmoil around him. The sniping fire was especially accurate that day and several of our men were hit. Then someone noticed that every time there was a shot, the Mexican's newspaper trembled in a curious way. A telescope was trained on him and he was found to have a gun concealed behind the newspaper. If the story was true, I suspect that man didn't live too long. I saw several men hanging from trees but as far as I know none were hung by us; they were supporters of Carranza and were hanged by the Huerta faction.

The plaza was in the center of the town. It was a large open space in the middle of which was a park filled with beautiful palms and other tropical trees and vivid with great red blossoms. There was a hotel here, and it was on the roof of this building that the Mexicans made one of their most determined stands. We climbed the narrow stairs to have a look at it.

As in the case of most of the houses, this roof was surrounded by a very thick wall of brick and plaster, but the high power Springfield rifle bullets of our men had not even hesitated at this obstacle; everywhere it was riddled with clean holes, the bullets passing not only through the walls but through the mattresses, pillows, and other "soft" resistance that the defenders had rigged inside. The roof was covered with torn, bloodstained clothing, discarded rifles, and other equipment. Everywhere on walls and mattresses were great splotches of blood while underfoot was a multitude of empty cartridge cases all of which, it may be mentioned in passing, had been manufactured in the United States. If it wasn't for us, I don't know where the Mexicans would get the ammunition to attack us.

Lastly, we went to the Naval Academy, where most of our casualties had occurred. This building was protected by walls of great strength, but never have I seen such utter ruin. Many shells had passed from room to room leaving jagged holes in the intervening walls and apparently not exploding until they reached the city beyond. One whole corner of the building was knocked off, a hole on the sea side was so large that a locomotive could have passed through it. The floors of the dormitories and recitation rooms were littered with broken furniture, clothes, toilet articles, books—everything in the greatest confusion. The recitation rooms, with mathematical formulae still on the blackboards, were a mass of plaster, bricks, stones, and every kind of debris. Our men had found and buried a large number of the building's brave young defenders. The *Chester* herself was struck nearly a hundred times during this bombardment and two men were wounded.

A few days later, we returned to Tampico. It is not generally known but Mexico had a navy; nothing to alarm our battleships but decidedly formidable when compared to destroyers. Her Navy consisted of a squadron of gunboats, their crews Mexican but the captains belonging to that more or less picturesque type "soldiers of fortune" of various nationalities.

The biggest of these gunboats, the *Zaragossa* was commanded by a Norwegian. She was armed with 4.7-inch guns, was of very sturdy build, and could have torn a destroyer to pieces; our largest guns were 3-inch. Indeed, had she caught a destroyer at anchor, she could have rammed and sunk the destroyer without firing a shot. Our main anxiety was that these gunboats might stage a raid on the army transports.

On April 24th, Captain Sims, who commanded our destroyers, issued an operations order:

"Three Mexican gunboats are inside the Panuco River at Tampico. Should these gunboats come out of the river they will be kept under close observation. Do not attack unless fired on. Vessels on observation duty be prepared to get underway on a few minutes' notice."

The *Warrington* was one of the observation vessels stationed at the mouth of the Panuco. Early the next morning, we sighted two vertical wooden poles that at first seemed to be the tops of dead trees. Then we saw that they were moving. On they came until they cleared the entrance; they were the topmasts of the *Zaragossa* and she was heading for us at her utmost speed. General Quarters was sounded and our guns manned, orders being given simultaneously to weigh anchor. Then we discovered, to our horror, that we couldn't weigh anchor; it was caught in something on the bottom and our anchor engine, always a little weak, was incapable of breaking it out.

On came the *Zaragossa* heading directly for our broadside, the water foaming around her bow; she evidently intended to ram us. Those of our guns that could bear were trained on her, as she was bow-on it was almost impossible to hit her with a torpedo. Then, just as we were about to let go a salvo, we saw activity on her bridge and a moment later an international signal was run up to her yard arm. Feverishly I grabbed the signal book and fumbled through its pages, my fingers all thumbs. After an eternity of suspense I found and interpreted her signal: "HAVE YOU GOT ANY ICE?"

We gave her our whole supply.

At one time it looked as though an advance might be made on Mexico City. We had a machine gun detachment on board the *Warrington* and I wrote to Captain Sims suggesting that, if the Army did advance, the Machine Gun Detachment, with me in command of it, go with them. Captain Sims replied that he "appreciated the spirit of the request" but that the Navy's work was on the sea. There was no advance beyond Vera Cruz and shortly afterward, orders came to return to the States. I received the Mexican Campaign Medal for "Services performed on the USS *Warrington*." I requested and was assigned a position at the Philadelphia Navy Yard, where I could be reunited with my wife and young son.

The First World War had begun in Europe and like all military men I was hoping the United States would join in the fray, but we had a president who was an ardent pacifist. In fact, for his second term in office the Democrats ran on the slogan, "He kept us out of war." So I was forced to content myself with routine duties at the Yard. I little thought that these duties would come very near to forcing me to resign from the service.

I had been promoted to Lieutenant Commander, and Polly and I moved into a pleasant little house in the Yard with a garden containing a large sandbox where young Dan liked to play. We did not see much of the "Navy Yard set" as Polly preferred her old friends in Philadelphia, and for my part I found parties on the big estates, evenings at the Academy of Music, and trips to the country more interesting than the stale gossip and constant "shop" talk that were typical of the Yard affairs. The Navy wives of my friends had a tendency to feel that our indifference constituted an insult. It was true that Polly, quite unconsciously, often behaved as though she were slumming when attending Yard dinners, even with the families of my superior officers. This naturally concerned me although I did not realize how dangerous it could be.

I did become alarmed when one afternoon Polly, who had been shopping at the Yard commissary in an unusual burst of domestic zeal, came bursting into our living room screaming with laughter to announce, "Pratt, did you know we have been put in coventry?"

It transpired that while shopping Polly had been approached by the fluttery new wife of a junior officer who asked her some questions about the commissary. The two young women entered into a conversation during which the new wife explained, "I want to be so careful what I do for George's sake. It would be just terrible if what happened to the Mannixes happened to us!"

"What happened to the Mannixes?" asked my astonished wife.

"Why don't you know? I thought everyone knew. They are so snobbish and stuck-up that now no one will speak to them. Oh, I would simply die if that happened to George and me!"

Polly thought this was screamingly funny. I did not. I made a few discreet inquiries and found that, yes, we had been ostracized. This was a serious matter. I had a heart-to-heart talk with Polly, and although I could not impress her with the importance of the situation and the damage it could easily do to my career, she did promise to be more careful in the future. We planned a dinner to which we would ask what few friends we had left and then try gradually to win over the others.

Before this could be done, disaster struck.

Like me, Dan had learned to read at an early age. I regretted that his favorite books were a series of fairy tales dealing with the magical land of Oz. I would much have preferred him to be reading Henty, *Frank on a Gunboat*, or Dumas as I had done but I took comfort in the fact that he was still very young and his taste would doubtless improve.

One afternoon, Dan was playing in the sandbox with the son of Captain Moses, commandant of the Yard. Dan was at his favorite game, conducting Dorothy, the Scarecrow, the Tin Woodman and the Cowardly Lion on their way to the Emerald City. Young Moses snatched at the little wooden dolls Dan was using as characters and Dan called him a "pig," the worst epithet he knew. Moses stared unbelievingly at this "lèse majesté" and then jumping up, ran to his father's office where Captain Moses was holding a conference with his staff. Bursting in on them, the boy blurted out, "Danny Mannix called me a pig!"

Captain Moses instantly rose, buckled on his sword, got out his cocked hat and followed by his staff marched down to the sandbox where Dan was still playing. Captain Moses stood towering over him in terrible silence while Dan, all unconscious, was busy shepherding Dorothy down the Yellow Brick Road. Finally Captain Moses said in an awful voice, "Did you call my son a pig?"

"Yes I did," replied Dan without looking up. "And you're another pig."

Captain Moses turned on his heel and strode back to his office trailed by his staff. Here he ordered, "Tell Mannix to report to me immediately." Then he started dictating to his yeoman. I received the message and all unsuspecting reported to his office. Captain Moses handed me a paper saying grimly, "This is your fitness report. According to Naval Regulations I must allow you to read it before putting it on file."

I read it and knew I was finished in the Navy. With a report like that on my record, there was no longer any hope for me.

I am glad to say that I never mentioned this matter to Dan nor showed him by any word or act how dearly he had cost me. I have seen too often men take out their own frustrations on anything weaker than they are. Dan learned about the incident many years later from his mother. Meanwhile, I went about stunned. A few brave souls openly came up to offer me consolation; most avoided me like a leper and I could hardly blame them. I thought of resigning but what would I do? I was trained for nothing but a naval officer's life. The future seemed hopeless.

Looking back, I believe I can understand Moses' actions. He was a Jew and the Navy didn't like Jews. As a young officer, he had undoubtedly been constantly subjected to sneers about his race which he had endured in silence but which had embittered him. Now that he had reached command rank, he was savagely determined to pay back anyone who insulted him. As to a Jew, a pig is an unclean animal, he took for granted that Dan's remark to his son was in the nature of a religious insult. He may have thought that I put Dan up to it.

None of this occurred to me at the time. All I knew was that I was ruined and all my hopes for advancement in the service were crushed.

Then the miracle happened. In April 1917, President Wilson asked Congress to declare war on Germany. People were cheering, bands playing, and every experienced man was desperately needed. Moses' vicious report could not hurt me now; like all regular naval officers I had suddenly become invaluable. I am not a religious man, but when I heard we were at war, I fell to my knees and thanked God for His mercies. I was quickly promoted to full commander and my future was assured.

CHAPTER ELEVEN

World War I (1918)

At fall of dusk we softly steal
From out each firth; and forth
Seeking the aid of night's dark tide
To strike hard from the North.

Nightly the North Sea knows our screws
By their muffled, careful beat,
While we strew the sudden death unseen
For our foes' unwary feet.

—Mine Force Poet

AUTHOR'S NOTE: The North Sea Mine Barrage was kept such a closely guarded secret that even after the war little was known of it. There are few mentions of it in histories of the First World War. Yet Capt. Reginald Belknap reported that the British Admiralty Staff told him that the surrender of the German Fleet and the collapse of the submarine warfare was due to the barrage as the German ships were unable to leave port. As long as the deadly U-boats controlled the seas, it was impossible for the United States to send troops and supplies across the Atlantic. This is the only eyewitness account of how the barrage was laid, written by one of the men who took part in the actual laying.

THERE WERE several German ships interned at the Yard, the largest of which were the *Eitel Friederich* and the *Kron Prinz Wilhelm*. There were at least two thousand men in their crews, and while the breech plugs of their guns had been removed, their rifles and small arm ammunition had, for some curious reason, been left on board. As their crews, composed of veteran seamen, could have seized the Yard and held it long enough to destroy the drydocks, machine shops and everything else of any value to our war effort, they presented a serious menace.

There were constant fires in the Yard, especially, so it seemed to me, when I was officer of the day and obliged to turn out and attend them. These fires, and most of our other troubles, were the fault of the civilian dockyard workers who were both lazy and incompetent. As they were all unionized, none of them could be discharged without a general strike so we were helpless to deal with them. I had noticed that the German seamen had been observing the slipshod methods of these men with increasing irritation. Perfectly disciplined themselves and highly efficient, it obviously infuriated them to see valuable equipment ruined by these men's gross carelessness.

Shortly after our declaration of war, I had the duty and at two o'clock in the morning, the phone rang. I answered and it was our regular nightly fire. I was greatly apprehensive that the Germans would take advantage of the chaos resulting from these constant alarms to stage a "coup de main" so I immediately alerted the guard and then called the Power House to make sure everything was in order. For some time there was no answer and I supposed everyone was asleep, which would have been typical. Finally someone at the other end took the receiver off the hook and with a pronounced German accent, inquired: "Vell, vat iss it?"

I was so stunned I didn't know what to do. Breaking the connection, I called the guard again and then hurried down to the Power

House, the heart of the whole industrial network. There I found the German sailors busy putting out the fire under the capable direction of their officers. It seemed they had become so disgusted with our incompetence they had taken over the situation and were putting matters to rights.

I was in a quandary. All my instincts were to have them confined on board their ships but, on the other hand, they were the only people available who knew what they were doing and to remove them would have resulted in the loss of much of the installations. I finally allowed them to go ahead and when the fire was out, thanked them in my best German and escorted them back to their ships. Something about my speech amused them very much and when I asked what it was, one young officer explained that I had been addressing them all in the feminine gender. "I wonder under what conditions you learned your German," he remarked. I thought it better not to tell him.

Meanwhile the situation in Europe was growing more critical. By far the greatest danger came from the U-boats, "the stiletto of the Seas" as they were called. Conventional naval tactics against them were useless, and they were sinking 800,000 tons of shipping a month. The subs presented a special danger to the United States for slow-moving transports, loaded with men, would have been the ideal target for the torpedoes of the deadly underwater ships and plans were already underway to send thousands of American troops to reinforce the reeling allies in France. As long as the submarines controlled the Atlantic, any efforts we made to aid England and France were doomed.

At this time I learned of highly secret plans to lay a mine field across the North Sea from Scotland to Norway, a distance approximately as far as from Washington to New York, the greatest undertaking of its kind in history. The English Channel had already been successfully mined by the British, thus blocking it to the U-boats but they could still issue from their docks along the German coast and swinging north of the British Isles, attack the shipping lanes.

To block this wide passage would require a mine field 250 miles long and 900 feet deep. This meant a total of 400,000 mines. There were not enough mines in the world for such a field and no chance of manufacturing such a vast number in the time available, yet already an announcement had been made in the House of Commons that Great Britain had only enough food for another month. A new type of mine was needed that could be used in deep water and did not actually have to be struck by a ship in order to explode. Such a mine had indeed been devised. It was attached to an anchor by a long copper cable and if a submarine touched the cable the mine exploded. A hundred thousand such mines would be sufficient to form an effective barrage.

The mines were to be loaded with a new and terrible explosive, far more deadly than dynamite, called TNT. Little was known about TNT and its effects. Both the British and the French had found the substance too dangerous to use, so there were few volunteers for a mine-laying squadron especially as professional sailors disliked mine laying on principle; it was often referred to as "rat-catching" and lacked the glamor of shooting it out with broadsides from the big guns. There was also the consideration that if you were beaten in ship-to-ship conflicts you could always surrender. If while mine laying one of your mines exploded, that was it. "You made a hole in the water that it took three months to fill up" was the popular phrase.

I saw a great opportunity here for advancement so I volunteered for the Mine Laying Squadron. I was accepted and given orders to proceed to New York where I was to take command of the *Jefferson*. I had no idea what the *Jefferson* was but when I arrived in New York, I quickly found out.

She was an old ex-merchantman with canvas-covered decks like a ferryboat and all her internal fittings were of wood. For twenty years she had carried passengers and freight between New York and Norfolk, Virginia. As her engines were completely shot, she had been retired from service. I could not believe that this frail ship was supposed to cross the Atlantic, weather North Sea gales, be rocked by terrific explosions, and actually survive the ordeal.

When I took command of her she was lying in the Erie Basin, South Brooklyn. Her ancient insides had been torn out, lounge rooms and dining salons transformed into long reaches of bare decks on which were laid complete systems of railway tracks with switches and turntables. In her stern had been cut two great "barn doors" through which the tracks passed, ending in a downward curve over the water. A 5-inch gun was mounted aft and two 3-inch anti-aircraft guns were on her forecastle; this was the extent of her armament. Her white paint was being changed to a mad futuristic orgy of color called "camouflage" which was supposed to confuse the eyes of submarine commanders and she had been rechristened *Quinnebaug*, a name dating back in Naval Annals to the Civil War. She was one of ten ships called

"Raiders of the Night," which were supposed to stop the overwhelming force of Germany's famed U-boats.

I protested that this old, discarded vessel could never get across the Atlantic; that even when she was new she had been designed for nothing but coastal work. My answer was that no other ships were available and that unless Germany's unlimited submarine campaign could be stopped, the war would be over in a few weeks. As I had asked for this assignment, I could not now very well refuse it. I could only bless the dear American public who in time of peace economized on naval expenditures and then in time of war expected ferryboats to cross the ocean and fight the Imperial German Navy.

Officers and men began to assemble. Our complement of the former was eighteen; only three of these, including myself, were "Annapolis men." The others consisted of an ex-merchant skipper over fifty years old, two young college men who had never been to sea before, a "millionaire" looking for excitement, and a tall Dane from the Geodetic Survey who was an authority on tropical flora. The rest were Navy warrant officers and merchant service officers.

I insisted that all hands, officers and men, be allowed to inspect the ship and know exactly what lay before them. Immediately quite a number of them developed ill mothers or aged fathers and were promptly sent back to the Receiving Station. I was glad to see them go. There could be no room for faint hearts in such a project as lay ahead.

The whole affair was cloaked in such secrecy that we were not permitted to tell even our families where we were going or what we were to do. As a result, the Mine Barrage, which was to play such a crucial part in the war, remained unknown to the American public and is ignored in history books.

We left the Erie Basin on April 15th and proceeded to the "Explosive Anchorage" in lower New York Bay, which all other vessels were careful to give a wide berth. There we remained for twenty-four hours loading mines and ammunition. The mines were great globes of steel three feet in diameter, containing three hundred pounds of TNT. Any one of them was quite capable of totally destroying our frail ship if a mishap occurred. Each mine was mounted on an iron box which acted as an anchor for the mine after it had been dropped into the sea. This box had four small wheels and ran along the tracks laid over the decks. A copper cable connected the mine to the box and could be set for different depths so a mine could be held just below the surface or close to the sea floor. A submarine, therefore, never knew when it might encounter the fatal cable.

As we were getting the last mine on board, we had our first thrill. This particular mine had become detached from its anchor-box, and we were hoisting the metal sphere with its explosive charge over the side. Just as it arrived at the top of the hoist and was being swung inboard the hook broke and the mine fell from a height of forty feet, struck the deck of the empty lighter, bounced along like a rubber ball and went overboard. I'm sure everybody was relieved to hear that splash; I know I was. Had it detonated we would have been as one of my officers remarked, "reduced to our constituent elements—a pinch of salt and three buckets of water." Also, New York would have learned what Halifax had experienced a few months before. A Norwegian ship had struck a French munition vessel loaded with TNT and the explosion wiped out two square miles of the town, killing 1,654 people and injuring 1,028. It also created a tidal wave which washed the ruins into the sea. Yes, I was very glad that that mine had hit the water without exploding.

We were due for another bit of excitement. We had left our anchorage and were heading south for Hampton Roads. I was on the bridge looking aft when suddenly the entire rear part of the ship burst into a sheet of flames which flared up as high as the mainmast truck. This would have been bad enough under any conditions, but loaded as we were with high power explosives, I thought it was the end. I stopped the engines, headed her away from the wind and sounded the general alarm. To my great gratification there wasn't the slightest panic. Officers and men manned the extinguishers, led out the hose, and put out the fire without any damage being done. Investigation showed that there had been a large accumulation of gas in our faulty forced draught system which, in some manner, had become ignited. What was particularly disturbing was the discovery that the asbestos that the shipyard had just put in burned merrily.

At Hampton Roads we anchored and a party of workmen carried on board a number of articles we vitally needed. One of the workmen casually spit on the deck as he went by. Perhaps a civilian cannot realize the enormity of this act. To seamen, their ship is their home and the decks are scrubbed scrupulously clean; long hours of holystoning keeps them spotless. To spit on a ship's deck is like spitting on the floor of a house. The boatswain promptly knocked him down. This natural act produced an outburst of fury from the dockyard workers who were, of course, all unionized and immune from the draft, their labors being regarded as essential. They proceeded to go on strike and refused to load the ship. To satisfy their indignation that one of them should have been struck, they were perfectly prepared to allow us to cross the ocean and enter a combat zone without adequate supplies. My answer was to distribute arms to a landing party and under cover of their weapons, I went ashore and directed the loading of the material by a detail of our crew. The furious workmen shouted, "Scab!" at us but they did not attempt to interfere; wisely for them.

As this would be our last home port for many months, leave was granted and a number of our men went ashore. To their annoyance, they were not welcome even by fellow seamen from the Battleship Squadron. Whenever one of them lighted a cigarette, the men ran away shouting that they could see the TNT under his fingernails. Already we had become pariahs even in our own country.

By now the ships that were to make up the Mine Force had assembled and were ready to put to sea. We proceeded up the coast to Provincetown, during which voyage we lost our radio aerial, a crack opened in the main condenser, we lost two thousand gallons of fresh water and as there were no baffles in the boilers, every time the ship rolled heavily the water went from the boilers to the engines and squirted out of every orifice. I could not imagine how we could cross the Atlantic, let alone brave North Sea storms and German submarines.

At Provincetown, we were sent to the Boston Navy Yard for repairs. I called on Commodore Reginald Belknap, and he told me regretfully that due to a press of shipping the commandant of the Yard had told him that the repairs would be long delayed. This was very bad news indeed as the *Quinnebaug* was due to make the transatlantic crossing with the rest of the squadron in a few days. I happened to mention that we had ninety tons of TNT on board. When I got back to the ship I found that a cordon of marines had been posted around her and the repairs were being completed with the most amazing speed. There was also a note from the commandant of the Yard in which he intimated that the sooner we got away from his Navy Yard the better. I have never seen such wonderful cooperation.

We rejoined the squadron at Newport and at a final conference the captains were told to get underway singly at midnight without signal and with their ships darkened in case there were submarines about. Outside the harbor the ships were to assemble and start for Scotland.

We reached the rendezvous at two o'clock in the morning, formed a double column and headed east. For the next few days all went well until we reached mid-ocean when we had our final and most serious breakdown. The main air pump flew to pieces necessitating the manufacture of a new pump rod and nuts in our little machine shop that had originally been a coal bunker. One of the other ships towed us for a day, using one of our anchor chains as a tow. We were able to finish the job, part of which required the cutting of a large hole in a steel deck in order to lift out the damaged pump rod. Just as we were completing it, a flank ship fired a gun—the agreed-on signal of a submarine attack.

We instantly cast off the tow, put on full speed, and our whole flotilla scattered. We saw a big collier astern open up with a regular fusillade, and everyone was seeing periscopes all over the place. Looking back, I think the whole business was a false alarm. No submarine captain could have failed to sink a twenty-year-old crippled ferryboat incapable of making more than a few knots.

Our course took us far to the north, nearly within sight of Iceland. It began to get colder and we saw the most wonderful color effects in sea and sky, the most brilliant and contrasted Northern Lights. The sun set later and rose earlier until soon it was never really dark, only a little hazy from midnight until one o'clock in the morning. Great schools of whales and blackfish appeared, some of them coming up between the columns of ships. I saw two whales, very close aboard, with a baby between them; the baby was about as long as our largest motor sailing launch.

Now we curved southward into the danger zone, and nobody was allowed to sleep or take off his clothes. Soon we would meet the British destroyers who were to escort us through Cromarty Firth to Invergordon. Our collier had been missing for three days and repeated radio calls had produced no response.

At daylight on a crystal-clear morning the little gray destroyers came skimming toward us over a glassy sea prompt to the minute, and at the same time our missing collier hove into view serene and safe. Greetings were cut short by the destroyer commander who urged us to put on all steam and make our utmost speed as submarines had been reported nearby. Our relief changed to intense excitement and the ships surged forward in a mass straining every nerve to reach the green landlocked harbor that lay ahead. The Englishmen handled their ships beautifully, swinging in circles ahead and on the flanks. Astern the collier was nearly having apoplexy rolling thirty degrees on a side; she looked like a fat man in a hurry. The commodore had the brutality to signal "Close up"; this to an ample party already going belly to the ground.

We ran along the coast of Scotland past high rocky cliffs smothered in veils of white spray, with stately snow capped peaks in the background and dimly glimpsed villages clustering at their feet. War seemed incredible in such a setting until we sighted the submarine nets ahead, vast webs that stretched across the harbor closing the funnel that forms Cromarty Firth. Outside lay the trawlers waiting to open the hidden gates of the net. The head of our column reached them and stopped; the trawlers gradually drew aside a section of the first net for us to enter. As we slowly ran through they opened another section of the second net, about half a mile south, and then, running south once more until they neared the wreck of the *Natal*, a big British cruiser that had mysteriously blown up a short time previously, they parted the third and last of the "naval barbed wire" and we came to anchor in the blue waters that meant, for a time at least, relief from anxiety.

The next day, after two hours' sleep, we motored to Inverness to call on the local authorities. We ran beside the sea over cobbles worn smooth with age, past little cottages with white curtains and turfed roofs where the grass grew thick and green, hedges and ivy and old stone walls covered with moss, some of them built by the Romans. The fields were full of Highland cattle, all shaggy with long hair hanging down over their eyes. A party of the Cameron Highlanders marched past us, their kilts swinging in unison. Just outside the town is Cawdor Castle and the "blasted heath" made famous by Macbeth, and Culloden where the clans made their last stand against the hated English. Further on is Nairn where Bonny Prince Charlie slept before the battle.

We called on Admiral Pears of the Royal Navy, who was very pleasant, especially considering that one of our men had just batted a baseball through his window while he was having tea. We returned to Invergordon that evening.

Invergordon was a little fishing village but the base of the famous

Seaforth Highlanders and the Royal Scottish Rifles. We saw many of these men just returned from France virtually every one of them wearing at least one wound stripe. Some of their drummers seemed about ten years old but they marched along under a full equipment which included a dirk carried in the right stocking. In the ancient town hall were the old flags of the Highland regiments embroidered with the names of the battles they had fought. I saw "New Orleans" rubbing shoulders with "Waterloo."

On July 13th we started on our first mining expedition. At dusk we passed through the submarine nets to meet our escort of fourteen British destroyers from the Grand Fleet and stood out for Muckle Skerry Light where we took our departure and headed for Norway. We were in a dense fog most of the night, but at sunrise it cleared and we could see aircraft darting about above us. On the horizon lay a division of battleships and light cruisers guarding against a sally by the German fleet while, on our flanks, the destroyers of our escort were deployed watching for submarines.

Our ships formed in two lines, one ahead of the other, moving on parallel courses five hundred yards apart. Of course, only the rear line of ships dropped mines; the front line stood by ready to change position with any ship in the rear that had a breakdown. The mines were carried on two of the lower decks, the "launching deck" and the "stowage deck." The railroad tracks on the launching deck passed through the "barn doors" in the stern of the ship where an officer was stationed in a soundproof booth. When the signal of execution was hauled down on the flagship we started to drop mines, one every eight seconds, while the ship steamed steadily on her course. The men lined up on both sides of the tracks, two to a mine and the mining officer moved a controller that illuminated an electric dial with the word PLANT. Immediately the first mine was pushed through the open door, its momentum carrying it to the end of the tracks and overboard. It was fascinating to watch them; they would go over with a great splash, bob around in our wake while the anchor-box gradually filled with water, then suddenly sink with a dull plop as though a giant hand had reached up from below and pulled them down.

We had been assured that a safety device on the mines absolutely prevented them from exploding prematurely. This device was a washer of compressed salt that fitted between the detonator and the firing pin; the mine couldn't "go off" until it had been in the water half an hour and this washer was dissolved. Even so, we watched with considerable apprehension as our first mine went over the side. Fine! We dropped the second. Still fine! Free from all anxiety, we let go the third. A crash like the Day of Judgment! An enormous column of flames, smoke, mud, and water rose just astern of us. Men a ship's length away were thrown on their faces and the entire ship quivered and strained so that it seemed impossible the rivets would not be sheered out of the side plating. On that first expedition about six percent of the mines exploded prematurely, in some cases detonating other mines that had already been successfully laid. There was something peculiar about these detonations of TNT; they were not like the explosions of gunpowder. They would be preceded by a deathly silence, then we would feel a heavy pressure on our chests and all the air in our lungs would be drawn away—sucked, toward the exploding mine. It wasn't just a tremendous noise like the discharge of a big gun; it had a quality of its own.

These repeated detonations began to get on the men's nerves and once, when we got slightly ahead of position so that our stern was abreast the foremast of the ship on our right, we received a prompt signal: "Please drop back." At one stage of the operation our ship had to drop from the leading line to the planting line, it required nice work for, had we lost headway too suddenly and dropped too far behind, we would have been on top of our own mines.

As mines were dropped from the launching deck those on the stowage deck were raised in elevators to fill the vacant places and to go overboard in their turn. We steamed at full speed dropping mines until the entire supply of eight hundred had been launched. The greatest accuracy and coordination was necessary and the physical labor was tremendous as, mining once started, there could not be a moment's let up until the last mine had gone over, otherwise there would be gaps in the mine field. The mines were laid at three levels, upper, middle, and lower, so that enemy submarines whether running on the surface or at ordinary submergence or as deep as 250 feet could pass through the barrage only at great peril.

When the last mine had gone over we headed back to our base. For a long time we could hear muffled explosions behind us. Curiously when they had become inaudible on the bridge they could still be felt by the quivering of the ship and could be heard in the engine room, the water transmitting the sound much further than the air.

The mining over, the tension should have been over also but there was still some excitement ahead of us. It grew damper and foggier. North Sea fogs are like nothing else in the world and soon it was impossible to see the forecastle from the bridge. Radio could not be used as it might attract the submarines. We were in two parallel columns five hundred yards apart. At three o'clock in the morning there was a rift in the fog and, straining our eyes, we suddenly saw a ship directly across our bow seemingly just under our forefoot. The quartermaster, without orders, spun the wheel and barely missed cutting her down. As we swung around, another ship cut under our stern disappearing the next moment in the fog while a third surged up on the quarter. We were in the midst of an enormous convoy. Then the whole outfit vanished leaving us, like the Ancient Mariner, "all, all alone."

There was a channel swept clear of floating and anchored mines a short distance ahead and I was faced with the pleasing alternatives of either going straight on, thus insuring our being in comparatively safe water but probably ramming somebody or being rammed, or, on the other hand, continuing down the coast outside and taking my chances with the enemy mines. I chose the latter danger.

Even overhead was misting closed while all around us crawled the thick white fog, impenetrable as cotton wool. I remarked optimistically to the navigator, an old merchant skipper, that it was still partially clear overhead. "Yes, but we ain't headed that way," was his encouraging rejoinder.

Leaning on the bridge rail and staring through the murky drip I could see nothing; the horizon had disappeared long ago and now sea and sky had blended into one indistinguishable and impenetrable gray. All sounds were deadened by the enveloping blanket and we unconsciously lowered our voices in speaking. The use of fog whistles, which would have enabled us to keep track of the other ships, was naturally forbidden as enemy submarines could hear them.

As the fog covered the horizon, it was impossible to take an observation in the regular way. I had a bucket of water taken to the bridge and a film of oil put on the surface, then I sat on the deck straddling the bucket and with sextant ready waiting for the sun to show itself. For a second only it peeped out but in that second I snapped its altitude using the bucket as an "artificial horizon." This observation placed us thirty miles to the eastward of the firth. Finally we came to the point where, if we were running on time, we should swing to the right to enter the firth. We turned and just missed colliding with the *Baltimore*.

Shortly after this near disaster, we were lucky enough to pick up the entrance buoy and headed in for the submarine nets. In the fog it was like threading a mystic maze; we would sight a heavy net close under the starboard bow, hear frantic whistles from the guarding trawler, put the rudder hard over, miss it by the skin of our teeth, sight another net under the port bow, reverse the process amid wild cries of warning in Cockney and Scottish, stop the engines to avoid entangling the propeller and trust to our momentum to slide through. Once we went so close to a trawler that our quarterboat touched her yardarm. We did get through, however, and, after sighting the range lights on the wreck of the *Natal*, anchored again off Invergordon. I wondered if every trip was to be this bad. No, most of them turned out to be worse.

The following week was spent in port. The premature explosions were a matter of serious concern as they left gaps in the minefield so the second expedition was delayed until certain changes in design had been worked out and the extreme sensitiveness of the mines somewhat reduced. The rain squalls became less frequent, and we began to enjoy those wonderful northern lights unlike anything in our latitudes. At ten or eleven o'clock the brilliant full moon would rise while the sun still shone above the horizon. Seen through the utter clarity of the cold air the green of the great mountains that ringed the harbor, the blue of the water and sky, all the little points of color, became intensified a hundred-fold into a splendor I have never seen equalled.

The British supplied us with a number of drifters, big motor barges, for transporting men and stores. One of these was commanded by a very grouchy Scotch skipper who furnished endless amusement for our men. One afternoon, as he came alongside the *Quinnebaug* somebody, entirely accidentally, threw a bucket of water over the rail which landed with the utmost precision. When we ventured an apology, we found the old fellow furious not on account of being wet to the skin but because his pipe had been put out.

Admiral Pears was always very gracious to us although he didn't approve of our enthusiasm for the local Annie Lauries, grimly observing, "And when will you start wearing the kilt?" I'm afraid his efforts were useless for I have never seen such lovely girls. There certainly wasn't anything "dour" about them, although I can't say the same for some of the men. I became very good friends with a girl named Aline and we were always together in whatever time I could spare from the ship. Aline mimicked my accent quite cleverly and amused herself by pretending to be an American. She and I were having breakfast at the Queensgate Hotel and I reached for a jar of marmalade on the table. It was snatched out from under my hand by the waitress who snapped: "Major McTavish's jam!" Aline remarked haughtily, "In America, people are more polite. Now tell me, are there any ostriches here in Scotland such as we have at home?" The waitress turned to a friend and made some remark, clearly uncomplimentary, in Scottish. The two women chatted sneeringly for a while until Aline burst into a tirade of broad Scots invective. They stared at her open-mouthed and then fled the room.

On our second mining expedition the weather was clear but the wind tremendously strong, even for the North Sea, home of the winds. It was impossible to walk upright and anyone trying to face it had the breath blown back into his lungs. The "prematures" were fewer in number, although they continued to take place at the most unexpected times. We heard a particularly violent explosion from the field we had laid on the first trip and the quartermaster asked me, "What do you suppose that was?" His question was answered a short time later when we passed the bodies of several German sailors floating on the rough sea. We had made our first kill.

The Germans were not long in responding. Obviously other submarines in the vicinity had also heard the explosions and now knew what we were doing. Suddenly we saw our escort destroyers make a dash toward the left flank and a regular Donneybrook Fair ensued, the Britishers weaving in and out at top speed, their guns depressed to the utmost limit hurling a continuous stream of fire into the apparently empty waters below while, at regular intervals, they let go depth charges from their sterns which sent cataracts of water into the air making our ships shiver violently. Fifteen minutes of this and silence fell. The escort commander, Captain Godfrey DSO, came slowly back to report that several submarines had been trailing us, paralleling our course and waiting for the right moment to attack. As all our mines had been laid we increased speed to the maximum and headed for home.

There was always a question in our minds which, luckily, was never answered. Should one of our ships be torpedoed with her mines still on board and be blown to atoms, would the explosion detonate the mines on the other ships and all of them go up together, just as the explosion of one mine in a field frequently detonates a whole line of them? The experts assured us that this couldn't happen, but with the prematures continuing to flourish we committed the heresy of doubting the experts.

One afternoon we were invited to tea by the Laird of Invergordon. His castle lay outside the town in the midst of a lovely wood. It was most attractive, enormous rooms filled with sunshine and flowers, very old furniture and china. One of his possessions was a great treasure chest taken from a ship of the Spanish Armada wrecked off the coast of Scotland; it was braced with beautiful ironwork and the keyhole was elaborately hidden. I felt sorry for the old Laird. He had served many years in the British Army, both his sons had been killed in the trenches of France, and a grateful government had taken most of his house to quarter munition workers imported from England. These people had killed all his deer and rabbits and he had no redress, although he was required to pay enormous taxes on land that any ragamuffin had the right to wander over at will. There was one thing certain about the war; no matter who won, the aristocracy on both sides were bound to lose.

At first our expeditions did not last more than a couple of days but as the barrage stretched farther and farther across the North Sea, we were out for five days or a week. Now we began to glimpse the ice-clad mountains of Norway. Our net was slowly closing around Germany.

I remember one trip especially. In order to avoid our own mines we were now obliged to run west into the Atlantic through Stronsay Firth which lay well to the north, go still farther north before turning east and then, running just south of the Orkney Islands, ease down until we were on the upper edge of the barrage where we were to start work.

Stronsay Firth is a narrow passage enclosed by great rugged cliffs that rise sheer from the sea. As we approached the entrance five enemy submarines were reported ahead. It was too late to turn back; the van of our column was already in the shadow of the cliffs.

As we went deeper into the passageway, there was a terrific roar from ahead and to port. A torpedo had been fired across our track, missing its target, and struck the high wall of rock on our left. The confined space made the noise indescribable.

The flanking ships opened fire with their guns and the destroyers raced to start smoke screens on both flanks, simultaneously dropping depth charges. In a moment we were running, loaded with mines, through whirling clouds of smoke. It was so dense that all we could see were the rocky pinnacles above us and, close alongside, the rough water covered with dead fish killed by the explosions. Then, for a moment, the smoke lifted and I saw the outline of a torpedo detach itself from the darker gray of the passage and rush toward us like a dog running across the road in front of a motor car. There was nothing we could do. Our guns would not depress enough to fire at it, and it was going so fast we could not possibly swing out of its way.

Abruptly the torpedo began to "porpoise," leaping up and down in the water as porpoises do before the bow of a ship. Something had gone wrong with its mechanism. It crossed our course to port and disappeared in a whirl of spray and smoke. At the same time not twenty-five yards off our starboard quarter, the thin, gray needle of a periscope rose above the water to study us. I simply crossed my fingers and waited.

The periscope stayed up for maybe five seconds, then the bow of a destroyer appeared out of the smoke. The periscope was jerked down just as the destroyer passed over it. Why the sub didn't fire a second torpedo at us, I will never know; perhaps she didn't have time. We made the rest of the trip through the firth in safety.

The presence of these submarines showed that our work was beginning to have its effects. No longer could the subs round the north of Scotland and head down to their bases; their only paths of return lay through the narrow firths like Stronsay and then south, hugging the coast until clear of the barrage. In the next few weeks we would close up these bolt-holes also.

One of our worst moments came about not through enemy action but because of our own faulty machinery. Shortly after we had started mining one day, the steering wheel rope jumped a pulley on the lower deck and started to scrape against a steel bulkhead. If the rope parted, being unable to steer we would run into our own mines and if we reported a breakdown and fell out it would mean a gap in the barrage. We had never yet failed the commodore so I stationed a man with a bucket of grease and a brush to keep the points of contact heavily coated and we actually laid six hundred mines with our steering gear in that condition. The last mine having gone over I sent Kellerhouse, our old merchant skipper, below with a crowbar. When he reported,

"Ready!" we suddenly put the wheel hard-a-port; this slackened the wheel rope and he deftly threw it back on the pulley before it tautened again. At the same time, on the bridge, the wheel was brought back to amidships before the ship could take a sheer.

While still eight hours away from home a second pulley did the same thing and the bucket of grease was once more requisitioned. Inspections were made every fifteen minutes to be sure the rope would last until we got in. About fifty miles from Inverness we ran into another group of submarines. The British destroyers deployed like so many pieces of clockwork, made their smoke screen, and dropped their barrage of depth charges while we forged steadily on through the darkness until their escort leader, the *Vampire*, resumed her station and the others, following their leader, slipped back to their regular positions on our flanks.

Several times we were guests at some of the great places near Inverness which now, I fear, are no longer occupied by their original owners. I remember especially going to Moy Hall to dine with the Mackintosh of Mackintosh, head of the Clan of Cathan, "the clan of the wildcat." We had a beautiful drive over mountains and down deep valleys. The heather was in full bloom covering the hillsides with purple and white. At the great gates of the castle we were met by the Mackintosh and his wife. He made a splendid and impressive figure in the scarlet and green tartan of his clan, a gray-haired man in middle life showing by his bearing the long years he had served as an officer of the Camerons.

The Mackintosh had recently lost his only son, an officer in the First Life Guards, who had been shot through the lungs. Even after being shot, he did not fall from his horse but by sheer willpower continued to advance at the head of his troops. They bred men in that part of the world.

The castle was a regular museum with enormous high rooms and all sorts of trophies from all over the world; tiger skins, heads of stags and of great gray wolves. I particularly enjoyed the many landscapes by Landseer, one of them, "Deer in October Woods," covering the entire end of a room. There was also a blacksmith's hammer mounted below the painting of a handsome woman. Bonny Prince Charlie had stayed in this castle and was nearly captured by the English. The laird of that day was away with the clans but his lady gathered the men on the place and, leading them out, fell on the flank of the searching party. The family blacksmith swinging his sledge downed the officer in command and the rest fled.

I expressed a desire to see the gardens at which the laird called: "Hey, Wully MacDonald!" and the head gardener appeared replying, "Yus, Mackintosh." You see, it would be an insult to say "sir" to him or any other title. He is THE Mackintosh. The gardens covered about five acres and were magnificent. While we were inspecting them, an old dog followed us around carrying an empty tin plate in his mouth; he wanted his dinner.

At table that evening we had ptarmigan, a bird which I was assured never comes below two thousand feet, and pheasant from the estate. There were several officers from the kilted regiments and after the ladies had left the table, they told reminiscences of their wars. One man who had just returned from France said that as his regiment advanced through a village they saw a live kitten nailed to a door. A sergeant tried to take it down and was blown to pieces by an attached bomb. Another had served in the Boxer Campaign. Two of his men were captured by the Chinese and later they were found lashed to posts, the natural orifices of their bodies plugged with red clay. Still another had served in the Sudan and was in the desert column sent out to punish the tribes after the disaster to Hicks Pasha, the English officer in the pay of the khedive of Egypt who led a force against the Mahdi and his dervishes. Hicks' force was ambushed by the dervishes at Kashgil and virtually wiped out. This officer told us, "for miles we marched past the bodies of Hicks' men staked out alive on the sands and left to be killed by the sun." I suppose these old Scottish families were an anachronism by 1918, but they certainly were a race of fighting men.

As our expeditions continued we met fewer submarines but a great many floating German mines. They were easily distinguished from our own as they had projecting points or "horns." Whether they were deliberately set adrift, a menace to both friend and foe, or had parted their mooring lines we never knew. At first each one sighted was promptly reported and efforts made to explode or sink it by rifle fire but before long they began to appear in such swarms that our attention was entirely occupied in dodging them. Had we attempted to sink them all there would have been no time left to do anything else.

Our main protection against *anchored* mines was the paravane. As this device was to play so important a part in our work I had better describe it briefly. A paravane resembled a torpedo and was towed by a line passing around the forefoot of the ship. A paravane, or "fish" as they were usually called, had horizontal metal fins which made it run along like an aquaplane except, instead of being on the surface of the water, it was fifteen or twenty feet below it. The motion of the ship through the water kept it clear of the side. If the ship slowed down the "fish" would come alongside and stick closer than a brother, in which position it was useless and had to be hoisted on board and relaunched by means of a small swinging boom.

In the nose of the paravane was a pair of very sharp steel jaws. When a ship met an anchored mine, the mine's mooring line would slide along the towing line of the paravane until it came to the steel jaws where it would be severed and the mine, cut adrift from its anchor, would come to the surface where it could be sunk by rifle fire. Each ship used two paravanes, one on either bow, when in mine-infected waters.

The paravanes cut down our speed about two knots and were very temperamental, constantly fouling themselves, but it was vitally necessary to use them.

Perhaps our worst day came on August 19th; I remember the date because it is my birthday. We were on a mining expedition when our starboard paravane ran in alongside the ship and stuck there. Thanks to the efficiency of Lt. John Price, it was hoisted on board without our having to slacken speed or lose position in the formation. Suddenly we sighted a big German mine about forty feet off the starboard bow. It seemed inevitable that we would hit it. I shouted to Price to get the starboard paravane over, any which way, even though I knew that the paravanes were useless against floating mines. It was our only chance. Assisted by several of the men, he lifted the heavy "fish," carried it to the rail and threw it over. It fell on its back, sank, righted itself and in a moment was running bravely alongside. I saw it pass directly under the mine and, miracle of miracles, the next second the mine, instead of continuing to approach us, was moving parallel to our course and about five feet from the ship's side. Leaning over the wing of the bridge I could look directly down on it. Apparently a mooring line hanging from it had caught in the jaws of the paravane and the ship was towing it through the water.

As the paravane swayed and plunged, it was inevitable that one of the horns on the mine would strike us. It was too close to be exploded by rifle fire; it would have taken us down with it. I was afraid to touch the steering wheel lest the slightest sheer bring it against our side. Helpless, I could only wait for the explosion that was sure to come.

At this moment a seaman ran up to me and reported, "Sir, the ship's on fire. The lower deck where the mines are stored is all in flames. The mines are going to explode in seconds."

I looked aft. Smoke was billowing up the midships hatch. Not only would we go, but with a full cargo of mines the whole squadron would probably go up with us.

A merciful Providence has so constituted the human mind that it can occupy itself with but one vital problem at a time. I forgot all about the fire as I watched that mine swing in toward our side. It was almost touching when it commenced spinning around like a top. Whatever held it to the paravane was worn through and I saw it drift clear. I glanced at my watch. We were due to start mining in two minutes. I shouted the necessary orders and then, and then only, remembered the fire.

The smoke had stopped. I could not leave the bridge so I sent my orderly below to find out what had happened. He came back to report that the fire was out. Five of our mess cooks had been peeling potatoes in the galley when they saw the smoke and flames rising from the mines stored nearby. Calmly equipping themselves with small extinguishers they crawled through and over tons of high explosives, put out the fire and then crawling back continued peeling their potatoes. Afterward, they were astonished when I recommended them for the Navy Cross.

Our adventures that memorable day were not yet over. Toward the end of the planting it became very dark and misty and we could only see signals with the greatest difficulty. I was anxious to get rid of our remaining mines as word might come at any time to suspend operations and it was considered a disgrace not to have planted them all. Sure enough, the message came down the line, "Get rid of all mines." We did it by shortening the launching interval until we had an empty hold.

It was pitch dark and raining when the word came to form double columns and return to port. I knew we belonged on the right-hand column behind the *Saranac* so I located her and followed her stern light like a bloodhound. All around us we could see ships exchanging call letters to find out who was who; it was crucial to maintain your correct place in line, otherwise you might find yourself in the mined area.

About one o'clock it was reported that a piston rod was red-hot, and we would have to stop to let it cool. There we lay while the other ships and the destroyers faded into the darkness ahead, leaving us to whatever fate happened to be abroad that night. There was one relief. When the last mine went overboard nobody bothered particularly about submarines. There is a considerable difference between having a ship sink under you and being blown to atoms. The rod took forty minutes to cool. Then we put on maximum speed and caught up with the squadron by three o'clock. Without wishing to seem sentimental, I sometimes think ships have souls. To hear our crippled engines straining, striving, doing their best to bring us safely in—surely they were something more than mere masses of metal.

When an explosion did occur, there was virtually nothing left of ship or crew. The next day we learned that a British minelayer which had been working with us had blown up, causes unknown. An officer's arm was found a mile from where the explosion took place. That was the only trace of her that remained. For the next week, if a door slammed, even in port, everybody jumped. I noticed a large box that had been left on the forecastle and ordered it taken below. The men lifting it let it drop with a slight thump. In two seconds there were fifty frightened sailors on deck.

Winter was coming and the sun was above the horizon for only six hours out of the twenty-four; from nine in the morning until three in the afternoon. Gales would soon be sweeping the North Sea, making mine laying impossible. We speeded up our work. Then on October 4th we started out on an expedition which very nearly became our last.

We successfully planted our mines and started back, congratulating ourselves on an easy trip. We reached the western entrance of Stronsay Firth at eight o'clock in the morning. Conditions were excellent; the weather was calm, the sky cloudless and brilliantly blue. Just as we arrived at the exit from the pass, with its high jagged cliffs only two hundred yards to leeward, we were struck by the most terrific tempest of wind that I have ever experienced.

The firth formed a regular funnel through which the wind roared like a thousand demons, and it is an actual fact that the men were thrown to the deck by the force of the wind alone. The sea rose in a series of huge combers. Our bridge was forty feet high but the water went over it. I thought we were done for. The destroyers barely missed swamping and were obliged to turn and run with the wind and sea astern to save themselves.

We slowed and tried to force our way against the wind that was blowing us down on the rocks to leeward. I have had years of service in destroyers, the most lively of all ships, but I never felt such pitching and surging; I could not believe our old ferryboat could hold together. In the midst of it a petty officer came to the bridge and shouted in my ear above the howl of the storm, "Captain, do you know our rudder is broken?"

If we could not steer, we were finished. I turned the deck over to Forgus, the executive officer, and ran aft where I saw that one of the two arms of the rudder yoke had broken sharp in two. The only thing left to control the rudder was the other arm which commenced to bend while I was looking at it. We had the most primitive type of steering gear and the only connection between the wheel on the bridge and the rudder was this yoke. If the second arm broke the rudder would be useless and we would be swept down on the rocks. In that tremendous wind and sea the ship would go to pieces in a moment and everyone be lost as the water was icy cold.

For a moment I had the mad idea of trying to repair it underway but the arm continued to bend and a crack appeared on the surface of the metal. I ran to the brige, we gave one prolonged shriek from the siren to warn the other ships that we were falling out of formation, and I put her before the wind heading down to get under the lee of a small island. It was touch and go but we rounded the corner and swung into Deer Sound just as the remaining arm parted.

I let go the anchor but it was a miserable place to lie with the wind howling and shrieking and the sea foaming and splashing around us One of the British destroyers gallantly risking her own chance of survival, ran in to guard us from hostile submarines as we were dead in the water and an utter "sitting duck."

While our very capable engineer, Lieutenant Antrobus, an ex-navy warrant officer, got to work with his men on the rudder we had an exchange of signals with the destroyer that reminded me of the comic strip characters, "Alphonse and Gaston" who were always elaborately polite to each other.

Quinnebaug: "We regret very much having delayed your return to port."

Destroyer: "Please don't mention it. It is a pleasure to be of service."

This when both of us expected to capsize at any moment. Oh well, we would have gone down like gentlemen.

In two hours our engineers had "fished" the broken arms with steel bars and horseshoe clamps which they made and fitted in our coal-bunker machine shop. We weighed anchor and had a terrible time getting it on the billboard. Every time the ship took a surge the anchor crashed into our side until I was sure it would knock a hole in us. Our paravanes, so vitally important to our safety, had both appeared on the same side of the ship with their lines inextricably scrambled. With great difficulty we finally hoisted them on board but as it would have taken several hours to get them in working condition again, we decided to chance the mines and make a run for it. Every moment was valuable as undoubtedly the Germans had picked up our radio signals and submarines would be headed our way.

We set out again into the gale, and I told Antrobus to give her all she had. Incredibly we made two knots more than the ship had done on her trial trip twenty years previously, although the poor old engines sounded as though they were tearing themselves apart. It was frightfully rough at first but, as we drew closer to the coast of Scotland, we found a partial lee.

About five o'clock we had an experience I will never forget. A cloud of smoke appeared which resolved itself into a fleet of twenty little trawlers out hunting subs. Kipling had aptly named them the Elizabethan Navy. They looked like a drove of small obstinate black pigs scudding along under their leg-of-mutton sails, cruising the North Sea in the teeth of the gale and in the face of the German Fleet ready to tackle anything that appeared. What courage and what seamanship! All these sailing ship captains were fishermen, the prototypes of the men who, under Hawkins, Howard, and Sir Francis Drake, drove the Spanish Armada on the rocks. I passed the trawlers close aboard in the heavy seas; their captains, in their high boots, standing firmly planted on the heaving decks, their pipes gripped between their teeth and, as we came abeam of them, I saluted and the Elizabethan Navy waved back.

Night fell while we were still twenty miles from our base and, as we approached the entrance to the firth we found none of the navigation lights were on; it was black as a pocket. I comforted myself with the thought that, at least, our accompanying destroyer knew her own coast. I looked around for her to guide us in and discovered that she had carefully dropped behind and was following our wake; her captain knew jolly well that we would run aground long before she did.

Abruptly there loomed up ahead of us a dark mass, blacker than the surrounding night. Hoping it was the high cliff at the harbor entrance we signalled: "Are you North Sutor?" A moment's wait. Then out of the darkness a pinpoint of light blinked the reply, "Yes." We were home safe and another link had been forged in the steel chain lying under the sea.

The next morning the commodore said to me: "I certainly was amazed to see you emerge from that whirlpool safely. We all thought you had gone on the rocks."

Our last expedition was on October 26th. For the first two days and nights there was a living gale blowing. It was impossible to lay mines so we ran up and down on the edge of the mine field waiting for the weather to moderate. On the second night our stack guys carried away and with every roll the high stack gave an excellent imitation of the Leaning Tower; we expected it to go overboard at any minute. As the stack shifted its position the siren, which was attached to it, uttered a series of shrieks that were audible for miles and guaranteed to attract every submarine within hearing. We finally got the steam turned off amid, I am sure, the curses of the entire squadron.

The next day it was calm enough to commence mining. In the midst of it a dense fog came down; we couldn't see the ships on either hand though they were only five hundred yards away. The searchlights were turned on and pointed at the bridge of our nearest neighbor in the formation. For a time these wavering dots of light guided us but, as it got thicker, even these disappeared and for two hours we ran through a dense wet blanket launching the mines at the prescribed intervals. One of the mathematical sharps on board reported that had any ship made an error of two degrees in her course and run at two revolutions more speed than her neighbor she would, at the end of the planting, have been directly ahead of said neighbor and dropping mines right in front of her.

That was our last run. The barrage was completed.

Two weeks later the armistice was declared. There was a great to do in the streets of Inverness. Crowds of people, all in civilian clothes, danced and shouted, many of them able-bodied young men. I saw a sergeant of the Gordons stride contemptuously through them. "Hi, Jock!" they shouted. "Haven't you heard? The war is over!" The sergeant retorted, "Which one?" Already he was on his way to another fight in some part of Britain's vast empire.

On the evening prior to our departure for the United States the Lord Mayor gave us a dinner. In his farewell speech, the old gentleman remarked, "After you leave there will be many wet eyes in Inverness." Noting the smiles that ran around the table he hastily added, "Na, na, I dinna mean only the shopkeepers and the lassies."

What had been the result of our summer's work? We had cruised 8,384 miles in submarine- and mine-infested waters without losing a ship. Of the 70,113 mines in the barrage, our ships had laid 57,470— the rest being planted by British mine layers. My ship, the *Quinnebaug*, had laid 6,045 of these and had taken part in ten of the thirteen expeditions. The entire barrage was 230 miles long and 35 miles wide.

How effective was it? Capt. Reginald R. Belknap, the officer in command of the mine-laying squadron, later wrote, "The German losses will probably never be fully known, but according to the German's own report they lost 23 submarines to the barrage. The British Admiralty staff told me that they believe the surrender of the German Fleet and the final armistice were caused largely by the collapse of the submarine warfare, this failure being admitted as soon as the mine barrage was found to be effective."

The moral damage done by the barrage was far greater than the actual number of U-boats it destroyed. Submarines began to disappear with no definite knowledge of what had happened to them. Crews became increasingly reluctant to go to sea. Finally the German Navy mutinied and the whole German war effort fell into ruins.

Captain Belknap generously recommended each of his ten captains for the Distinguished Service Medal, a decoration second only to the Congressional Medal of Honor. We were also recommended for the French Legion of Honor but never received it. Apparently some patriotic politician in Washington thought it was un-American for us to receive a foreign decoration. I have always deeply regretted it. I would have liked to have been a Chevalier like the Chevalier D'Artagnan! Well, it was not to be.

On our way back across the Atlantic we passed through the combined fleets lying in Scapa Flow. The British had arranged a little celebration for us. The crews of all the Allied ships were assembled on the upper decks, the bands played, and the men cheered us as we steamed slowly by. Vice Admiral Sir William Pakenham, incidentally a great grandson of the Pakenham who fell at New Orleans, signalled:

"You take with you the gratitude and admiration of the battle cruisers."

As we reached the surrendered German ships a dead silence fell. These were the ships whose crews had mutinied at the Kiel, refusing to put to sea. Strict orders had been given to maintain absolute silence while passing them; no jeers nor gibes of any sort. The orders were quite unnecessary. The predominant feeling of our crews was curiosity rather than hatred or exultation.

Close aboard, across the narrow space, our men and the Germans looked at each other as I have seen strange children look; wide-eyed, not attempting to hide their mutual interest. The German ships were in shocking condition, officers and men crowded together in nondescript uniforms or no uniforms at all. The decks were filthy and littered with gear. Ever since the mutiny they had been operated by "Committees of Sailors and Workmen." The best officers, those who hadn't been murdered, had refused to remain under such conditions. A number of these committees had stationed themselves on the quarterdecks and waved fraternally to us as we passed. I wonder if these men thought for an instant that our crews would have any sympathy for mutineers and traitors. At Santiago the Spaniards had fought to the death, and their defeat was as glorious as any victory. This was disgusting.

We sailed for New York anticipating a triumphal entry. After all, we had done something entirely unique in the history of warfare. Then our orders were changed. We were switched to Yorktown, Virginia. Running up Chesapeake Bay, we met a sister ship of the Old Dominion Line plodding along on her regular trip north. Despite our military mast and war paint she recognized us as the old *Jefferson*. There was a great scurrying around on her decks and her crew and waiters lined the rails waving their hats, towels, dish rags, and anything they could pick up. She dropped astern and our triumphal entry was over.

On arrival in port, the officers and men were ordered to other duty, the ship returned to her owners, and five days later I sailed for France to help bring home the Army. The Mine Force had ceased to exist.

CHAPTER TWELVE

Transport Service and Shore Duty (1919–1921)

I never sailed with a pirate crew
From Sombre ports of violet hue
Nor did my heart leap at the smile
Of the Peerless Lady of Lesbos Isle
For I was a man on a fighting ship
That knew the North Sea's mighty grip.

—`L'Envoi

Oh King, should you tire of your damsel fair
Well, here's an address at St. Nazaire.

—Transport Force Poet

ON THE AFTERNOON that the *Quinnebaug* was placed out of commission, I received orders to take command of the *President Grant*, sailing for France at nine o'clock the next morning to serve as a troop transport to bring our soldiers home. There was no time to pack. I left at once with only such clothes as could be stuffed into a suitcase.

I must say that I rather resented these peremptory orders. After several months of arduous and dangerous service I felt that I was entitled to at least a short leave. As it was, I was able to see Polly and little Dan for only a few minutes on the platform of the Broad Street Station in Philadelphia where my train stopped en route for New York. In my honor, Polly had gotten Dan rigged out in a sailor suit made by the famous Philadelphia tailor, Peter Thompson; in fact, these suits were known as "Peter Thompsons." I was not particularly impressed until I heard what the suit cost; I was impressed then. Polly and I scarcely had time for a kiss before I was on my way.

I was lucky enough to have with me my chief yeoman, Weiser, and my steward, Katoo, a highly capable Japanese. Both had been with me in the North Sea, and I cannot say how important it is to have men attached to you who thoroughly understand their duties and are efficient. Katoo knew exactly how I wanted things done, what my likes and dislikes were, and having him with me was the difference between constantly nagging irritations and blissful rest.

The *Grant* was lying at the Hoboken Dock. She was the second biggest ship afloat and had formerly belonged to the North German Lloyd Company. I was prepared to see a big ship but nothing like the reality. She was 650 feet long and displaced 35,000 tons. For some mysterious reason, one of her boilers had been removed which meant her best speed was about eleven knots and so it would take her twelve days to cross the ocean under ideal conditions. She had a troop carrying capacity of five thousand, the men to sleep in temporary bunks three deep. So in addition to the regular nautical problems of handling such a floating behemoth, I would also be acting as mayor of a small town with all the administrative problems that entailed; duties about which I knew absolutely nothing. As many of the passengers would be women, this greatly complicated problems.

I wasn't long in finding out some of the difficulties in handling a floating city. At nine o'clock the next morning all lines were cast off, a prolonged blast given on the big whistle and the engine room indicators swung to "Full Speed Astern." On the bridge I watched a range ashore to note the first indication of a backward movement of the ship. Nothing happened. Had the engines failed to function? No, when I called the engine room I was told that they were working perfectly. One minute passed. Two minutes passed. Then three minutes. Still we were dead in the water. Something was obviously very wrong. At last after six minutes, I saw that the ship was beginning to move slowly, almost imperceptibly, astern. Her bulk was so great it required that length of time for her to get underway. I wondered how long it would take her to heave to in an emergency but I soon realized that I wouldn't have to worry about that. Every vessel we encountered as we headed downstream fled from before us. As we couldn't keep out of anybody else's way, the world at large had better keep out of ours.

The next morning I began to familiarize myself with the enormous craft. She was so large that it was impossible to inspect everything on the same day so I organized several inspections spaced over a week. Some statistics might be of interest as few people realize how incredibly complicated the organization of these vast liners is:

In addition to the 5,000 men we would carry on each voyage, our crew consisted of 800 men and 50 officers. There were also 6 doctors, 60 nurses, and 2 dentists each with 4 assistants.

12 chaplains, including Catholic, Protestant, and rabbis.

5,000 loaves of bread had to baked daily and we manufactured a ton of ice every hour.

8 moving picture theaters gave 4 shows a day.

The troops purchased $30,000 worth of candy each day.

We maintained wholesale butcher shops where live animals were kept to be slaughtered.

There was a diet kitchen for the wounded where 125 meals were prepared at a time.

There was an enormous machine shop and also a printing shop where we published our own daily newspaper.

There was a hospital that comprised the whole after part of the upper deck. In it were several large wards, including one for "shell shock" and other mental cases, many of whom had to be kept under restraint. This section was barred with strong iron wire and the door was invariably kept locked.

On the good side, when we encountered some rough weather we found that the *Grant*, owing to her great size and slow speed, was as steady as solid ground. Apart from an almost imperceptible pitch there was no movement; she didn't roll a bit. Seasickness would not be one of our problems.

Katoo quickly made my quarters comfortable. He ripped out the narrow and uncomfortable bunk and stole one of the beds from the "General's Quarters" reserved for top brass passengers. So I was able to get a good night's rest when my duties did not require my presence on the bridge.

I had thought ferrying troops across the Atlantic in time of peace would be a dull, routine job. I was soon to find out differently. Our port of call in France was Brest on the coast of Brittany. It is an awkward place to approach in a fog and as summer advanced there always seemed to be a fog. Fortunately there is a big lighthouse, Ushant, outside of Brest which we were able to pick up before entering the harbor. This was crucial because soundings were of little use in determining one's position as the deep water extended almost to the cliffs; this made it impossible to anchor and, to make conditions still more unpleasant, very strong currents swept down the coast. I once read an article by an aviation enthusiast who wrote, "On a ship, if you are uncertain of your position, all you have to do is stop the engines and remain in the same position." If that gentleman thought that a ship remains in the same position after her engines have stopped, he didn't know much about ships. The moment a ship loses steerage way she commences drifting and your navigation data becomes useless.

Brest is a little Breton fishing village with a number of towers and other fortifications built by the Romans. There wasn't much to do there but on each of our visits I arranged matters with our engineer officer so that "necessary repairs" to the machinery would keep us in port long enough to give everybody a chance to stretch his legs ashore before starting the long twelve day trip back.

To my great relief, the troops we took on board behaved well, which was rather surprising as they all knew that they were to be

demobilized as soon as they reached port and so their officers had little
control over them. Also, many units came on board under the command of strange officers who didn't even belong to the same arm of the
service; aviators commanding infantry companies and so on. We naval
officers were not supposed to give any orders to the Army men but it
occasionally became necessary to do so. The soldiers could have told
us to go to hell, but they always obeyed promptly and cheerfully.

There were, however, two classes of passengers who did frequently cause us a lot of trouble. These were casual officers of high
rank and women.

The "casual" officers, not having any command, had nothing to
keep them occupied and some of them expected a lot of attention and
special privileges. We were simply not equipped to cater to their
demands. The women caused constant problems. Let me hasten to say
that I do not take a superior attitude about women. There were
a number of Army nurses who belonged to the regular complement
of the *Grant*, and I remember them with the greatest admiration
and respect. They were often more military and efficient than the
men. There was no monkey business about them even though they
were all young girls and most of them quite attractive. The women
who tended to cause trouble were the welfare workers, entertainers,
YWCA's and others who had gone to France to "dance with the
soldiers and show them how to amuse themselves in Paris." As if
anyone needs to be shown how to amuse himself in Paris!

We were not a passenger liner and when women are quartered on
a man-of-war the situation is difficult. Many of the ladies were of high
rank and, like the casual generals, demanded lots of attention. Others
were young and pretty and caused another and still more potent type
of trouble. In addition, there were the war brides: French, English,
and in one case, German.

The war brides seemed to fight constantly. The English women
wanted the ports open, the French wanted them closed. Also, they
didn't like each other anyway. As for the poor lone German girl,
surrounded by enemies, she literally had to fight her way across the
Atlantic.

In a number of instances the soldier husbands of these girls were
on board. The brides were "cabin passengers" while the husbands
were quartered with the troops, an unpleasant arrangement but one
rendered necessary by the vast number of people on board.

I recall one especially potentially unpleasant situation. The weather being clear and no ships in sight, I took the evening off and went to the main salon to see a motion picture. During the intermission, Courts, the executive officer, said to me, "Captain, would you like to see an extraordinarily pretty girl?" I naturally said Yes and he indicated a young lady sitting in the gallery surrounded by a group of young officers. She was pretty all right and it was only too obvious that the officers recognized it. They could hardly keep their hands off her; in fact, several didn't try.

I asked Courts, "Has that girl a husband?" He replied, "Yes, her husband is an enlisted man with the troops on board."

I foresaw trouble and I was right. The next morning the unhappy young husband presented himself at "Mast" with a complaint. The officers were being too familiar with his wife. The poor fellow had evidently been "joshed" by his comrades. I didn't know what to do. I sympathized with the man yet I had no jurisdiction over Army officers. The perfect solution would have been for the young lady herself to have told her admirers to get lost, but she was obviously enjoying the attention she was receiving and if her husband had no influence over her, neither would I. I was especially worried that the husband, in a fit of jealousy, would take a swing at one of his wife's followers in which case he would have been guilty of striking a superior officer which, technically at least, is a capital offense. There was no way of putting her and her husband together in a separate cabin. He was bunking with the troops and she with a number of other women.

After some thought, I called the officers together and explained the situation to them. "I can't order you to let this woman alone," I told them. "But in forcing your attentions on her which her husband cannot resist, you are abusing your rank. I hope you will behave like gentlemen."

I am glad to say they did and left the lady to her own devices for the rest of the voyage.

We had another crisis involving a lady, but it was more comic than tragic although the woman involved was prepared to have my head. She was an elderly maiden lady and what she was doing in France I can't imagine. However, she seemed to be someone of importance, at least she obviously so regarded herself, and was given a comfortable deck cabin. Trouble developed the first night at sea. A number of soldiers seated themselves on the deck just outside her open port and, unaware that they were overheard, proceeded to recount their amorous experiences in Paris. Finally the lady could stand no more. Sticking her head out the port, she screamed, "YOU NASTY THINGS! In the morning I will report you to the captain and see that you are all severely punished!" A deep voice answered, "Pull in your ears, we're coming to a tunnel!"

Sure enough, in the morning she appeared at "Mast" shaking with fury and demanded that I avenge her on the miscreants who had not only offended her virgin ears but then told her to pull them in. "And you'd better do it too," she warned. "For I have powerful friends in Congress."

I asked the lady if she could identify the culprits. She assured me that she had no idea who they were; it was up to me to find them. I pointed out that unfortunately our passenger list did not include Holmes, Lecoq, or Dupin. She replied that she had never heard of any of these gentlemen and what did they have to do with the matter anyhow? Assuming my most judicial aspect, I promised her I would leave no stone unturned in tracking down the villains. At intervals for the rest of the trip she kept coming to me demanding to know if I had found the transgressors and was going to have them hung at the signal yardarm. Each time I assured her that I was closing in on them. Unfortunately the scoundrels remained anonymous. However, I am sure they all came to a bad end long ago.

Another situation that looked potentially sticky concerned an Army nurse. Nurses ranked with enlisted men but this nurse was given a room by herself and a "Mex" major found out about it. By a "Mex" major I mean that he wasn't a regular major; he had that rank only temporarily. The major was sharing a room with another officer but now he "pulled rank" and demanded that he be given the nurse's room.

I asked him, "What do you expect us to do with her?"

The major retorted, "Put her in the bunk house with the rest of the enlisted men."

That would have made for an interesting voyage all right. Ridiculous as it was, the major was technically right. He was entitled to better quarters than an enlisted "man." I asked the other officers at mess if they had any suggestions but except for suggesting that the nurse and the major get married or we throw the major overboard, they could think of nothing. I had just about decided to tell the major his demand was impossible and let him report me to the War Department (as he was threatening to do) when the medical officer asked to see me.

"Captain, I have just examined the nurse and she is very ill. So ill that she can't possibly be moved," he told me with a straight face.

We shook hands and I relayed his message to the furious major. The day before we arrived at New York, we gave a dance. I was especially struck by one lively young thing who was doing the Charleston, the Bunny Hug, and the Shanghai Gesture to great applause except on the part of the major who was glowering at her.

"Who's that woman?" I asked the medical officer who happened to be standing near.

"That's the nurse," he explained. "Just this morning she was at death's door. Most remarkable recovery I've ever seen."

Do you wonder I preferred having a bachelor ship?

Admittedly not all our unusual characters were women. One of my orderlies was a Texas cowboy and how he ever got into the Navy I can't imagine. He knew as much about nautical matters as I did about running a ranch. Once after having checked the smooth log, I rang for him and said, "Orderly, take this to the Navigator's Office." He took the log book and started off with it. Shortly afterwards he returned, stuck his head in the cabin door and said with a puzzled expression, "Did you say the Alligator's Office?"

A more serious problem was the vast number of ships on the Atlantic that had been built by the Shipping Board. They had been turned out wholesale in the shortest possible time and the result was that they were constantly breaking down and sending out SOS signals. We had to stand by one such ship for several days which, of course, ruined our schedule. This was far more serious than it sounds. We were supposed to make the round trip without taking on additional fuel and frequently had just enough to get back to New York. If we continued answering SOS calls we might have to send out one ourselves. So when we cleared Brest and began hearing SOS signals we always waited a few minutes before answering, hoping somebody else was closer to the broken down ship.

A nuisance—and on one occasion more than a nuisance—in Brest was that we were required to take on a French pilot before entering the harbor. We soon found these men weren't pilots at all but local fishermen. In other words, it was a racket whereby we were forced to pay for the privilege of returning our soldiers to the United States.

Ignorant as these men were, it is difficult to ignore the suggestions of a pilot who supposedly knows his home waters better than you do.

One evening we were entering Brest Harbor at the time President Wilson was in Paris attending the Peace Conference. His ship, the *George Washington*, was in Brest and just ahead of her was the great liner the *Leviathan*, moored to a buoy. The tide was flooding strongly, carrying us in with it. I felt that we were going in too fast and spoke to the pilot about it; he intimated that he knew what he was about and I, weakly, hesitated before interfering with him. Then, before we realized it, we found ourselves broadside to the bow of the *Leviathan* and rapidly drifting down on her. I shoved the pilot out of the way, put the wheel hard-a-starboard, rang up emergency speed on the starboard engine and backed full speed on the port engine. Simultaneously I heard Lieutenant Pearson on duty amidships sing out, "Stand clear of the port side!" There was a terrific crash as we slid past the *Leviathan*. We hadn't hit her but we did hit her buoy. As soon as we had room for swinging we let go an anchor. The pilot, with a series of shrugs, disclaimed all responsibility.

We waited anxiously for the sun to come up so we could see what damage had been done. As soon as there was light, we levelled our glasses on the bows of the *Leviathan*. Everything seemed to be all right and her anchor chain, securing her to the buoy, was intact. Then, getting a shore range behind her, we saw that both she and the buoy were slowly drifting astern and coming down on the *George Washington*. We commenced signalling frantically and it seemed an age before the *Leviathan* answered. We signalled, "Look at your buoy." Somebody ran up on their forecastle, saw that the mooring chain was intact, and signalled back, "Everything O.K." We signalled again, "You are adrift." Finally they woke up to the fact that they were coming down on the *George Washington* and their buoy was adrift. They let go an anchor and checked her drift but a cargo barge alongside the *Washington* was smashed.

Thereafter no French pilot ever came on board my ship. I paid the pilotage fees—I was forced to—and found that that was all they wanted.

All told we brought home 50,000 American soldiers without the loss of a life. There were nearly 6,000 people on board during the western passage and, while we had a lot of boats, life rafts, and so on, we didn't have nearly enough to accommodate everybody. Besides, these people were not seamen, many of them had never seen the ocean before being inducted into the Army (like one of Roosevelt's Rough Riders who while en route to Cuba, lost his hat overboard and exclaimed, "Ma hat jest blew into the creek!") and I had no idea how they would behave in an emergency at sea. I was constantly haunted by the possibility of a bad accident with heavy loss of life. One of my worst moments occurred off Fire Island during a dense fog with the forecastle invisible from the bridge and whistles blowing all around us. A collision seemed inevitable and I was waiting for the shock when I got the following message from New York, "Understand you have the 29th New York Division on board. Be sure to arrive promptly on time as a great celebration has been prepared." That was one order I did not obey.

The *Grant* was put out of commission in 1921, and I was assigned to shore duty in New York City. I was designated, "Legal Officer, Headquarters Third Naval District." I knew nothing of law and frankly cared less, but I was glad of the opportunity to be reunited with my wife and children for I now had a little daughter. We took an apartment on Park Avenue and I entered into my new duties. It is said that a naval officer must be prepared to do anything, anywhere and at any time, so I might as well be a lawyer and a judge as anything else.

My offices were in the old ferry building at South and Whitehall streets, extending out over the water and commanding a fine view of New York Harbor. I had been on several court martials but, as I soon learned, civilian courts are something else again. Lawyers and judges seem to regard naval officers who are involved in legal work as their natural enemies. My first experience with this was when I was called to appear as a witness for a young sailor who had become involved in some trouble. Dumas speaks of "lawyers who delight in humiliating soldiers" and I found myself, in full uniform with my combat ribbons, being screamed at by a civilian judge while a crowd of court hangers-on listened with grinning faces. I had to stand there and take his abuse. To have done anything else would have hurt the unfortunate young sailor who had trusted me.

To one used to the cut-and-dried, undramatic methods of a military court, the conduct of civilian lawyers came as a surprise. I remember one case we investigated which involved pilfering in a big government establishment employing hundreds of civilians. One of the accused, represented by a "real lawyer," not a naval officer, was a middle-aged woman with a face that looked as though it had worn out five bodies and a jaw like the ram on a Roman trireme. Her lawyer rose to address the court. Taking out his handkerchief, he buried his face in it. Then, overcoming his emotions, he said in a low, moaning voice, "Look, gentlemen, at this sweet-faced young girl!" For a moment we thought he was trying to "run" us. Then we realized this was merely his regular technique.

We were not brought into contact with many lawyers as most of our cases involved naval personnel only, and Navy men almost always depend on their officers to see that they have a square deal. However, we did learn to guard against a certain type of lawyer who, by making objections, taking exceptions, and delaying the proceedings at every point, attempts to irritate the court until it commits some error in the proceedings. Then the entire case has to be thrown out when it arrives at the JAG Office in Washington, the court is reprimanded, and the culprit goes free.

Occasionally, possibly by mistake, the Naval Department behaves like a human being. A member of the crew of a battleship wrote the department a letter in which he said, "this ship is a madhouse and our captain a Dutch son-of-a-bitch." The letter was forwarded to us with the notation, "You need only investigate the first charge."

We heard of another case, although I cannot vouch for it, where a man was tried for calling the executive officer of his ship "An old Portugee son-of-a-bitch." The court found the specifications "Proved except the word 'Portugee' for which the court substitutes the word 'Greek!' "

Even regular seamen did not always show us the respect due to our exalted rank and judicial presence. We were trying a very bibulous Irish sailor and he was asked the standard question, "Do you object to being tried by any member here present?" The Irishman replied frankly, "I object to the whole lot of yez." His objection was overruled.

Even though my opinions of the New York judges and lawyers were in general not of the highest, I did have a greatly increased admiration for the Police Department, especially the uniformed men. My duties naturally brought me in frequent contact with them and they impressed me as doing a difficult job extremely well. I acquired several friends among the force and this later turned out fortunate for a young Puerto Rican who spoke no English and had been arrested for "making indecent advances" to a young woman in a motion picture theater. In such cases, the word of the woman is usually automatically accepted and the man, helpless, alone in a strange land and unable to speak the language, was thrown into prison. Pictures of both the man and the woman happened to cross my table and I didn't think the frightened young fellow looked like the type that paws strange women. I showed the pictures to my assistant Haughey, who was a born and bred New Yorker and had worked in a number of government jobs over the years. He took one look at the woman's picture and said, "Why, Captain, I know her. She used to have a job here and accused everybody in the district, from the commandant to the office cat, of trying to seduce her." The affair wasn't our business but we looked up the lady's case history and took it down to Police Headquarters. After examining it, they released the young Puerto Rican in our custody. We had all we could do to keep him from kissing us.

I have said that naval personnel usually depended on their officers for help rather than the civilian authorities. One case did come up before our board when I, at least, was prepared to be much harder on the transgressors than the civilians. The Navy was running a line of transports to the West Indies, and we discovered, to our incredulous amazement, that certain "Mex" officers on these ships were smuggling in liquor, not to drink, not to give to their friends, but to sell. This was during Prohibition and large sums could be made in this way.

To a man with my silly old-fashioned ideas and service background this was not merely serious, it was appalling. And it was being done by men wearing the same uniform I did; the uniform that I had been obliged to serve four years and pass countless exams before I earned the right to wear.

The local prohibition agent wasn't a bad fellow. He called at my office and said, "Now, Captain, I don't want to be too hard on you Navy fellows." In other words he was putting me in the same category as the whisky smugglers. I bowed ironically and thanked him for his forbearance but the irony was lost on him. I regret to say that when we staged a surprise inspection of the ships, the "officers" involved had evidently been tipped off ahead of time because we found only a few bottles which they had put in a supposedly secure place. Even so, we stopped the traffic and as for the men involved, well, it was with considerable satisfaction that we "wound up their little ball of yarn."

One constant source of trouble we had was with "land sharks" who would sell sailors some expensive article on the "installment plan." Many enlisted men are just kids and are easily victimized. I cannot believe that any honest merchant would persuade a twenty-year-old boy to buy a diamond ring and obligate him to pay heavy installments out of his pay for an indefinite number of years in the future. Once the sailor was at sea, the "land shark" no longer had any hold on him so the "shark" would then demand that we withhold the sum he claimed was owing him from the seaman's pay. When we received such a communication we would reply, "This office is not a collection agency." We had to do this so often that we began to get letters starting out, "We KNOW you are not a collection agency but . . . ." I am afraid that I never had any sympathy with these people.

Part of our duties was to attend official parties. Most of these were bores but I remember one which was delightful. Ancient Rome could have done no more. On arrival we were ushered into a private suite where there was an enormous punch bowl and half a dozen private bars, all this during Prohibition. The banquet hall featured a long table for the Brass Hats with other tables perpendicular to it. During a long and very elaborate dinner, a different wine was served with each course, stars from the various Broadway shows did their skits, and a particularly charming ballet of pretty girls danced up and down between the tables.

The next morning I went into the commandant's office with some papers and he asked me, "Did you go to that affair last night?" I replied, "Yes, sir" and was about to add, "Wasn't it GREAT?" when the commandant continued, "Simply disgusting! A lot of drunken men and those horrible naked women dancing around between the tables!" I hurriedly swallowed my words and erasing the cheerful expression from my face muttered, "Horrible! Horrible!"

This was the height of the pacifist craze. The League of Nations was to make wars impossible. All armed forces would be demolished. The resulting saving in taxes would be used to benefit the poor and needy. The climax of this business was the Disarmament Conference that was held in Washington. The foreign delegates to the conference landed in New York and somebody in Washington, presumably with a sardonic sense of humor, arranged for the naval officers stationed in the city to escort them to their hotels. It reminded me of the old nursery rhyme, "Dilly, Dilly, come and be killed."

My group of delegates came from a certain European country, a very little one, that had no navy. They were insulted at being met by a naval officer in uniform (we were ordered to wear our uniforms). The chief of the delegation, a little fat man, informed me that he was "a man of peace" and I "no better than a hired assassin." I called a taxi to take them to their hotel and the chief delegate got into a terrific row with the taxi driver over where he was to put his suitcase. As a dove of peace he was the most bellicose person I've ever met.

Great capital was made of the fact that this conference was to be run by civilians only; we Navy men were ordered to be present but were to keep quiet. As we had no power I don't know what good it did to force us to be present except to humiliate us. The United States delegation to the conference was indeed composed entirely of civilians but this was hardly true of the other groups. I saw the Japanese delegation arrive and instantly recognized an admiral I had met in Tokyo, although he was in civilian clothes with an unfamiliar bowler hat perched on his bullet head. The delegation of another country arrived. They also were in civilian clothes but I immediately recognized one of them; he had been a military attaché with our Army during the Santiago Campaign. Meanwhile crowds were cheering these people, eager to put the fate of the United States in their hands.

Everywhere in the city was the same anti-militaristic attitude. Even walking in the streets, I was met by scowls and often muttered imprecations. This happened to all men in uniform. It seemed to me that they deserved better of their fellow countrymen after risking their lives for them. I am sure a number of these "pacifists" would have attacked me if they dared. Many of them carried foreign language newspapers and had clearly come to the United States only recently to escape the crushing conditions in their homelands. Obviously they felt that their first duty was to change matters in the nation that had given them shelter.

One evening, as representative of the Navy, I was required to attend—in full uniform—a large, formal dinner given by the English Speaking Union. The speaker was Mr. Arthur Balfour, the famous British statesman. In his speech he assured us that the United States did not need a Navy; we could depend on England to protect us. His remarks about our Navy were so abusive that people turned to glare at me. I felt that I should have vanished like the devil in a pantomime through a trapdoor but unfortunately none had been provided. I thought how different our reception had been in Great Britain a few years before. Of course, at that time they needed us.

At the end of his speech, the audience gave him an ovation. A number of them, both men and women, rushed up and actually kissed his hand. I watched his aides during this performance. They were barely managing to keep their faces straight.

A high dignitary of our own Episcopal Church turned to me and said enthusiastically, "A wonderful speech, was it not?" I began to wonder whether I was crazy or whether everyone else was. How that bishop could possibly imagine that an American naval officer would approve of abolishing the Navy and turning over the defenses of our country to a foreign power.

In Washington at the conference we agreed not to fortify our island possessions in the Pacific. The Japanese agreed to the same thing and of course went ahead and did it anyhow. Other nations gave similar assurances and likewise broke them. Meanwhile we had either sunk or dismantled the ships that would have made us the first naval power in the world.

Perhaps I was unduly embittered by the Disarmament Conference, but it seemed to me that I accomplished very little by my year's shore duty in New York. However, shortly before I was detached and given sea duty again, I received the following letter from the Navy Department:

From: The Chief of Naval Operations
To: Commandant, Third Naval District.
Subject: Activities of Legal Department.

1. The following comments of the Judge Advocate General is quoted for the Commandant's information.

"The work done by the legal department of the Third Naval District had been of invaluable assistance to this office and it is suggested that an organization in other Naval Districts, patterned on the Third, be established."

Well, I suppose that I did do something useful.

Although I was glad to have been able to spend this time with my family, I was eager to get to sea again and see new lands. Polly, I knew, was equally eager to return to her familiar life in Philadelphia, and young Dan, who had developed a curious passion for animals, hated New York and could not wait to get back to The Hedges and his pets. So everyone was delighted when my orders came through to take command of a Destroyer Squadron bound for a two-year cruise in the Levant. This was to turn out to be the most interesting and varied duty I ever had.

CHAPTER THIRTEEN

The Levant
(1922–1924)

Awake! for Morning in the Bowl of Night
Has flung the Stone that puts the Stars to Flight:
And Lo! the Hunter of the East has caught
The Sultan's Turret in a Noose of Light.

—The Rubaiyat of Omar Khayyam

THE READER who has stayed with me thus far will know that I have always enjoyed seeing exotic lands and meeting interesting people. The Levant, my last foreign tour of duty, was by far the most picturesque and unusual place I have ever seen—not excepting the Orient.

I took command of the Destroyer Squadron's "mother ship," USS *Denebola*, in June 1922. We had six destroyers already in the Levant and I was to bring twenty more with me for Turkey and Greece were at war and it was vital that the passage to the Black Sea be kept open. Already half a dozen European nations were rushing warships to the trouble spots.

I have never had the deep attachment for any ship, or any place, that I developed for the *Denebola*. When she was put out of commission some years later, I paid a special trip to New York to say goodbye to the old lady. It nearly made me weep to see her rusty hull, dirty decks, and broken ports. During the years when I was in command of her, she was kept up like a gentleman's yacht and you could have eaten your meals off her deck. That she should have come down in the world like that! Ah well, perhaps it's as well we cannot see into the future.

First, let me fill you in with some background of the Middle East of the time. Turkey had been an ally, albeit a rather reluctant one, of Germany in the First World War. When Germany was defeated, it was natural to assume that Turkey also was defeated especially as Constantinople (we hadn't learned to call it Istanbul in those days) was occupied by the troops of Britain, France, and Italy.

However, certain of the Turks refused to admit defeat. Instead of remaining in Constantinople under the supervision of the Allied troops they took to what, in the Philippines, we used to call the "bosque," that is to say the wild country in Asia Minor and here more and more of these irreconcilables began to gather. They included discharged soldiers whose occupation was gone, farmers driven from their farms, police whose duties had been taken over by the Allies, tramps, criminals of varying degrees of criminality and a hodgepodge of others who, for one reason or another, had no intention of submitting to the rule of the Western nations.

This ragtag and bobtail array needed someone to weld it into an effective fighting unit and to inspire it with the patriotism necessary to oppose the foreign soldiery then occupying their country. They found that someone in a truly great man, Mustapha Kemal. Kemal has always reminded me of George Washington. Some of my Constantinople friends have told me that he had certain private habits that were not a bit like Washington but no matter. In his official life he most certainly was "first in war and first in peace."

By 1922, the Allied nations were fed up with war. They didn't want to send an expeditionary force into the hills of Asia Minor against an array of brigands who would scatter at the first impact and then harry the Allied troops all the way back to the shores of the Bosphorus leaving the situation exactly as it had been before the expedition started. Still, the Allies had a partner ready and, presumably, able to take on the job . . . Greece. Over the centuries Greece had suffered greatly from Turkey and now was the chance to take her revenge. A Greek army was landed in Asia Minor under the guns of an Allied fleet and then left to its own devices. Kemal promptly defeated the Greeks and then drove them across country to the Mediterranean port of Smyrna. In the course of these operations a large part of Smyrna was destroyed by fire. The Greeks said that the "Unspeakable Turks" had done it. The Turks retorted, "Why should we have burned a city that already was in our possession?" I was inclined to agree with the Unspeakables.

The first thing the Greek Army did on returning home was to escort their cabinet to an open place and shoot them. When I was in Athens, about a year after the event, I discussed this affair with a Greek Army officer and intimated that the punishment was, perhaps, a bit drastic. He replied, "Those men betrayed their country; due to them, Greece has suffered a national humiliation and the bones of thousands of our young men are bleaching on the hills of Anatolia. In England or America they would have gotten away with it; we made up our minds not to let them get away with it here. If every group of politicians who embark on a war that plainly cannot be won was shot instead of the soldiers who had to fight it, there would be fewer senseless wars." Perhaps he had a point.

This campaign resulted in the deaths of thousands, the paying back of countless old scores, the burning of Smyrna and the advance of the victorious Turkish Army (it had become an army) to the shore of the Dardanelles. It was feared that Russia—which had recently become a communist nation with the murder of the Tzar and killing or exiling of the old nobility—might move in and occupy the straits. We were involved because American business interests were imperiled and also the life of every American in that part of the world.

While in New York I looked over the length of time at sea of the captains of the various units and noticed that the skipper of the *Denebola,* my old classmate Vic Tomb, was due for shore duty. I immediately got on the telephone and in a few hours received telegraphic orders to report on the *Denebola* as his relief. I was given twenty-four hours leeway in which to start but left in five minutes after receiving my orders, afraid the department might change its collective mind.

The *Denebola* was an old ship and presented problems. As a tender, she had been loaded with auxiliaries and these took a lot of steam to run. When these auxiliaries were turned on, there wasn't enough steam to run the engines so like the little tug whose engine stopped every time she blew her whistle, we were dead in the water. I solved that by disconnecting as many of the auxiliaries as possible and leaving them disconnected. Even so, she couldn't make more than eight knots but, as our engineer force gained experience, we were able to bring it up to ten. This proved to be important when we had to fight the fierce current in the Bosphorus.

We had movies every night in the big machine shop and they were very good, previews most of them. I remember that some of them were Douglas Fairbanks in *Robin Hood*, the Gish sisters in *Orphans of the Storm, Blood and Sand* with Rudolph Valentino and *The Prisoner of Zenda* with Alice Terry and Lewis Stone. The ship turned out to be very comfortable in a seaway; she had an easy roll and pitch. There was some trouble with the drinking water caused by rust in the tanks but the medico devised a filter and, while the water tasted a little like the medical department smells, it became crystal clear and presumably healthful.

On November 12th we raised the Azore Islands. By noon we had dropped the islands astern and had started our great circle to Cape St. Vincent Light on the southern end of Portugal. From there we took our departure for the final leg to Gibraltar. Here I made a formal call at the palace and met some old friends I had known long ago in London. I remember one was Sir Walter Cowan, Bart., who had a long string of letters after his name. Cowan was on Togo's flagship as a naval observer at Tsushima and a man was killed alongside of him and his white uniform covered with blood. Cowan rushed below and the Japs thought he wouldn't appear again but he reappeared in a clean white suit and continued making notes of the battle.

We sailed for Constantinople the next morning. Coasting along Africa we had a fine view of Algiers and great mountain ranges fading off into the distance. At Gibraltar, I had been warned that a British Navy oil tanker had been fired on by a French battery in the Dardanelles two weeks before. She had attempted to pass through at night and they thought she was Turkish. To guard against misunderstandings, I determined to arrive at the Dardanelles in full daylight, to have the men dressed in their best uniforms and also to have our largest American flag flying at the gaff and our longest pennant, the universal sign of a naval vessel, at the truck. Then came a rumor that the Turks had seized the Dardanelles and were not permitting any foreign vessels to pass. Just in case this was so, I arranged to have two chests filled with rifles and small arm ammunition located conveniently and inconspicuously on deck and to mount our machine guns (we didn't have any other guns) with some old canvas thrown over them and the gun crews lounging casually in the vicinity. Also, most important of all, a fire hose was laid out in each gangway and maximum pressure to be kept on the fire main. If any attempts were made to board us, the boarders would receive a bath. I didn't intend to look for trouble but it might have been ugly if a body of armed men got on our decks.

As we entered the straits, we saw on our right the wrecks of two French cruisers, sunk by the Turks, and a great collection of old ruins along the shore. Among them, perched on top of a hill, was the fort of an old Turkish corsair. From this vantage point he could see approaching ships a long distance away and decide which ones he wanted to plunder. It was hard to believe that here in the twentieth century we were making preparations to repel boarders much as other vessels had done since time out of mind.

As we approached the narrows it began to snow; horizontal snow with a gale of wind behind it. At the Chanack, which is the narrowest part and where there is a sharp turn, we could see a lot of British battleships and cruisers and also a crowd of merchant ships. No sign of the French battery that had supposedly fired on the British oil tanker and no Turkish warships. Still, we went very slowly expecting to be intercepted at any moment but nobody paid the slightest attention to us, so I rang up full speed and kept on.

Just beyond the Chanack is the famous Hellespont. I found it especially interesting because I am fond of swimming and according to legend, Leander, who lived on the Asian side of the strait, used to swim it nightly in order to be with his sweetheart, Hero, a priestess of Venus who lived on the European side in the town of Sestos. One night there was a storm and Leander drowned. Hero, in despair, killed herself. According to Bulfinch's *Mythology* Leander's feat was long regarded as fabulous as swimming the strait was considered impossible because of the rip current running from the Sea of Marmora into the archipelago, but in 1818 Lord Byron made the same swim, thus proving he was a crack athlete as well as a great poet and lover. Possibly two or three other men have made the swim but, as far as I knew, no American had even attempted it. Studying the strait from the bridge of the *Denebola* and watching the set of the current, an idea popped into my mind which had its fruition a year later.

We passed the town of Gallipoli, scene of the grisly British disaster in the First World War when they had tried to take the place with landing parties but were disastrously defeated by the Turks. The snow kept getting heavier and it was hard to see anything. We finally emerged into the Sea of Marmora and the weather got better; it still snowed but we could see. In about an hour we sighted one of our six destroyers. It was the *Bainbridge*. We exchanged greetings by signal.

When it got dark our troubles began. For some reason, few of the navigation lights listed on our chart were burning. About two in the morning, I sighted ahead a glow of lights that looked like Broadway on a Saturday night. My navigator said, "According to the chart, sir, that's not Constantinople. It's a town this side of it." I couldn't believe that any small town would be so brilliantly illuminated. I went to the starboard wing of the bridge to see better and there, looming close aboard, were three dark blotches, a little darker than the night. The young officer of the watch told me, "Those are three ships anchored without lights, sir." While he was still talking I stopped the engines and rang full speed astern just in time to avoid the objects whatever they were. We took a sounding and the officer of the watch reported, "Twenty fathoms. You see, I was right, sir. We're well within the channel."

"We'll wait here until morning," I told him. "I want to see what those things are by daylight." When the sun rose, we found that we were cozily nestling against three rocky little islands. Beyond them was Constantinople. We made a careful swing at slow speed around the islands and headed for the city.

I mention this matter not to show that I am always right— unfortunately that isn't the case—but to stress how careful the captain of a ship must be never to take unnecessary chances. If anything goes wrong, by Naval Law it is always the captain who is responsible; never a subordinate. There is no "passing the buck." You may not always be right but you're always the captain.

As we approached the city, the rising sun shone full on it. It was the most beautiful sight I have ever seen. Constantinople covers the hills on both sides of the Bosphorus and was a mass of towers, mosques, and minarets, most of it brilliantly colored and all sparkling in the sun. It was like nothing in Europe or America. It was like something out of the Arabian Nights or out of a dream.

As we rounded the Golden Horn, we passed four British battle-ships, a flotilla of destroyers, two French cruisers, a Spanish cruiser and several Italian warships with all of whom we exchanged bugle salutes. We saw the other five of our destroyers at anchor and they began signaling us, "Have you our spare propeller?" and so on. I gave orders not to answer any of them until we were anchored ourselves.

I took good care to anchor next to a British ship. The British have their faults but they are seamen, which is more than I can say for some other European nations. The current running down the Bosphorus from the Black Sea is so swift that ships, except those anchored close inshore, don't swing but they frequently drag their anchors. If anything like this happened, I wanted to be next to a vessel whose crew knew what they were doing.

I shifted into full dress and called on our admiral on the *Pittsburgh*, our flagship. He filled me in on local conditions. Our men were allowed liberty but not in Stamboul, the native quarter, after dark. They were not to leave the city limits. If they did they were liable to be captured and held for ransom by various brigands that infested the suburbs. "A number of men have been murdered in the city," he told me. "Mainly English. The Turks don't like the English. They like Americans but occasionally mistake our men for Britishers which is unfortunate for our men. There are a lot of Russian refugees, many of them aristocrats, in the city who fled the Bolsheviks. Many of the restaurants employ only Russian girls as waitresses. The city is divided into quarters: the British have one quarter; the French another and the Italians a third. They don't like us to trespass on their territories. Watch out at all times for the current; it's like a millrace and even in a small boat you're not always safe."

The next morning I went with my officers to pay an official call at our embassy. We landed at the Dolma Bagtche wharf, a spot that was to become as familiar to us as our own deck, and engaged two fezzed Levantines to drive us to the embassy in a battered Ford. The streets were crowded with every nationality under the sun; Turks, Russians, French, British, Italians, Greeks, and all the Near Eastern peoples. Everyone wore his national costume so it looked like a fancy dress ball. There were trams, on which the women passengers were segregated many of them being veiled. At the embassy we were met by a gorgeous person who we thought was at least a Turkish general but he turned out to be the kavass, or doorman. I had a pleasant talk with the chief of staff and learned that I was to have charge of all repairs to the ships based here.

The next morning a destroyer came alongside for overhaul and her executive officer turned out to be Taylor, who used to be with me at the Third Naval District. He offered to show me around the Stamboul bazaars that afternoon. We got into my gig—being in command of the Destroyer Squadron I was entitled to my own private power boat— and ran down the Bosphorus and across the harbor through masses of anchored shipping to the landing in Stamboul. The bazaars cover several square miles. They are enclosed overhead and have little open shops on both sides of the streets. There were crowds of beggars and street vendors, some of whom were unpleasantly aggressive. There were beautiful Persian shawls, samovars, brass work, and loads of rugs. You had to haggle and I had no idea of the articles' value.

I noticed that all the British we met carried arms but nobody else had weapons. Taylor told me that their general had ordered it since a number of British soldiers had been assassinated in the city. I think the British tend to antagonize many people. They carry themselves with an arrogance that annoys anyone not used to it. Of course, at that time they still "owned half of creation" as Kipling boasted and showed it in their behavior.

Except for China, I have never seen such poverty. Homeless and penniless wanderers crowded the streets, most of them Russian women, poor things. Many were in rags and lay in the gutters prepared to spend the night there. Taylor hailed a coach by shouting "Arabatche!" and we drove to a restaurant named the Muscovite which had two enormous Cossacks as bouncers. The patrons were of every race and nation conceivable, some of them decent enough looking individuals while others seemed to be cutthroats. The waitresses were all refugee Russian girls chosen obviously for their good looks. They were all in black with little white aprons. On demand, they had to dance with any man who took a fancy to them, first rolling up their aprons so they would not show. There was something tragic about it, being obliged to entertain a lot of drunken brutes night after night.

The food was excellent but the only drink was vodka which I have never liked. The headwaiter was a reduced Russian gentleman with a black beard who looked like Rasputin and kept assuring Taylor and me that "we could be as wicked as we liked." After my long voyage over the Atlantic and across the Mediterranean I wasn't up to being very wicked. It got rougher as it got later and a lot of the men, some in uniform, made fools of themselves. I asked Taylor if all the cafés were like this. He said, "No, this is one of the better ones." I left as soon as I could, shouted, "Arabatche!" and told the driver, "Dolma Bagtche." I fell into my gig and nearly embraced the coxswain I was so glad to be there.

I soon found out that in the American colony the women ran everything and no man was supposed to associate with what one lady who took me in charge called "furrinors." I also discovered that seniors were supposed to dance and talk only to the older women; no associating with any of the young girls, Americans or not. I paid no attention to these rules and as a result was heartily disliked by the ladies' contingent. They took a petty, and it seemed to me rather a cruel, revenge by writing letters to Polly saying that I was being unfaithful to her with half the female population of Constan and they also did what they could to hurt me with the admiral, claiming that my immoral conduct was disgracing the United States Navy. The admiral never said anything to me although his manner was rather cool, especially when his wife was present as she was not surprisingly influenced by the American ladies' views.

There was no sultan in Turkey since the last one, with all his lady friends, left for Malta. The highest Turkish official was the Caliph, a sort of Moslem Pope. He was to officiate at a special ceremony at the mosque and we were invited to attend. To my astonishment, I actually had to order the officers on my ship to attend the service. They would rather have attended one of the American women's parties or sit around playing cards. I felt it was a unique opportunity to see something of another civilization, and it turned out that I was quite right.

Friday is the Turkish Sunday. There were three "Sundays" in Constan: Friday for the Moslems, Saturday for the Jews and Sunday for the Christians. We landed from my gig at Stamboul and went to the mosque which was built in 1460. There was a beautiful gateway where the Caliph was to make his entrance and we waited there. There was an enormous crowd almost entirely Turkish, the women all wearing the veil, although I noticed that the veils of the younger, prettier women were transparent.

Presently there was a great clatter of horses and through the arch trotted two hundred Janisseries. They were big, husky men and wore red breeches, hussar jackets, and Astrakhan hats. At the ends of their lances were little red and green pennants. The Caliph was in an open carriage with four horses and outriders in scarlet and gold. We saluted him and he returned the salute, giving an order to one of his aides. This man came to us and said that we were to be given special places in the mosque. The Caliph had evidently recognized us as Americans and Americans were the only foreigners popular in Turkey at the time; we had never fought them.

When in a cloud of dust and glory the Caliph and his Janisseries had passed, the aide conducted us to an open coach which was to take us from the gateway to the mosque proper. Apparently half the population of Constan had decided to attend the ceremony for with a wild whoop billy goat carts, old Fords, camels, water buffalos, and everything that had wheels or legs joined our motor car in a rush for the entrance. Our driver did his best to keep ahead of them, and I swear that at times as we cut around corners all four of our wheels were in the air at the same time. Most of the way a racing dromedary had his head resting on my shoulder while some queer animal in front kept decorating my face with mud as it leapt the puddles with careless grace. We passed some little gray donkeys who promptly had hysterics; one of them jumped over a fruit stall and through a shop window, panniers and all. At the mosque's entrance was a battalion of the Palace Guard in bright scarlet, a battalion of sailors and one of the troops of the line in khaki. In addition, there were three bands and a large number of British, French, Spanish, and Italian officers.

At the mosque, one of the court officers came to greet the foreign contingent and show them to their places. The Europeans treated him with the utmost contempt, why, I have no idea. Perhaps it was with the idea of "keeping him in his place." When he approached me, his face was frozen with anger and he walked stiffly, trying to control himself. After he had spoken to me, I smiled, bowed, and thanked him. He stared at me unbelievingly and then positively beamed and taking my arm, escorted me in as though I were the guest of honor. I can understand why the Turks don't like Europeans; they object to being spoken to as though they were dogs.

When the Caliph entered, his horses were decorated with tiger skins and bright silver mountings. The troops presented arms and the bands played. Meanwhile, the Europeans were talking loudly among themselves, pointed to various individuals and remarking, "Look at that old fool" or "Isn't that a fat one?" If they had behaved this way in a Christian church they would have been immediately put out but the Turks ignored them.

Probably the main reason why the European nations look down on the Turks is because of their chaotic political system. When a sultan dies his son doesn't become sultan but his oldest male relative. It hasn't been unknown for an ambitious man to assist the sultan's demise. The natural result has been that some of the sultans, when they took office, promptly locked up or killed all possible candidates before the candidates could kill them. One of them kept his only brother locked up for thirty years. Polygamy doesn't help matters as each wife is eagerly backing her own children for the throne and as they were locked in a harem and had nothing to do except amuse themselves plotting, they were extremely adept at it.

Later that same day I went to the native quarter to see the howling dervishes. I believe this sect has now been abolished; at least they are not allowed to perform their rites in public. I found them most interesting. About thirty men in all styles of turbans and costumes were seated in a circle moving their bodies back and forth and intoning the ninety-nine known names of Allah (the hundredth name he told to the camel and that is why all camels are so haughty). The dervishs kept on and on and then commenced inhaling and exhaling all together until it sounded like the exhaust from a steam engine. Then they went from chant to chant swaying violently with one hand palm up, to receive blessings and the other hand palm down, to give blessings. They swayed their heads so violently it looked as though their necks were dislocated; it seemed to be a form of self-hypnotism.

A brazier filled with glowing charcoal was brought in and they heated irons in it. The priest stripped the upper part of his body and, after licking a red-hot iron, seared his body with it. I could smell the burning flesh. Then he took a sword and struck himself repeated heavy blows on the head. He placed the point against his stomach and, putting the hilt on the ground, rested the whole weight of his body on it. Afterwards he placed the edge across his middle and the others jumped on it. Lastly, he took a spiked iron ball hanging from a chain and beat himself with it.

A wild-eyed, long-haired creature ran across the room and plunged headlong against the wall shaking the entire building. A sick child was brought in, laid down and the priest walked up and down its body. Finally something happened that I know could not possibly be a fake as it took place not four feet from me. The priest put one of his followers against a wall and thrust a long, thin dagger through both of the man's cheeks and hammered it into the wall. After a while he pulled it out and blew into the man's mouth. At first there was no sign of blood and then I noticed a slight trickle. I think some of the tricks could have been clever sleight of hand but not this. I could have touched the man nailed to the wall and I know well that I wasn't hypnotized.

A few days later I was invited to dinner at the home of a Turkish official who had married an attractive Russian woman. Apparently as a tribute to me, the couple had also invited a number of young American women, all the wives of officers. I was wearing a dinner jacket and the women obviously did not know that I was a captain in the Navy for they commenced discussing their husbands' commanding officers with the greatest of freedom, laughing heartily at those who had paid them any attention and speculating on what they could get for their husbands by encouraging the old fools, at the same time expressing confidence in their ability to "handle them." It reminded me of the lady in *Charlot's Review* who used to sing, "I can't imagine what he wanted—but he didn't get it." Any commanding officer who was fool enough to put himself in the power of that flock of harpies deserved anything he got. Why anybody should bother with this crew in a city teaming with beautiful, intelligent, willing women I can't imagine.

On Christmas, we gave a big party for the refugee orphans, five hundred of them as well as some little Turks. I was somewhat concerned about having the Turkish children attend a Christian festival but no one minded, least of all the children. The *Scorpion*, our "stationaire" had been moored in the Golden Horn for fifteen years and looked more like a yacht than a war vessel; fine rugs, hangings, and so on, covering her, so I turned the details of the party over to her captain and he did a magnificent job. Officers and men all chipped in to buy the presents. The men had just given five hundred dollars to the Red Cross but when asked to help the children they gave a thousand more, money they could have used having a good time ashore.

The children came out in four of our big boats and the men stationed themselves down the gangway ladder and passed them up from hand to hand. Many of the poor little tots had no shoes and nearly all were in rags. I don't think any of them were more than six or seven and there were several babies; one boy carried his baby sister all the afternoon. In addition to the presents, we had a tree beautifully decorated and a dinner.

Probably the toughest member of our crew was the blacksmith, an enormously powerful man with a bad temper and a propensity for drink. The week before he had gotten drunk ashore, knocked down several of the military police, then after being locked up, kicked open the jail door and liberated all the prisoners, civil and military, brought them out to the *Denebola* and presented them to me. During the party he carried one little girl up the ladder who was too small to walk. She was doing her best to be a lady but the excitement proved too much for her and she began to cry. When the blacksmith found out what the trouble was he took her behind the smokestack, took off the offending garment, laid it on the hot metal until it was dry and then pinned it on again. He was under sentence of court martial for his conduct on shore but his case is still "pending."

The next day I dined with the Leavitts; he was American and she a very charming English woman. They lived 'way up the Bosphorus, nearly to the Black Sea. On the way there I saw a lot of Russian refugees being put ashore from a British merchant ship. They were in terrible condition, most of the women so denuded of clothing that they were virtually naked. Some of them had been able to retain only a tiny bit of cloth no bigger than a handkerchief and they used these strips of cloth to cover their faces so no one would know who they were. I stopped to see if we could be of any help but the ship's captain said there was nothing anyone could do. He pointed out a little girl, about ten years old, who had been raped and her right arm pulled out of the socket. I wanted to have her sent to Sick Bay on the *Denebola* but she didn't understand English and was afraid to leave her fellow Russians who apparently thought I was trying to kidnap her. The English captain told me, "I don't know who mistreated them so, but it is unfair to blame all this on the Turks. Nobody could be worse than some of the Near Eastern people who profess Christianity for political purposes." I went on to my dinner with the Leavitts but was unable to eat. Somehow the sight of a child in pain is far worse than seeing an adult suffer.

A week later I was with a party that went to Maxim's on Taxim Square, a place run by an American Negro, Thomas, who was in Moscow for many years and was driven out by the Bolshis. I heard that he had done a lot for other refugees and was generally liked and respected. A little later, I saw two drunken Englishmen abusing a Russian attendant. One of them struck the man in the face. He made no effort to strike back. Then the Englishman struck him again and this time the Russian returned the blow. Instantly both Englishmen went into a perfect spasm of fury, yelling and waving their fists in a frenzy of rage. By now Thomas had come up and he asked mildly what the trouble was. One of the men, shaking his fist in Thomas' face, screamed, "He struck an ENGLISHMAN!" Thomas replied grimly, "You shake your fist in my face again and I'll strike another." The Englishman recoiled in open-mouthed astonishment while his friend turned to stare at Thomas unbelievingly. A few seconds later both left the café, still seemingly in a daze.

It was an object lesson to me of the tremendous power Great Britain once had that no one anywhere in the world dared to lay a hand on an Englishman for any reason whatever. If anyone transgressed against this law, the whole enormous force of the British Empire was brought to bear no matter at what cost of men and money. It was in an attempt to emulate this prestige that Roosevelt had issued his famous proclamation, "Perdicaris alive or Raisuli dead." Today it is hard to believe that any nation could once have had such power.

Our motion picture films were in great demand, not only with the fleet but with American institutions ashore. We were asked by the Woman's College to send them some films "suitable for young girls." I instructed the chief petty officer in charge of films to send them something innocuous and he said he would. Fortunately I checked the first shipment. Heading his list was "Damaged Goods," a picture about venereal infections and how they are spread. I asked him why he picked that one. "Isn't it about department store distribution, sir?" he asked me.

I saw a great deal of British Army and Navy men, hoping to renew old acquaintances from London and Scotland. They were fine fellows but what a difference from the magnificent men I recalled having seen on our 1903 cruise. All those men had died in the war—the pick of British manhood. I recalled reading somewhere that the French had never recovered from the Napoleonic wars. I believe that everyone of the Old Guard was over six feet. Very few modern Frenchmen reach that height. They are the descendants of the "second raters" that Napoleon rejected.

I happened to mention to these men that I had seen the battle flags of the Forty-second Highlanders with "New Orleans" embroidered on them. "Ah yes, that was one of our minor victories," one man remarked. I didn't correct him. Most of them had never heard of the engagement, nor had they ever heard of the War of 1812. I didn't dare ask them if they had ever heard of the American Revolution.

I hasten to say that although physically the English were not as impressive as I remembered them, they still retained their skill at seamanship. I have mentioned that I have always made it a point to anchor near a British vessel if possible. One night the wind blew up into half a gale and it began to snow heavily; the current was very strong and I went forward to make sure we were not dragging our anchor. I had only taken a few steps when I saw a Spanish collier coming down the straits toward us utterly out of control. I turned out the watch and by heaving on the anchor chains we managed to veer out of her way. It was only by great good luck that I happened to see the collier when I did, and I glanced over at the Britisher wondering when her officer of the deck would notice the collier and man the chains. To my astonishment, I saw her anchor watch had already been mustered forward and had cast off her chains even before ours had. The English may not know much about history, but in a tideway I would rather be anchored next to them than any other nationality. Both of us avoided the errant collier who then proceeded to smash into an anchored French vessel, sliding along her side with a series of grinding clashes. She smashed a gun, a whole line of ports, and sank a big motor sailing launch that was lying alongside, crushing it flat. Then she dropped astern disappearing in the darkness.

It seemed to me ridiculous that so many of my officers spent all their spare time at Novatni's and Maxim's when there was so much to be seen. At last when we received an invitation from the British high commissioner and his lady to attend an afternoon reception, I ordered several of them to accompany me, to their intense disgust. The affair was very pleasant though a bit formal and toward the end of the afternoon I noticed that they were looking very unhappy and restless. I asked them if they were enjoying the affair. One of them said in horror, "Captain, they gave us TEA to drink!" I remembered then that to many Americans tea is an effeminate drink suitable only for women. I recalled that when in Scotland during the war, even I thought it was amusing to have the rough British navies stop work every day at four o'clock to drink tea. I commiserated with my unfortunate officers but was secretly relieved that our hosts had not offered us anything stronger. Men who have had a few drinks are liable to say things which to them seem merely good-natured joshing but are only too likely to give offense to strangers.

As I took many trips up the Bosphorus in my gig with guests, I had the ship's carpenter make and install a comfortable bench on the gig's deck with lifelines on either side so we could sit in the open instead of in the cabin and enjoy the scenery. To have such a seat was contrary to Naval Regulations and would not have been permitted in the Big Fleet but we were a long way from the Big Fleet and mine was practically an independent command. Some of the happiest days of my life were spent on that bench watching the ancient ruins, wild hills, and lovely towns slip by. When I left the service, I took the bench with me and had it installed around a great tree by the swimming pool at The Hedges. I used to spend long hours sitting there dreaming that I was back in Constantinople with the pretty women and interesting people of that wonderful city.

At this time we received a very pleasant compliment from Doctor Black of Roberts College. He asked permission to address the *Denebola*'s crew during religious services on Sunday. He pointed out that we had saved thousands of lives in the last few months because, ever since we had arrived, we had been sending all our spare food to the various refugee camps in the vicinity. "Not only the fifty thousand

Christians in Constantinople are grateful to you, but also the Turks," he added. "I have talked to many of them who say your actions have given them a new slant on Christian nations they never had before."

A few weeks later we were able to recommend ourselves to our Turkish hosts in an even more effective manner. The Contantinople Volunteer Fire Department was a standing joke. They wore fantastic costumes, carried an ornamental and useless hand pump on a long pole and at night illuminated their progress with paper lanterns. They used to dash down the streets falling over dogs, street merchants and each other yelling: "Yan Gin Var!" (Fire, there is!) and "Haidee!" (Gangway!). Arriving at the scene of the fire they would start haggling with the property owner before attempting to put it out.

On February 27th the *Denebola* was moored off Orta-Keuy where there is a beautiful little mosque whose stone work looked like fine lace. Near the mosque was a big building crowded with refugees. At ten o'clock that morning this building suddenly burst into flames, apparently caused by the ignition of kerosene or gasoline. Our Fire and Rescue Party was called away and in five minutes a fifty-foot motor sailing launch left the ship with twenty-five men commanded by Lt. Allan Smith. This party was equipped with wrecking tools, buckets, extinguishers, and heaving lines. Ten minutes later a second sailing launch with thirty men commanded by Lt. Lars Peterson left the ship. This boat carried handy billies (hand pumps), lengths of fire hose, an extra long suction hose, spanners, reducers, nozzles, buckets, and axes. Immediatedly after the second boat I shoved off in my gig with an orderly and a signal man to see if I could be of any help.

I saw at once that the burning building and another directly behind it were crowded with refugees. We entered the burning building, climbed to the top floor, got the refugees out and then proceeded to save their property (bundles of clothes), by throwing them out the windows. One squad climbed to the roof to determine the possibility of starting a bucket-line prior to the arrival of the pumps. Owing to the height and the heat and extent of the flames, I decided this was not practicable. The axemen occupied themselves with clearing away wood that was not yet on fire.

Our men on the ground experienced considerable difficulty in keeping the women refugees from running back into the burning building in an effort to get the clothes, their sole earthly possession. They did not realize that our men were rescuing their bundles and as none of them spoke English and we did not know any Russian, we could not communicate with them. I am glad to say that all their clothing was saved.

Upon the arrival of our second boat, the handy billies were landed, a line of fire hose run out and in a few minutes we had a strong stream playing on the flames. Shortly afterwards the Constantinople Volunteer Firemen arrived but were unable to produce a stream of water larger than that from an ordinary garden hose and this could not reach the fire.

Immediately to the east of the burning building and separated from it only by a four foot stone wall was a large white wooden house. I had no idea what it was or to whom it belonged but in anticipation of a possible shift of wind I directed the bucket men to leave the fire itself and drench those portions of the house that were nearest to the blaze. It was fortunate I did so for within minutes burning embers and large fiery sections of wood were falling on it and this building would certainly have gone up too.

There was great confusion in the neighborhood, for the refugees were rushing around, upsetting people, weeping and getting in the way. At first it appeared that no one had been hurt, but I came across a sixteen year old girl who was lying in the street and in danger of being trampled. We got her up and under the cover of a portico in spite of a Turkish soldier who threatened us with his bayonet and attempted to force us back into the street. For awhile I thought I would have to call on some of our armed Shore Patrol to handle him but fortunately a Turkish officer who could speak French came up and very courteously complied with my request that we be permitted to remain. Our hospital corpsman had started to give her first aid when we discovered that one of her eyes had been torn from the socket. As soon as we saw the shocking nature of her injury I sent the orderly to the ship for a medical officer and he shortly returned with Lt. John Cloyd who applied dressings.

Meanwhile Miss Allen of the Near East Relief joined us. As I have made a number of slighting comments about the American woman in Constantinople, I would like to say that Miss Allen was one of the finest people I have ever met. Her knowledge of Turkish and her attractive personality were invaluable in dealing with the Turkish police who were greatly annoyed at our bothering with these infidel refugees. We had considerable difficulty in getting a car to take the injured girl to a hospital. One woman who had driven up to watch the fire said that her chauffeur had disappeared. Lieutenant Smith then offered to drive the car but the woman pretended she didn't understand him. Eventually Miss Allen got a car. In lifting the injured girl she became deathly sick and vomited all over Miss Allen who continued to support her and did not flinch in the slightest. She accompanied the girl to the hospital.

By now the fire was under control and we could safely leave it in the hands of the regular fire department. I had the men fall in and marched back to the boats. En route we passed through the gardens of the large white house that had so nearly burned also. As we went through a gentleman wearing a fez and with a monocle in his eye came up and said in French: "Their Imperial Highnesses wish to express their appreciation of the protection of their property by the American officers and men." I thanked him and after he left I asked a Turkish newspaper man who the gentleman was. He told me that the big white house was a palace and was occupied by two Turkish princesses, Vaima Sultane and Zekie Sultane. "That man is their Highnesses' chargé d'affaires," he added. I thought little of the matter at the time.

A few days later I received a letter from Admiral Bristol, our high commissioner, enclosing a note from the Princesses. Here is a translation:

Her Imperial Highness Zekie Sultane presents her compliments to Admiral Bristol and wishes to inform him how grateful she is for the valuable assistance rendered by the *Denebola* on the 27th instant when a fire broke out next door to her Palace at Orta-Keuy. She is of the opinion that had it not been for the assistance of the *Denebola*'s crew her Palace would certainly have been destroyed.

Later I was presented to Her Highness, who personally thanked me for our help.

I received a letter of commendation from Admiral Bristol that was put on my record. As a result of this episode, I was asked to dine with Talat Bey, an important Turkish official. The Turkish titles are first "effendi" (which really means "gentleman"); then "bey" which includes ranks as far up as General and Admiral, then "pasha" and finally "prince," "caliph" and "sultan." We talked in a curious mixture of Turkish, Greek, French, and German. He made no bones about his hatred for western Europeans and showed me his piano which had been smashed by them. "And the men who did it were not private soldiers but officers" he assured me. He said he was never going to have it repaired but intended to keep it as a monument to Christian perfidy. Then, more to the point, he went on to say "Because of your thoughtfulness in saving the Royal Palace I will see that your American businessmen will be given a lot of concessions not extended to the Europeans. I hope that you will believe that we Turks are not 'terrible' or 'unspeakable' but very like other people." I assured him that I thoroughly agreed with him.

Talat Bey was as good as his word, and I later received a number of calls from grateful American businessmen who found that their relations with the Turks had enormously improved. As American trade with the Middle East was growing in importance, the United States taxpayer got a return on the cost of sending our Destroyer Squadron to the Middle East. Personally, I received an unexpected dividend. The vicious letters concerning my love life which Polly had been receiving suddenly stopped. Obviously someone had put a flea in the ear of these self-appointed censors and told them to mind their own business; I suspect the businessmen were involved. Upholding America's high moral code is one thing but it can't be allowed to interfere with profits.

As a result of the fire, I became fairly well known in Constantinople and received a number of invitations. One was to a reception given by a delightful Russian couple named Mr. and Mrs. Henie. Mrs. Henie had been a countess before being forced to flee Russia. They had a beautiful apartment with a balcony overlooking the Golden Horn. As I entered I noticed a large photograph of a charming young lady dressed "à l'Anglais" in a smart tailored suit with a rolled up umbrella under her arm. She was the younger sister of my hostess. I did not realize it at the time but I was looking at a picture of my future wife. I met her thirteen years later in Switzerland after Polly's death. We were married the following year.

To anyone not personally involved, the different *mores*, beliefs and customs of the various peoples in Constantinople would have made a fascinating study. However, as I was responsible for the well-being of several thousand men, plus my country's prestige in the area, this confusion of attitudes presented a constant threat. There were a number of lepers on the streets who wore white veils over their faces.

No one thought anything of it and did not seem to fear infection. On the other hand, the Turks were shocked at the sight of drunken men. Of course, their religion does not permit them to indulge in alcohol in any manner and they regarded drunks not only with revulsion but also alarm, never being sure what a man under the influence might do.

I remember especially an affair at Petit Champs that nearly developed into a free fight. There was dancing and among the couples was a Jamaican Negro and a white girl. Near our table—I was there with a French girl—was a young American naval officer with an American woman. This woman kept protesting in a loud voice, "A white woman dancing with a nigger! I never saw anything so disgusting in my life. It's an outrage! Why doesn't somebody do something about it?" My companion and I were discussing a ballet which had taken place earlier in the evening and I tried to ignore my fellow countrywoman but her escort, poor kid, finally was goaded by her into the role of knight errant. Before I could say anything, he had walked over to the Jamaican and ordered him off the floor.

To be a successful knight errant you should have the build for it. The young officer was decidedly weedy while the Jamaican was over six feet and built like a bull; he could have broken the American in two and showed every indication of being willing to do so. I got up at once but before I could interfere, several other young American officers had gone to their comrade's help, simply because he was their comrade I am sure. Instantly an English Army officer, followed by several tommies, moved up to back the Jamaican who was shouting, "You come here from America a thousand miles away and think you can tell us what to do!"

As I came up, the English lieutenant said to me, "I am the British officer of this district and I will handle this affair." As he was fifteen years my junior in age and four grades my junior in rank I found it hard to control my temper. I merely reminded him that the United States was a sovereign power and he had no authority whatever over an American citizen. Still it was ridiculous to make an international incident over the conduct of a silly young woman and a stupid young man who had seen fit to interfere in a matter which was absolutely none of their business. So instead I turned to the American officer and said, "We cannot lay down rules of conduct for these people."

"Why, Captain," said the young officer with a strong Southern accent. "There are American women in this place. They should not be exposed to a sight like this."

"If they don't like it let them go somewhere else," I brutally retorted. Then seeing he was about to make some reply I added, "You are not under my command but if you don't drop this dispute I will report you to Admiral Bristol."

He hesitated for a moment and then turned and left. His friends were inclined to linger on so I said, "I think I'll report him anyhow. What is his name?" They hastily said, "We don't know" and vanished. As the Jamaican had disappeared, I said to the Englishman, "I realize that officer had no right to interfere but you must realize that in most parts of America we strongly disapprove of a black man dancing with a white woman." Much to my surprise, he answered, "So do we but he is a British subject and I was bound to defend him."

Curiously, not a person in the café understood my reason for butting in. The Jamaican thought I was acting as his champion. I was told later that, while I was wigging the young American officer, he was making deep bows behind my back and saying, "Thank you, Captain, thank you!" The Turkish gentleman in the café thought I was defending the Rights of Man and congratulated me on taking a strong stand against racial intolerance. As I left one Turk said to me approvingly, "You were perfectly right, Captain. What would happen if a black man should get up in a New York night club and say, 'I will not allow two white people to dance together?' " I assured him quite truthfully, I trembled to think of what would happen. The young American officers thought I was an old fool to interfere in an affair that was none of my business and then side with an Englishman against my own countrymen; they concluded I was some sort of an Anglo-maniac. The Englishmen thought I had officiously broken up what promised to be a most entertaining fracas and was afraid they'd hurt the American officers. It never occurred to anyone that I was merely trying to prevent what could easily have been an ugly international incident.

I have described this incident in some detail because I think it is a good example of how different ethnic groups can react to the same situation and how each of them can be quite convinced that they are in the right and there is no other possible point of view except their own. It also illustrates how often a group feels perfectly justified in forcing their own standards on others. I have heard a great deal about "hands across the sea" and "all men are brothers," etc. It seems to me far more important to realize that an American Southerner, a Jamaican Negro, an Englishman, and a Turk have very different attitudes, and it is crucial to realize in international affairs that what is perfectly permissible to one group may be exceedingly offensive to another.

The Balkan peoples are an excellent example of these differences. To me, they have the same naturalness as children and the same inability to hide their feelings; in this they are the exact opposite of the English. One afternoon, about tea time, I called on an attractive Hungarian lady. Shortly after my arrival another guest arrived. He was in the diplomatic service of one of the Balkan states and, of course, an educated, upper-class man. When he saw us he stamped his foot in a rage, hit the table with his fist and then shouting, "I cannot stay, I must go!" turned and literally ran out of the room. He had expected to be the only guest and, like a child, could not hide his disappointment.

On another afternoon at Tokatlians an Army officer from the Balkans was sitting at a table with a Russian girl. One of our men, a big lieutenant from Kentucky, came into the room and, as he knew the girl, stopped as he passed her table and commenced talking to her. The Balkan officer acted exactly like a small boy; he commenced wiggling in his chair and showed unmistakably that he wanted the American to go away. You may have seen small boys, when bored by the conversation of other small boys, take the bore by the shoulders and endeavor to push him away. Something very like that happened. The Balkan, perhaps unconsciously, picked up his napkin and flicked it across the American officer's face in an effort to drive him away. The American stood staring at him unbelievingly and then knocked him completely through a small table where two Englishmen were quietly having their tea. When the shower of tea and buns subsided the Russian girl had fled and the Englishmen were disclosed sitting on the floor, applauding frantically and demanding an encore. The Balkan officer was knocked unconscious but several of his friends came running up, drawing their swords as they did so. Their way was blocked by the other patrons who had jumped up and were crowding around to see what was happening. In the ensuing confusion, we got the lieutenant out of the café and around the corner. Just as the Kentuckian could not conceive of someone hitting him in the face for no reason, so the Balkan officer obviously had no idea that the American would retaliate. If he resented the action, the correct procedure would be to issue a challenge to a duel.

With the best will in the world, one had to be constantly on one's guard to avoid giving offense. I met a Captain Rawlings on the British

Aircraft Carrier *Pegasus*, whom I had known in Scotland and we renewed our old friendship. Rawlings asked me if we had any motion pictures the *Pegasus* could borrow and I sent to the *Denebola* for a few. He had me over to dinner on the carrier and, in front of the crew before the picture show, presented me with a silver cup to be used as a prize in athletic competitions on the *Denebola*. I said a few words of thanks, the men applauded, and we sat down to enjoy the show. Suddenly I remembered that for some reason a number of the pictures we had been receiving were violently anti-British. I don't know if this was because they were slanted to the Irish-American audiences or because there was resentment among the Jews over the British mandate in Palestine. I did know that if one of these pictures was to be shown, the entire crew of the *Pegasus*, officers and men, would consider it a deliberate insult. Thank heaven the picture turned out to be quite innocuous and before leaving I carefully checked the others.

As summer approached we spent more and more time out of doors, most of it on the water. Constantinople is the most wonderful summer resort in the world, especially if you have a power boat. It is never really hot there and, unlike New England, the water is warm and perfect for swimming. The Bosphorus forms a sort of funnel from the Black Sea to the Sea of Marmora and there was nearly always a cool breeze coming down from the Russian steppes. At intervals along the shores, both of the Bosphorus and the Marmora, there are little cafés extending out over the water and provided with boat landings. Here we would run alongside, step from my gig, sit down at a table and have tea. There were countless such places but Moda became our favorite. It is on the Asiatic shore of the Sea of Marmora, not far from the Tower of Leander, where the legendary Greek hero performed the amazing feat of swimming the Hellispont. After passing through the entrance to the Bosphorus and rounding the breakwater, we would head in at slow speed, sounding with a boathook, until we were in about five feet of water and let go the gig's anchor. The girls would go down into the cabin and shift into swimming clothes while we were changing up forward and then all hands would go swimming off the boat.

I had a wooden ladder rigged to hang over the side so we could get back on board without too many gymnastics. After swimming we would get up anchor, run across the bay and have tea and dance at a little Russian café on the end of the breakwater, returning to Constantinople after dark. Ah, those were golden days, the happiest time of my life.

I remember a couple of amusing incidents connected with these trips—at least, they seemed amusing to me. Once I was accosted by an old fellow who started to talk to me in Turkish which I did not understand. One of the girls with us, an Austrian, began to laugh. I asked her what the man was saying and she replied, "He says that the Turks like Americans but they cannot stand those accursed Christians."

On another occasion I was confronted by one of the American ladies attached to our embassy who looked with strong disapproval at our female companions and asked angrily, "What do you see in those furriners?" I told her "They have nice manners and are pretty and interesting." She retorted, "They don't look like real folks" and turned away with an angry sniff. I felt put in my place.

We were forced to shift our anchorage to one off Bostanjik in the Sea of Marmora. As the peace approached, the natives got more and more aggressive and several of our men were stabbed in the streets at night. As we had been on very friendly terms with the Turks, I was entirely unprepared for this sudden change in attitude. I don't know whether this belligerancy was because the Turks thought our men were Western Europeans or whether in a burst of national pride over the peace treaty they delighted in attacking any strangers, but the embassy wanted to get the Destroyer Squadron away before a general battle took place and to clear the Bosphorus of ships as far as possible.

We left our old berth and shifted to one about half a mile from the shore of Asia Minor. After anchoring, I went to a conference at the embassy; an hour's run for my gig. The city was adorned with Turkish flags and all foreigners were being evacuated. It looked like the beginning of the end.

I held a conference with the fleet navigator of the British Squadron and we discussed various plans for mutual support if the trouble became acute. The next day I discovered that two of our men were missing. They had gotten into a fight on shore and when the Shore Patrol had gone to their help, the patrol had been beaten up too. According to my informant, everyone had been drunk, including the Shore Patrol, which was outrageous. I went to Pera that afternoon with a group of armed sailors. As we tramped down the main street of Bostanjik apprehensive heads appeared at the windows. Through some of my Turkish friends I was able to obtain the men's release.

Except for some broken heads, none of them was seriously injured. After that, I stopped all shore liberty.

Again through my friends in Constantinople, I was warned that conditions in southern Russian were "uncertain" and there might well be fighting at any time. This was something I didn't want to get involved in unless it was absolutely necessary to protect American lives. I went ashore in Varna and called on the captain of the port, the mayor and the British consul general hoping for more news; we had no diplomatic or consular representative there. What they told me was not encouraging. They all agreed that the Bulgars and the Serbs were "les vrai sauvages" and trouble between them and the Turks after the European warships left was inevitable. The British consul's wife was a Polish woman, who spoke twelve languages as well as several gypsy dialects and kept abreast of all the rumors. Her companion was a Bulgarian girl who had been secretary to Stambouliski, the Bulgarian statesman who had sided with the Allies during the war and later been deposed and shot by a military coup. She told me that he wasn't simply shot; the revolutionists had first cut off his ears and then tortured him to death. "If there is trouble, don't let those people take you alive," she warned me. I promised her to avoid it if possible.

Of course, as long as we stayed on our ships we were in no danger but if it became necessary to send landing parties ashore to take off American citizens, the situation might become sticky. I made a few visits on shore and noted that almost all foreign uniforms had disappeared and there were many more fezzes. The most gruesome aspect of the whole business was the plight of the refugee Russian girls who worked in the restaurants and cafés. Many of them had been helped by the foreign officers and men. Now that the Allied Forces were leaving, the girls were faced with the alternative either of being "nice" to the scum of the Near East or starving to death. Many did not even have that choice. While I was there I heard of one girl who, reduced to the last extremity, attempted to drown herself. She was pulled out of the water by a gang of laborers who, after doing what they wanted with her, threw her back again and stood laughing as she drowned.

I personally witnessed one of these tragedies. There was an officer on the *Denebola* who disliked all women intensely and who never failed to be rude when he was forced to speak to them. His sole recreation had been to go ashore once a week and drink beer with his cronies at Novatni's. One morning he came to my cabin with a face as long as the maintopbowline and asked my advice. It seems there was a young Russian girl who was very much in love with one of our seamen and was hoping desperately that he would marry her—her only chance to escape the city. She had tried hard to see her sweetheart but this officer had callously turned her away. She had then come back with a little bunch of flowers she had picked somewhere and presented them to the officer in a despairing effort to win him over. Even this misanthrope was touched by the poor child's pitiful gesture and he had allowed her to see her lover. One of the American women saw him take the flowers and had written a vicious letter to the man's wife. (I could not imagine his having a wife), saying he was receiving flowers from women. Except for the fact that the officer was almost out of his mind with anxiety the affair would have been amusing as he had never looked at a woman except to insult her. He said he was going to write a scorching letter to his wife for presuming to doubt him. I advised him simply to laugh at the affair for if he and his wife had a falling out it would be just what the writer of the letter hoped for. In retaliation for the trouble she had caused him, I later learned that he had refused to allow the Russian girl on the ship and, as all shore leave had been cancelled, she was never able to speak to her lover again, although she used to stand on the wharf and wave to him. Whether after we sailed she drowned herself or was forced to become a prostitute I never learned.

This morning we have received our evacuation orders. Everybody was to get out not later than October 4th and on the 5th the Turkish Army under Mustapha Kemal would march in. At first it was not expected that we would leave at the same time as the Europeans; we have never been at war with Turkey and there was not the same feeling against us. However, a regular campaign was started by the local foreign language newspapers such as the *Levant News* and *Le Journal*. Their headlines screamed, "Why do the Americans stay when we must leave?" and so on. Finally, apparently to shut them up, the Turkish authorities requested us to leave at the same time.

I had a final luncheon at the "Summer Embassy" at Therapia. All the Near East Relief people had fled and the YMCA was preparing to leave with the Navy. For several days the *Denebola*'s radio had been our only means of communication with the outside world and we were the only means of rescuing the remaining Americans. I helped evacuate several of the women who had been complaining about me to

Admiral Bristol and strangely enough they couldn't have been more agreeable. I wonder why. Our businessmen ashore didn't seem to be apprehensive as they knew how to get along with the Turks. We sailed at five o'clock the afternoon of October 4th with a long, home-wardbound pennant flying at the main truck. All our ships were to be away before the entrance of the Kemalist Army. At seven o'clock we anchored in Suvula Bay opposite Chanak. That afternoon I did something I had long wanted to attempt—swimming the Hellespont.

For months now I had been studying all the available literature on this famous strait including tide tables, sailing directions, charts, and the encyclopedias. The first step was to locate accurately Sestos and Abydos—the two points on either side of the strait where both Leander and Lord Byron had made the swim. In one of the encyclope-dias I found the following, "North and east from the town of Tchanck Kalesi is a low strip of land called Nagara Burun projecting into the sea. This spot has been fixed upon as the site of ancient Abydon and a similar projecting point corresponds to it on the European shore. Here Leander swam across the strait from Abydos to Sestos and Lord Byron swam the same distance on May 3, 1818."

This information checked with the standard Navy Hydrographic Office chart of the Dardanelles for, while there are no traces of the ancient towns there is a "Sestos Point" on the European side and an "Abydos Point" on the Asiatic, and behind these points the chart shows the "Sites of Ancient Sestos and Abydos."

The current at this point flows southwesterly with a force of from one to four knots depending on the strength and direction of the wind. The shortest distance between Europe and Asia is very nearly one and one-eighth nautical miles but because of the current it would be impossible to swim directly across; I would have to swim diagonally across the axis of the current so as not to experience its full force.

I had arranged to have a small pulling boat follow me. There were two reasons for this: one, in case I couldn't make it at least I wouldn't drown. Secondly, I wanted to have witnesses to the stunt if I succeeded.

The day I decided to attempt the swim there was a fresh breeze blowing from the southwest or directly against the current. This had raised a choppy sea with waves about two feet high. I was obliged to decide either to swim with the current and against wind and sea or vice versa. I had heard so much about the strength of the current that I decided to go with it and buck the waves. As soon as I got clear of the shore the waves began slapping me in the face and before long the little following boat was half full of water and the crew had to start bailing. When I had been in the water about an hour I began to get cramps, first in one leg and then in the other, but fortunately they didn't get too bad.

I did all right until I approached the Asiatic shore where I encountered a counter current flowing strongly up toward the Sea of Marmora. When I first put my feet on the bottom they were snatched out from under me by this counter current and I found it impossible to stand up until I got closer inshore but I finally made it. I did not try to establish a time record as we were under orders to sail that evening and there would have been no opportunity to attempt the swim again in case I failed the first time. The state of the sea, indeed, made any fast swimming impossible.

When we got back to the ship the crew of the following boat signed a certificate of the swim. Here it is:

> Office of the Commanding Officer
> USS *Denebola*

This is to certify that, on October 5, 1923, Captain D. Pratt Mannix, US Navy, swam across that part of the Dardanelles known as the Hellespont, from Europe to Asia, between the ancient sites of Sestos and Abydos. Distance, one and one-half nautical miles; elapsed time from shore to shore, one hour, thirty-five minutes, seven seconds. Sea, choppy, wind South West, force five.

> John J. Smith
> Boatswain, US Navy
>
> Oswald H. Lucke
> Chief Boatswains Mate, US Navy
>
> Anton Eminger
> Boatswains Mate First Class, US Navy
>
> Herbert D. Van Voorhis
> Coxswain US Navy

An account of my swim was published in the *Naval Register* but otherwise it attracted little attention. Two years later, the writer-traveler Richard Halliburton claimed to have made the swim and announced that he was the first American to do so. His account was widely publicized. I wrote to the newspaers pointing out that whether or not Halliburton did make the swim—and several of the feats he claimed to have performed were highly questionable—he was certainly not the first American to do so. Halliburton, however, continued to make his claim and many people believed him. Whether or not I was the first American to perform this stunt I do not know, but while the newspaper controversy between Halliburton and myself was raging, no one else made a prior claim so I suppose I was the first American to duplicate Leander's feat.

After a short stay in Athens, we proceeded homeward. We had been absent for two years. There is always a thrill in coming home! As we passed Fire Island Light, a radio message was brought to me on the bridge. I must admit I was touched. Clearly it was a "Welcome Home" and meant that the Department remembered us. It is pleasant to feel that you are not forgotten. Wiping my eyes which, I am ashamed to say had become moist, I read it by the light of our binnacle. It was from the Big Flagship:

> You will report in writing your reason for
> violating section seven-eleven Paragraph four-
> eleven-forty-four subhead QXR of Radio Communi-
> cation Manual WJZ as amended on the umpteenth instant.

Then I KNEW we were home!

POSTCRIPT

My father retired from active service in 1928 and lived with my mother, my sister, and myself at The Hedges, Rosemont. He redid his own sitting room to make it resemble a ship's cabin as much as possible; installing portholes for windows, having charts on the walls, and hanging up pictures of the various ships on which he had served. He went out very seldom, having little in common with the people who lived on the Main Line. He spent most of his time reading books on travel and corresponding with his naval friends.

My mother died in 1932. Soon afterwards Father began to take long trips to Europe where he always felt more at home than in the United States. Father was always ready to die for America but he disliked living here. As he often pointed out, it was the only country in the world where an officer in uniform did not meet with automatic respect. I remember once in New York he was standing in full dress outside our hotel when a lady approached him doubtfully and, obviously mistaking him for a doorman, asked, "Is you from Gimbels?" Furious, Father replied, "No, I be from Macy's." He never got over this insult.

On one of his European trips, Father encountered his old Constantinople friends, Mr. and Mrs. Henie, who were now living in Switzerland. Here he met Mrs. Henie's younger sister whose picture he had seen in Constantinople: Countess Claudia Bougroff. Claudia's father had been an aide to the Tzar before the Revolution but he had managed to escape from Russia with his family and part of his fortune. Claudia and Father were married in 1937. For a few years they lived at The Hedges but shortly after World War II they moved to Claudia's estate in Geneva.

Father had always dreamed of obtaining the rank of admiral but because of his unfavorable Fitness Report from his tour of duty at the Philadelphia Navy Yard he never rose above the rank of captain.

However, a high ranking naval officer was going over the records of retired officers and came on father's name. According to the story I heard, this man exclaimed, "I had no idea that Pratt Mannix was still alive. I remember when I was a young ensign I wanted to go ashore to meet my girl but our commanding officer was an old sundowner (martinet) and refused permission. Pratt Mannix was officer of the day. When the Old Man had gone below, Pratt Mannix said to me, 'Go ashore, youngster, and see your girl. I'll cover for you.' I've never forgotten that." A few weeks later, father received his promotion to Rear Admiral, his life's ambition.

Having known him as "captain" since I was ten years old, I later sent him a letter to Geneva addressed to "Captain D. Pratt Mannix." I promptly received a cable reminding me that he was REAR ADMIR-AL Mannix and not to make that mistake again.

My father died September 17, 1957. At his request, he was buried at Arlington with his naval forebears. Cannons fired salutes, white horses drew the hearse, and the Naval and Marine guards were paraded. Shortly before his death, I had an opportunity to talk to him. I was a lieutenant in the Navy at the time and we discussed the atomic bombing of Hiroshima on August 6, 1945. "This is the end of the Navy," he told me. "No ship can defy those damned flying machines armed with bombs like that." There were tears in his eyes.

It has not been the end of the Navy. The Navy has changed but it still remains our first line of defense as it was in his day.